The Languages of Addiction

The Languages of Addiction

Edited by

Jane Lilienfeld
and Jeffrey Oxford

St. Martin's Press
New York

THE LANGUAGES OF ADDICTION

ISBN 0-312-21850-8

Library of Congress Cataloging-in-Publication Data

The languages of addiction / edited by Jane Lilienfeld and Jeffrey Oxford.

p. cm.

Includes bibliographical references and index.

ISBN 0-312-21850-8

1. American literature—20th century—History and criticism. 2. Alcoholism in literature. 3. Drinking of alcoholic beverages in literature. 4. English Literature—History and Criticism. 5. Narcotic habit in literature. 6. Drug abuse in literature. 7. Alcoholics in literature. 8. Authors—Alcohol use. 9. Compulsive behavior. I. Lilienfeld, Jane, 1945- II. Oxford, Jeffrey Thomas, 1966-

PS228.A58L36 1999

810.9'355—dc21 99–22567

CIP

Design by Letra Libre, Inc.

First edition: October 1999

10 9 8 7 6 5 4 3 2 1

08 07 06 05 04 03 02 00 01 99

Dedicated to the memory of my mother,
Edna R. Lilienfeld, 1907–1990;
to my husband Steven MacNiven Jerrett;
and to my students in
"Alcoholism and Literature."
J. L.

Dedicated to my wife, Raquel,
and my parents, J. T. and Kathleen Oxford.
J. O.

Contents

III
Teaching Interventions

IV
Addiction and Literature

Acknowledgments

THIS COLLECTION OF ESSAYS DEVELOPED from discussions with Professor Stephen Infantino. Our scholarly approaches to the use of literature to study the subject of addiction were so at variance, that the incongruities in our methodologies and basic assumptions were illuminating. These incongruities also mirrored, in literary theoretical formulations, the divergent discursive practices in medical discourses of addiction and alcoholism. Professor Stephen Infantino and I agreed that a collection of essays in dialogue about literature and addiction would be a useful addition to literary studies of the field. Professor Infantino and I began this volume together, and I want to thank him for his contributions to it.

When Professor Infantino's schedule did not permit him to continue as co-editor, Professor Jeffrey Oxford stepped forward to share editorial duties with me. Jeffrey Oxford's humor, hard work, and excellent editorial skills have been indispensable to the completion of this work. I want to express my deepest thanks to him. We have shared in all editorial decisions, and this collection is the product of a greatly rewarding and egalitarian scholarly endeavor.

My work on alcoholism and literature began in my classrooms in the 1980s. Working with students in traditional and nontraditional settings deepened my understanding of how to use literary texts to teach about alcoholism and drug addiction. To my students at Boston University, Assumption College, and Cambridge Center for Adult Education, I want to express my gratitude for their questions and willingness to share their insights into the topic with me and with one another.

I had the privilege of team-teaching a course with Ben Adams, an alcoholism counselor, on the topic of addiction and literature.

His knowledge of the field and his wide reading deepened and sharpened my approach. I learned as much from our differences in definitions and interpretations as from our arguments, and I thank Ben Adams for many stimulating hours of discussion.

Additionally, I want to thank all those who took time to help me gather bibliography, hone my insights, and answer my questions about alcoholism and addiction. I gratefully acknowledge the help provided by Ben Adams, M Ed; Elaine Black, CAC, LICCS; Tommy Bower, MA; Celia Dulfano, MSW; Sally Ann Duncan, MSW; Priscilla Johnson, MA; the late Mark Keller; Sally O'Leary, RN, MA; Amy Stromsten, MFA, and Susan Waldstein, CAC, MSW. I thank Rosemarie Johnstone for allowing me to read the manuscript of her dissertation, written under the direction of the university of Minnesota, English Department, entitled *American Declarations of Dependence: The Alcoholism of the Text.* Special thanks to Marcia Deihl, Staff Assistant, Tozzer Library, Harvard University, for her tireless help with checking sources, finding rare books, and tracking down the sources of obscure quotations. My thanks to Norma Luebbering of Lincoln University for help with proof reading the manuscript. My thanks as well to Professor Hilde Hein of the Department of Philosophy, College of the Holy Cross, Worcester, MA. They are not responsible for my choices of emphasis or interpretation.

I would like to thank my family for the generous financial assistance that sustained my researching the topic of alcoholism and literature: my mother, Edna R. Lilienfeld, my uncle, Joseph Meyerhoff, and my cousin, Harvey Meyerhoff, all of Baltimore, Maryland.

—Jane Lilienfeld

Being given the opportunity to join this project at mid-stream and shape the overall dynamics of the anthology was certainly not what I envisioned when I initially submitted my paper to Jane and Stephen. By chance coincidence, however, fate determined that I would ultimately step in and contribute in more ways than simply a chapter. Consequently, I owe a debt of gratitude to Jane for allowing me to help shape the project to represent fully my views, beliefs, and feelings about the direction that this project—which was not initially mine—should take.

Additionally, I would like to thank my wife, Raquel, for the constant support and understanding that she gives when late-night editing and/or proofreading sessions turn into hours of absence. I owe her a lot!

Finally, I would like to acknowledge Charles Barnes and ITP for the interest in addiction studies that they have brought me. Hang in there, Charles! You're an inspiration to many!

—*Jeffrey Oxford*

Both editors would like to thank our editors, Maura E. Burnett and Kristi Long, and the members of the Production Department of St. Martin's Press Scholarly and Reference Division. In addition, we would like to thank the following for permission to reprint articles as chapters in the present work:

Dionysos, for their kind permission to reprint Kathryne McDorman's "Ngaio Marsh and the 'Drug Scene' of Detective Fiction" in volume 8.2 (Summer 1998) pages 5–25.

Humanitas, for their kind permission to reprint Gregg Franzwa's "Degrees of Culpability: Aristotle and the Language of Addiction" in volume XI, 1 (1998) pages 91–102.

International Third World Studies Journal & Review, for their kind permission to reprint Nancy Bazin's "Alcoholism in Third World Literature: Buchi Emecheta, Athol Fugard, and Anita Desai" in volume 4.2 (1992) pages 13–17.

Plenum Publishing Corporation, for their kind permission to reprint Edward Khantzian's "Self-Regulation and Self-Medication Factors in Alcoholism and the Addictions: Similarities and Differences" in *Recent Developments in Alcoholism,* volume 8 (1990) edited by Marc Galanter, pages 255–271.

St. Martin's Press, for their kind permission to reprint Jane Lilienfeld's "I Could Drink a Quarter-Barrel to the Pitching": The Mayor of Casterbridge Viewed as an Alcoholic," an excerpted and condensed essay from her *Reading Alcoholisms: Theorizing Character and Narrative in Selected Novels of Hardy, Joyce, and Woolf* (1999).

INTRODUCTION

Jane Lilienfeld

ALCOHOLISM THEORY IS A CONTESTED SITE. This anthology is organized to bring into conversation the many differing views of alcoholism.

Medical, sociological, cultural, and psychological discourses of addiction contest the definition, causes, and treatments of alcoholism. Each of these approaches formulates its questions and answers very differently. Is alcoholism different from addiction to narcotics? (Miller and Chappel, 197) If so, how and why? Are alcoholics physiologically compelled to drink? If so, are they accountable for their behaviors? Is alcoholism a disease? (Vaillant, *Revisited,* 42–119, 376–93; Levin, 92–98) If so, what kind—a disease of the psyche, of the body? (Bean, "Denial") Are there psychological areas of vulnerability that lead to addiction to drugs and alcohol? (Vaillant, *Revisited,* 380–82; Khantzian, "Treatment") If alcoholism is a disease, can it be cured? (Vaillant, *Revisited,* 382–88; Levin, 249–50) What treatments, if any, are most effective? (Zinberg and Bean, "Introduction," 23–30; Vaillant, *Revisited,* 380–82; Levin, 189–195; Frye) Does alcoholism take different forms in women? (Vaillant, *Revisited,* 120–24) Can social conditions and cultural practices lead to alcoholism and addiction? (Single; Godfrey and Maynard) Are there views of alcoholism that are sensitive to cultural differences? (Heath, 359–66, 380–92; Barrows and Room, "Introduction," 7–12) If so, how are these formulated? (Heath; McGoldrick; Gusfield, 7–8) How and why has Alcoholics Anonymous (AA) become a media joke? (Hirshey) Historically, how do societal and media responses to alcoholism treatment differ across time, gender, and social class? (Sournia)

These questions are raised and examined in the essays in this book. The essays thus enter an already existing critical conversation about alcoholism, addiction and literature. Most current literary approaches to this topic focus either on exploring the AA model of alcoholism or study alcoholism as a linguistic event removed from the experiential lives of alcoholics and addicts. For example, *Equivocal Spirits: Alcohol and Drinking in Twentieth-Century Literature* and *The Thirsty Muse* rely on an AA model or medical model of addiction, moving simply between fiction and biography. *The White Logic: Alcohol and Gender in American Modernist Fiction* and *Pleasures and Pains: Opium and Orient in Nineteenth-Century British Culture,* on the other hand, analyze form, tropes, and metaphor to examine alcoholism and addiction as the organizational strategy of literary works. Similarly, sociological models of addiction focus primarily on symbolic meanings of the cultural phenomena of addiction, not on how alcoholics and addicts experience themselves and their needs and choices (Barrows and Room; Gusfield; Lanza). Our anthology incorporates these varied approaches, bringing them into conversation with one another.

Who is authorized to speak "for" the alcoholic? In North American media culture discursive practices include arguments based on self-disclosure. But self-disclosure is problematic in North American intellectual discourse, often leading to heated debates about "essentialism," "identity politics," and epistemological Balkanization. The question of who is empowered to speak is central to alcoholism discourse in literature and in medicine.

From its inception as a form of North American literary criticism, discussions of literature and addiction depended on self-disclosure. Donald Newlove's subtitle informs the reader that his book, *Those Drinking Days: Myself and Other Writers,* arises in part from his experiences drinking and sober. Similarly, Thomas Gilmore suggests in the introduction to his book, *Equivocal Spirits,* that his personal experience has deepened his scholarly work on the topic. However, other books on addiction and literature do not disclose whether or not the author is or was a problem drinker. There is no mention in Barry Milligan's *Pains and Pleasures* or John Crowley's *The White Logic,* or Tom Dardis' *The Thirsty Muse* of a search for sobriety.

Several essays in this anthology use the self-disclosing narrative stance of recovering alcoholics as the basis for an analysis of the emotional experiences of alcoholism and addiction, either by citing the experiences of the essay's author, or by citing the collection of transcribed oral histories to be found at meetings of the 12-step group of Alcoholics Anonymous. One essayist in this volume refers to herself as a witness to an alcoholic seizure, an experience that revealed to her her own ignorance about addiction. She was galvanized by such witness into learning and teaching about alcoholism and addiction. Recently, David Bleich argued that self-disclosure is a function of that classroom practice which seeks to model an ethical search for truth. His is not a universal response to self-disclosure. Interestingly, the anonymous writer of *Alcoholics Anonymous* apologized for the self-disclosures on which the book is based in a passage which, by its embarrassed tone, seems to validate the cultural bias against self-disclosure:

> We have concluded to publish an anonymous volume setting forth the problem as we see it. We shall bring to the task our combined experience and knowledge. . . .
>
> Of necessity there will have to be discussion of matters medical, psychiatric, social and religious. We are aware that these matters are, from their very nature, controversial. Nothing would please us so much as to write a book which would contain no basis for contention or argument. We shall do our best to achieve that ideal. (*Alcoholics Anonymous,* 19)

Summarizing the approach of the volume, the author concludes with another apology:

> We hope no one will consider these self-revealing accounts in bad taste. Our hope is that many alcoholic men and women, desperately in need, will see these pages, and we believe that it is only by fully disclosing ourselves and our problems that they will be persuaded to say, "Yes, I am one of them too, I must have this thing." (29)

What is apparent in these quotations from *Alcoholics Anonymous* is that the author anticipated that self-disclosure might enable other readers to identify with the people whose stories are recounted in the volume, and thereby recognize themselves. Seeking self by reading others is an established methodological tool of Reader-Response Theory (Fetterly, xi-xxvi; Schweickart). However, the writer was correct, too, in arguing that using discussions of personal experience to substantiate theories, to persuade others of the validity of one's intellectual position, and to find truths remains highly controversial. If this were not the case, what is now dismissed as "the memoir boom" would not be receiving the drubbing it is getting in the middlebrow and elite North American media (see, for example, McDowell).

Other essays in this volume approach an analysis of the feeling and thinking modes characteristic of alcoholism from a more distanced vantage than self-disclosure. Dr. Edward J. Khantzian's analysis of addiction as self-medication for structural deficits in the self grows out of his compassionate interactions with his clinical patients as well as the evidence of other clinicians and medical researchers. Khantzian's view of alcoholism and addiction as being comprehensible through scientific discourse combined with humane, respectful listening and participation as both a psychiatrist and a fellow human being, in fact, might be said to serve as the unacknowledged model for other essays in the volume, such as those of Jeffrey Oxford or Jane Lilienfeld, which rely on the biopsychosocial interpretation of addiction. Still other essays in the volume problematize medical models that presume that such a model, even one based on empathic entrance into the experiences of another, marginalizes the addict. For example, Sandy Norton's essay asserts that "the language of even a very compassionate [medical] analysis . . . still performs [the] cultural work" of "othering" the addict. The essays of Gregg Franzwa, Lawrence Driscoll, and Stephen Infantino interrogate language and textual discourse practices, an approach that turns on philosophical speculation rather than the experiential bases for knowledge.

This dialogue of methods replicates the many voices heard in medical discourses of addiction. It is common for medical and sociological texts on alcoholism to note that definitions of alcoholism depend on the training and professional methodology of the researcher (Levin, 87; Zinberg and Bean, "Introduction," 3–4 ; Gusfield, 32). Noting the variations of explanation, George Vaillant states:

> Scientists and clinicians do not always agree about the best model for conceptualizing alcohol abuse. No other habit or culturally determined behavior pattern creates more medical problems than does alcohol abuse; no other social "deviance" leads to more somatic pathology. But at the same time, there is no other so-called disease in which both etiology and cure are more profoundly dependent upon social, economic, and cultural variables. (Vaillant, *Natural,* 15)

This anthology replicates the contested nature of addiction discourse by representing a variety of literary critical voices in dialogue with one another.

As far back as Plato's *Ion,* the divinely inspired madness of creativity has been a staple of discussions about the artistic process. Plato's *Ion* clearly links the artist's inspiration to the orgiastic rites of Bacchus, or Dionysos, linking possession by the Muse with drinking:

> So it is also with good lyric poets; as the worshiping Corybantes are not in their senses when they dance, so the lyric poets are not in their senses when they make these lovely lyric poems. No, when once they launch into harmony and rhythm, they are seized with the Bacchic transport, and are possessed . . . for a poet is [a] light and winged thing, and holy, and never able to compose until he has become inspired, and is beside himself, and reason is no longer in him. (Plato, 32)

Whether alcohol and drug use sustain or impede the creative process has thus become a question that must be confronted in the emerging field of addiction and literary studies. Tom Dardis in *The Thirsty Muse* argues forcefully against the idea that alcohol and drugs improve creativity, demonstrating clearly that addiction stops or mars the creative production of great writing (Dardis, 7–11 and ff; see also Goodwin, 46–48).

The ambiguous ending of James Baldwin's "Sonny's Blues," with its alcohol tingling on the top of the blues piano, and Baldwin's own reliance on alcohol "to get through some of the more traumatic moments of living in a racist culture" (Norton, n4), are interrogated by Roger Forseth's analysis of Malcolm Lowry's and Jack London's convictions that their creativity was enhanced by the products of the vine. Similarly, Matt Djos raises important questions about John Berryman's complex depiction of the myth of the artistic potency of intoxicating substances. Ellen Lansky's reading of alcoholism strips it of romantic glitter. The plots of the characters' lives in Ernest Hemingway's and Djuna Barnes' novels replicate the misery Lansky defines as alcoholism—a foggy, self-defeating repetition of futility, unsatisfied longing, and anguish. These essays offer both a respectful acknowledgment of the allure of alcohol and drugs, and a powerful antidote to the myth of creativity fueled by drink and drugs.

The first section of this collection presents a range of theoretical approaches to alcoholism. It focuses on all the approaches to addiction and literature utilized by the essayists in this collection. This section begins with "The Alcoholic Writer by Any Other Name" by Roger Forseth, one of the founders of the North American discourse on addiction and literature. Forseth humorously presents the clash of views about terminology and definition in addiction studies, contrasting the medical, the AA, the cultural studies, and the psychoanalytic approaches. Using examples drawn from American, French, and British literature, Forseth explores the meaning of the concept of denial, that of the alcoholic and that of the literary critic. As does Forseth's, Gregg Franzwa's essay, "Aristotle and the Language of Addiction," interrogates the meaning of the word addiction by examining specific passages of Aristotle's *Nicomachean Ethics*. Franzwa demonstrates that Aristotle's analysis avoids simplistic divisions between "sin" and "sickness" models, dissolving the binary oppositions between these by offering a rational, inclusive way to delineate those behaviors and emotions now termed addiction. His conclusion moves Aristotelian categories of analysis into current discourse, exposing the persistent cultural denial that underlies the drawing of "moral distinctions between addictive behaviors of differently situated individuals." "Fingarette, AA, and the

Disease Concept of Alcoholism," Ben Adams' essay, indirectly responds to Franzwa's linguistic analysis, locating the problem of addiction in the body of the alcoholic rather than in discursive practices. In questioning Fingarette's misrepresentation of the program of Alcoholics Anonymous and its relation to the medical model of alcoholism, Ben Adams' essay also challenges much of the previous literary analysis of this topic, in which the AA model of addiction and the medical model are seen as synonymous.

Dr. Edward J. Khantzian's essay, "Self-Regulation and Self-Medication Factors in Alcoholism and the Addictions: Similarities and Differences," studies the psychological and emotional experience of addiction. Entering into his patients' feeling state, Khantzian presents their views of the logic of addiction, suggesting that addiction to "the [substance] of choice" is a comprehensible response to the interior life of an addict. Through its compassionate attention to the particularities of human experience, the essay demonstrates connections between alcoholism and drug addiction, thus sustaining the dual focus of this collection. Further, the essay substantiates Forseth's and Adam's arguments that medical views of alcoholism are more than the simplified clichés presented by their detractors, and elaborates on both Roger Forseth's and Ben Adams' analyses of the medical model. The essay's depiction of the experience of addiction is pertinent to the study of many writers analyzed in this collection, among them, John Berryman, Ernest Hemingway, James Baldwin, and Djuna Barnes, and the fictional figures, Michael Henchard, Sherlock Holmes, and Father Garnette.

The second section of the anthology presents one major aspect of addiction studies, the focus on language and symbolism. Khantzian's view—a refusal to moralize about addiction, but instead to view what addiction might mean to the addict—despite arising from an entirely different philosophical stance, has similarities to Lawrence Driscoll's approach in his essay, "'Something Strange but Not Unpleasant': Freud on Cocaine." Speaking through the persona of the cocaine-using Sigmund Freud, Driscoll challenges the hypocrisies that underpin the moralizing approach to the use of drugs in North American public policy debates (Bertram and Sharpe; Reed, 171, 181–82). Driscoll deftly allows his own adversarial position to be deconstructed by his inclusion of E. M. Thornton's scathing dismissal of Freud's view of cocaine and, hence, of the theoretical work Freud did during the period when he used cocaine. This daring inclusion of a dissenting echo voices the possibility that Driscoll and his Freud might be uttering the very voice of addiction itself in its endless denial of its own lack of choice.

Through his linguistic analysis rather than through a medical or psychological investigation, Driscoll's essay demonstrates an approach that Forseth interrogates in his essay. A similar focus on the concept of addiction as a literary event rather than a product of disease animates Stephen C. Infantino's rereading of sexual desire in *Tristram and Isolde* and *Madame Bovary.* Infantino's essay, "Female Addiction and Sacrifice as Pretextual Communion," elegantly sets up a chain of signifiers in which imbibing/consuming women are themselves consumed by men and by desire (what other essays in this anthology might suggest is addiction itself), a desire unslaked by the attainment of that which is desired. Although focusing on contemporary issues, Infantino's essay reveals historical literary precedents in the Western world of gendered attitudes toward and treatments of addicts and their "substances."

Yearly, the University of Michigan releases the results of its epidemiological studies of North American adolescents' use of alcohol and drugs. One recent study tracks 21 graduating classes of high school seniors from 1975 through 1995. The researchers found that both "occasional heavy drinking" and the use of heroin by these group members have begun to rise with statistically visible increases (Johnston, O'Malley, and Bachman, *Secondary,* 108–9). Further, although "college students and their age peers have equal prevalence rates for lifetime use of *alcohol* (88%) . . . [t]he most important difference lies in the prevalence of *occasional heavy drinking* . . . which is 40% among college students vs. 34% among their age peers" (Johnston, O'Malley, and Bachman, *College,* 131; emphasis in original). These statistics document what many university teachers have found: that the use of alcohol and the peer pressure to drink are widespread on college campuses nationwide. "The official response [to increased deaths, date rapes, and severe physical damage sustained by students as they participated in campus drinking rituals] on many campuses is an all-out war on underage drinkers. Some education is in place, but the primary focus of our conservative state administrations will be on punishment" (Bazin, "Teaching," 3).

Faced with increased harm to students and what many might perceive, as does Nancy Topping Bazin, to be an incomplete administrative-directed intervention strategy, teachers may ask: does the role of the college educator include that of raising students' awareness about alcoholism and addiction? If so, how might such teaching objectives shape lesson plans? Like so many classroom teachers, Nancy Topping Bazin and Krista Ratcliffe confronted the effects of students' use of alcohol. Each decided to take action, to challenge received opinions about alcoholism, and to demonstrate these challenges through careful analysis of both literary texts and students' responses to such texts. As part of this endeavor, Bazin and Ratcliffe deconstructed the North American media encoding of alcoholism and addiction as a nonwhite, non-middle-class epidemic. In teaching literature by Africans and by Native Americans, these teachers challenged their students to recognize and grow beyond the unexamined stereotypes that underlie so much media misinformation about addiction to alcohol and drugs.

Nancy Bazin's essay, "Alcoholism in Third-World Literature: Buchi Emecheta, Athol Fugard, and Anita Desai," and Krista Ratcliffe's essay, "A Rhetoric of Classroom Denial: Resisting Resistance to Alcohol Questions while Teaching Louise Erdrich's *Love Medicine*," interrogate simplified models of addiction. In their hands, the medical model of alcoholism is complicated by the recognition of the cultural norms of cultures other than those of white, middle-class, late twentieth-century America. Sensitive to the impact of colonizing practices on the formation of the gendered, racialized self, Bazin and Ratcliffe situate alcoholism in the texts they discuss as simultaneously a personal and as a familial and cultural practice in a hostile social environment.

As does the first section on teaching, the concluding section of the anthology examines texts and authors heretofore left out of such discussion. Continuing to push the boundaries of those texts usually included in analyses of addiction and literature, the papers in this section of the anthology examine popular as well as elite literary forms.

In “Ngaio Marsh and the ‘Drug Scene’ of Detective Fiction,” Kathryne S. McDorman analyses Marsh’s focus on drug addiction in context of the genre of detective fiction, a form in which plot not characterization predominates. Using the lens of social and political history, this essay contextualizes the cultural differences between British and American views of narcotics addiction. An intertextual comment on Nancy Bazin’s analysis, McDorman’s essay suggests that in Marsh’s fiction all addicts and pushers are marked as “Other,” as people of color or foreign born, definitively not British. Noting this, McDorman demonstrates that British international antidrug police alliances may be illuminated by reference to British colonial ties. As does Bazin’s and Ratcliffe’s essay, this one also expands the model of addiction, placing an individual’s use in context of the social circumstances sustaining of narcotics addiction. Elaborating on the question of the similarities and differences between drug and alcohol addiction, the essay points to a form of cultural denial certainly on view in North American media constructions of drug addiction: alcoholism appears “benign” in context of drug addiction.

“To Keep from Shaking to Pieces,” by Sandra Norton, investigates the presentation of the narrator in James Baldwin’s classic short story, “Sonny’s Blues.” Arguing that the narrator’s obdurate self-protective inability to hear his brother’s suffering and the underlying causes of his addiction, the essay connects itself to the arguments of Lawrence Driscoll and Edward J. Khantzian, which also model a way to listen to the voices of addiction while not entering into addiction. Norton’s essay establishes a metanarrative that hopes to speak to a combined “us.” Not all readers may find themselves included in this interpretive community, for Norton risks the possibility that some will find that her methodology practices rather than eschews appropriation. Strategically, her essay mimics the intent of Baldwin’s story: she seeks a listening reader just as Sonny seeks a listening heart. Just as Baldwin’s short story refuses to sentimentalize addiction, but instead, deconstructs the stereotypical view of the African American male, particularly the African American male jazz and blues musician, so Norton's essay models reader identification with Sonny's suffering by making sense of it as similar to the life experiences of all readers who have been hurt, or suffered losses, or been afraid to acknowledge or share their deepest feelings and experiences.

Jeffrey Oxford's essay, "Alcoholic Implications: A Catalyst of Valencian Culture," examines Vicente Blasco Ibáñez's naturalistic fiction from the combined perceptive of the medical model of alcoholism and the recognition of the cultural construction of drinking. This doubled rereading deepens characterization and theme in Blasco Ibáñez's fiction. Frequently compared to Zola, Blasco Ibáñez's perspective on the force of alcohol in class struggle is a tragic one. He reminds readers of the complex presentation by the middle class of the European working class as always-already alcoholics and drug addicts, a perspective interrogated by Franzwa's arguments that note the current North American popular cultural denials of the differences between the poor and the wealthy addict and alcoholic.

From the international perspective of the preceding essays, the concluding essays take on additional resonance. Matts Djos' essay, "John Berryman's Testimony of Alcoholism through the Looking Glass of Poetry and the Henry Persona," analyzes the harsh and colloquial utterances voiced by Berryman's Henry persona. Arguing that Berryman's attempts to achieve sobriety through the 12 Steps of Alcoholics Anonymous encourage a critic's use of that material as a frame of reference, Djos analyses the Henry persona's poetic form and his self-hating self-division with reference to AA studies of the alcoholic personality. Scrutinizing the poetic conventions of the dramatic monologue from the point of view of AA's definition of alcoholism, Djos seems to underline Ben Adams' arguments that insist on the complexity of the AA construction of the disease model of alcoholism.

Additionally, these concluding essays of the volume highlight the relation of gender to discourses of alcoholism and addiction. "The Barnes Complex: Ernest Hemingway, Djuna Barnes, *The Sun Also Rises* and *Nightwood*" by Ellen Lansky challenges the feminist and media dismissals of the concept of codependence as merely another means to blame women rather than a useful method by which to analyze women's complex behaviors. Lansky deepens the use of the medical model of addiction because her essay interrogates gendered views of dependence. In doing so, her work suggests that the predictable behaviors resulting from alcoholism, as read by the medical model, rather than conventional sexuality animate Hemingway and Barnes' intertextual alliances. Her insightful explanations of codependency deepens from another vantage Stephen C. Infantino's investigation of female sexual desire in classical French texts.

Jane Lilienfeld's "'I Could Drink a Quarter-Barrel to the Pitching': The Mayor of Casterbridge Viewed as an Alcoholic" historicizes alcoholism in Thomas Hardy's family, in his social and historical milieu and its fictionalization in the novel that many critics view as one of Hardy's finest (Millgate, 269). Michael Henchard's behavior and feelings about himself and his difficult, complicated relationships to those on whom he depends are not tangential to his alcoholism, Lilienfeld argues, but are manifestations of it. This view of alcoholism as a unified yet many-faceted series of inchoate thinking and feeling states, of unconscious choices and responses to those unwilled choices, and of the intense suffering such an illness brings illustrates the biopsychosocial definition of alcoholism. The essay demonstrates that the AA model is not the only one, or even the most useful one, for an analysis of the disease of alcoholism as depicted in literature. As such, the essay refers back to the divergent, complex readings of the texts analyzed in the present collection, thus interrogating the dependence of literary criticism on a simplified construction of alcoholism.

Varied discourses of alcoholism and addiction structure the essays in this volume. From an international perspective that does not privilege whiteness, the essays in this volume also deconstruct the North American media's racialized constructions of alcoholism and addiction. Although few solutions are offered to the questions echoing throughout the discourse of addiction and literature, the questions raised and the intertextual resonances from these divergent texts enlarge the readers' awareness of how one might understand alcoholism and addiction as they are created in literature.

BIBLIOGRAPHY

Alcoholics Anonymous: The Story of How Many Thousands of Men and Women Have Recovered from Alcoholism. 3rd ed. New York: Alcoholics Anonymous World Services, Inc., 1976.

Barrows, Susanna and Robin Room. "Introduction." *Drinking: Behavior and Belief in Modern History.* Ed. Susanna Barrows and Robin Room. Berkeley: University of California Press, 1991. Pp. 1–29.

Bazin, Nancy T. "Teaching about Addiction in English Classes, a Response." The Prose and Poetry of Addiction, Stigma and Symbol Panel. Midwest Modern Language Association Convention. St. Louis, MO. November 3, 1998.

Bean, Margaret. "Denial and the Psychological Complications of Alcoholism." *Dynamic Approaches to the Treatment and Understanding of Alcoholism.* Ed. Margaret Bean and Norman Zinberg. New York: Free Press, 1981. Pp. 55–97.

Bean, Margaret and Norman Zinberg, eds. *Dynamic Approaches to the Treatment and Understanding of Alcoholism.* New York: Free Press, 1981.

Bertram, Eva and Kenneth Sharpe. "The Drug War's Phony Fix: Why Certification Doesn't Work." *The Nation.* April 28, 1997. Pp. 18–22.

Bleich, David. *Know and Tell: A Writing Pedagogy of Disclosure, Genre, and Membership.* Westport, CT: Heinemann, Boynton/Cook, 1998.

Chaudron, C. D. and D. A. Wilkinson, eds. *Theories on Alcoholism.* Toronto: Addiction Research Foundation, 1988.

Crowley, John. *The White Logic: Alcohol and Gender in American Modernist Fiction.* Amherst: University of Massachusetts Press, 1994.

Dardis, Tom. *The Thirsty Muse: Alcohol and the American Writer.* New York: Ticknor & Fields, 1989.

Fetterly, Judith. *The Resisting Reader: A Feminist Approach to American Fiction.* Bloomington: Indiana University Press, 1977.

Frye, Robert Vaughn. "A Multimodality Approach to the Treatment of Addiction." *The Addictions: Multidisciplinary Perspectives and Treatments.* Eds. Harvey B. Milkman and Howard J. Shaffer. Lexington, KY: D. C. Heath and Co., 1985. Pp. 175–82.

Gilmore, Thomas B. *Equivocal Spirits: Alcoholism and Drinking in Twentieth-Century Literature.* Chapel Hill: University of North Carolina Press, 1987.

Godfrey, Christine and Alan Maynard. "An Economic Theory of Alcohol Consumption and Abuse." *Theories on Alcoholism.* Ed. C. D. Chaudron and D. A. Wilkinson. Toronto: Addiction Research Foundation, 1988. Pp. 411–35.

Goodwin, Donald. *Alcohol and the Writer.* New York: Penguin, 1988.

Gusfield, Joseph R. *Contested Meanings: The Construction of Alcohol Problems.* Madison: University of Wisconsin Press, 1996.

Heath, Dwight B. "Emerging Anthropological Theory and Models of Alcohol Use and Alcoholism." *Theories on Alcoholism.* Ed. C. D. Chaudron and D. A. Wilkinson. Toronto: Addiction Research Foundation, 1988. Pp. 353–410.

Hirshey, Gerry. "Happy [] Day to You." *The New York Times Magazine.* July 2, 1995. Pp. 20–27, 34, 43–45.

Johnston, Lloyd, Patrick M. O'Malley, and Jerald G. Bachman. *National Survey Results on Drug Use from the Monitoring the Future Study, 1975–1995.* Volume 1, Secondary School Students. U.S. Department of Health and Human Services. Washington, DC: GPO, 1996.

——. *National Survey Results on Drug Use from the Monitoring the Future Study, 1975–1994.* Volume II, College Students and Young Adults. U.S. Department of Health and Human Services. Washington, DC: GPO, 1996.

Khantzian, Edward J. "Some Treatment Implications of the Ego and Self Disturbances in Alcoholism." *Dynamic Approaches to the Treatment and Understanding of Alcoholism.* Ed. Margaret Bean and Norman Zinberg. New York: Free Press, 1981. Pp. 163–88.

Lanza, Joseph. *The Cocktail: The Influence of Spirits on the American Psyche.* New York: St. Martin's, 1995.

Levin, Jerome David. *Introduction to Alcoholism Counseling: A Bio-Psycho-Social Approach.* 2nd ed. Washington, DC: Taylor & Francis, 1995.

McDowell, Deborah E. "A Brief History of Autobiography." Review of *When Memory Speaks: Reflections on Autobiography,* by Jill Ker Conway. *The New York Times Book Review.* April 19, 1998. P. 14.

McGoldrick, Monica. "Irish Families." *Ethnicity and Family Therapy.* Ed. Monica McGoldrick, John Pearce, and Joseph Giordano. New York: Guilford, 1982. Pp. 310–39.

Miller, Norman M. and John N. Chappel. "History of the Disease Concept." *Psychiatric Annals.* 21.4 (April, 1991). Pp. 196–205.

Millgate, Michael. *Thomas Hardy: A Biography.* New York: Random House, 1982.

Milligan, Barry. *Pleasures and Pains: Opium and Orient in Nineteenth-Century British Culture.* Charlottesville: University of Virginia Press, 1995.

Newlove, Donald. *Those Drinking Days: Myself and Other Writers.* New York: McGraw-Hill, 1981.

Plato. *Ion.* Tr. Lane Cooper. *The Critical Tradition: Classical Texts and Contemporary Trends.* 2nd ed. Ed. David Richter. New York: Bedford Books, 1998. Pp. 29–37.

Reed, Ishmael. "Bigger and O. J." *Birth of a Nation'hood: Gaze, Script, and Spectacle in the O. J. Simpson Case.* Ed. Toni Morrison and Claudia Brodsky Lacour. New York: Pantheon, 1997. Pp. 169–95.

Schweickart, Patrocinio. "Reading Ourselves: Toward a Feminist Theory of Reading." *Gender and Reading: Essays on Readers, Texts, and Contexts.* Ed. Elizabeth A. Flynn and Patrocinio Schweickart. Baltimore: Hopkins University Press, 1996. Pp. 31–62.

Single, Eric W. "The Availability Theory of Alcohol-Related Problems." Ed. C. D. Chaudron, and D. A. Wilkinson. *Theories on Alcoholism.* Toronto: Addiction Research Foundation, 1988. Pp. 325–51.

Sournia, Jean-Charles. *A History of Alcoholism.* Tr. Nick Hindley and Gareth Stanton. London: Basil Blackwell, 1990.

Vaillant, George. *The Natural History of Alcoholism: Causes, Patterns, and Paths to Recovery.* Cambridge, MA: Harvard University Press, 1983.

———. *The Natural History of Alcoholism Revisited.* Cambridge, MA: Harvard University Press, 1995.

Zinberg, Norman and Margaret Bean. "Introduction." Ed. Margaret Bean and Norman Zinberg. *Dynamic Approaches to the Treatment and Understanding of Alcoholism.* New York: Free Press, 1981. Pp. 1–35.

Part I

Theories of Addiction

CHAPTER 1

THE ALCOHOLIC WRITER BY ANY OTHER NAME

Roger Forseth

THE LITERARY REPRESENTATIONS OF THE CULTURE of drink take many forms. In his poem "Wine," Raymond Carver wrote that Alexander the Great, "after / a long night of carousing, a wine-drunk (the worst kind of drunk— / hangovers you don't forget), threw the first brand / to start a fire that burned Persepolis" (32). We know that Carver was an alcoholic because he said so. Was Alexander? To ask the question, let alone answer it, is to confront its complexity.

Alcohol abuse is a behavioral disorder; whether it is also a moral defect, a disease, or a joke depends not only on the individual doing the describing but also on the culture within which that description takes place. More than a version of scholastic nominalism is involved here for the use, and abuse, of alcohol is a deeply embedded cultural practice. The British, for example, don't wish to label a chronic drinker an alcoholic because this disease-label might deprive him of his pub culture. The French don't think it is polite to describe a person as an alcoholic, no matter what the circumstances—especially if he or she is an intellectual. In America and the Scandinavian countries, on the other hand, "alcoholic" is the proper term, if preceded by such adjectives as "recovering" or "hopeless."

This pluralistic Babel, combined with a general resistance on the part of critics and biographers to the finality of the "alcoholic" designation, has resulted in considerable critical confusion.

It is—to me—a fascinating confusion, for out of it has come progressively sophisticated discussions of both artist and art. A case in point is the highly productive Literature and Addiction Conference, which was held at the University of Sheffield in 1991. A wide-ranging international gathering, it presented at once the rich potential of addiction studies and a rush of often contradictory ideas concerning the critical and scholarly inquiries into the subject. At one point in the conference, for instance, after a somewhat uproarious—and creative—exchange about the use of the word "alcoholic" (such as, "You Americans have to label every little thing!"), I asked Jean-Charles Sournia, vice president of the French government's Commission on Alcohol and author of *A History of Alcoholism,* why the French, as he had asserted, avoided the "alcoholic" label. His answer: "Because we French don't think it a nice thing to do." That is a culturally rich statement: not an act of psychological denial, but an observation drawn from the courtesy books, an assertion that etiquette overrides the clinic. Indeed, one reality displaces another reality, for in the world of alcohol consumption—both historically and geographically—there are more things in heaven and earth, Horatio, than are dreamt of in *The Diagnostic and Statistical Manual of the American Psychiatric Association.*

Theoretical or universalized speculations, then, on alcoholism, creativity, and literature are at the present time problematic. Clinical and cultural models of alcohol abuse are not designed to be the same, but perhaps in the present state of the art there is a distinction without a difference; behavioral disorders simply do not remain static long enough to be scientifically defined. Yet there is at least one notion that is a potentially unifying cultural theory: the idea of "denial."

The tendency now is to put the term "denial" in quotation marks, since, with the proliferation of 12-step programs accompanied by a vulgarized jargon, to be "in denial" has become, for all practical purposes, the normal human condition. Lost in this psycho babbling is the insight that denial, as Anna Freud demonstrated, may be a powerful and overriding defense mechanism of survival. Though Freud has as her particular objective the explication of the various means children employ to defend their mental integrity or psychic peace or simply their sanity, her ideas also have striking explanatory power in the analysis of alcohol abuse in a cultural context. She observes, for example, in *The Ego and the Mechanisms of Defense:*

> In [the] struggle to preserve its own existence unchanged the ego is motivated equally by objective anxiety and anxiety of conscience and employs indiscriminately all the methods of defense to which it has ever had recourse in infancy and during the latency period. It represses, displaces, denies, and reverses the instincts and turns them against the self; it produces phobias and hysterical symptoms and binds anxiety by means of obsessional thinking and behavior. (147)

Anna Freud's psychoanalysis of childish deviance bears a striking resemblance to the behavior of adults when faced with drunkenness, which itself often manifests as childishness. Since the complexities of art and therefore of the artist directly contradict the simplicities of children, it is understandable that we tend to repress, displace, deny, and reverse the irrationalities of intoxication that are plainly before us.

Denial like survival, appears in a number of shapes, some of them creative and all of them complex. In a recent article in the *Wall Street Journal* titled, "Fatal Attraction / How Sex and Drugs Brutally Ripped apart Hot Hollywood Team / Troubled Don Simpson Split with 'Top Gun' Partner, Then Was Found Dead / Heidi Fleiss at the Memorial," an account of a alcohol/drug/sex-induced "flame-out" of a prominent Hollywood producer, it was observed that Simpson "became consumed by the darker, more dangerous side of life. The demons that helped destroy him, some friends think, may have been responsible for his success" (King and Lippman, A1). The connection between "darker . . . dangerous . . . destroy" and "success" has been with us at least since Dionysos and Icarus, and embedded in this connection is the Phoenix bird: creation rising from fire—or, in this case, a "flame-out." Denial—or at least the rationalization—of destruction, then, becomes necessary to art. Booze causes great poems. This line of thinking, at any rate, is richly illustrated in the histories of a multitude of writers, regardless of their cultural origins.

Jack London, for instance, in spite of ample evidence to the contrary, believed alcohol presented him with only moderate difficulties. He wrote *John Barleycorn*—judged "one of the most moving and dramatic histories of the making of an alcoholic in the literature of drinking" (Anderson, 50) and at the same time recognized as "a classic study of the drinker in denial" (Crowley, 20)—after an extended cruise that he took in order to dry out. Yet London was convinced he was not an alcoholic. Furthermore, as John W. Crowley points out in his study of *John Barleycorn,* "[t]rue believers in Jack London have taken him at his word. The mere suggestion that their hero was an alcoholic is fiercely resisted by the London cult, a band of literary devotees both inside and outside the academy" (20). London managed to convince himself, through a tortured definition of "dipsomania," that *real* alcohol addiction was somebody else's failing, for to admit to such an affliction would be to admit to an unacceptable weakness of character. Rather, alcohol for London the artist instilled a Nietzschean power: "Through the necromancy of John Barleycorn, London's values undergo a comprehensive transvaluation as he gains an occult knowledge undreamt of in the philosophy of his conventional upbringing" (Crowley, 31). Through booze, then, the manly, two-fisted drinker is transformed into an aesthete. And London's devotees aren't subjected to the confusion of literature with pathology.

In the world of drink, if Jack London was the first of the modernists, Evelyn Waugh was the last of the Victorians. As John Bayley put it, he "was in the great tradition of English eccentrics and Victorian follies" (3). In Great Britain, of course, odd behavior by people of Waugh's position is customarily described as "eccentric," never as "crazy." There is a kind of spiritual secretiveness in Waugh's use of drugs and alcohol that reminds one of the Victorian pornographers, a created world of vivid, prurient indirection. Thomas B. Gilmore, in his chapter on Waugh in his *Equivocal Spir-*

its: Alcoholism and Drinking in Twentieth-Century Literature, concludes that "although at some periods of his life Evelyn Waugh was certainly a heavy drinker, I am not convinced that he is an alcoholic" (17). Now, it's true that George Eliot did not have to be a man in order to create Daniel Deronda, nor did Henry James require a sex-change to give us Isabel Archer; but the author of *The Ordeal of Gilbert Pinfold* and *Brideshead Revisited* was surely coming from rich experience. Pinfold's "ordeal" is an addiction to bromides, that is, bromide psychosis or "bromism," and the author's clinically accurate description of this form of addiction is so detailed and precise that Pinfold would be "useful in the education of psychiatrists and neurologists" (Hurst and Hurst, 263). And, as Gilmore demonstrates, Waugh's depiction of the terrifying physical and spiritual dimensions of Sebastian Flyte's alcoholism in *Brideshead* is one of the more powerful of such creations in literature. Waugh did not get his material from a book. It can be argued that in his time, social class, and culture he was not perceived as an addict or alcoholic, but now he would have some difficulty staying clear of Hazelden or Betty Ford.

If in America the defense against the "alcoholism" label is bluster, and in England it is rationalization, in France it is nationalized defiance. In his essay on Simenon in *Alcohol and the Writer,* Donald W. Goodwin tells a story of a French alcoholic describing himself:

> My name is Pierre. I am not an alcoholic. I do not know alcoholics. There are no alcoholics in France, except tourists.
>
> I have drunk wine since I was a child. Wine is good for you. I drink it with meals and when I am thirsty. Since I was a young man, I have drunk three or four liters of wine every day. I also enjoy an occasional aperitif, especially on Sunday mornings and after work. I never drink more than this. I have no problems from alcohol.
>
> Once, when I was in the Army, no wine was permitted. I started shaking all over and thought bugs were crawling on me. I think it was the Army food. My doctor says my liver is too large. My father and grandfather had large livers. It probably means nothing. (Goodwin, 93–94)

That among the French denial of a drinking problem is more a cultural than a class phenomenon is suggested by a glance at the alcoholic behavior of those celebrity intellectuals Jean-Paul Sartre and Simone de Beauvoir, who, one senses, without much modification could adopt Pierre's resignation to the side effects of the National Beverage.

Alcohol and drug abuse permeated their lives, though it was not until their last years that they paid the price. In her memoir of Sartre, Beauvoir writes of him shortly before his death:

> [O]ne Sunday morning at the beginning of March Arlette [Elkaim, Sartre's adopted daughter] found [Sartre] lying on his bedroom floor with a terrible hangover. We learned that he got his various young women, who knew nothing of the danger, to bring him bottles of whiskey and vodka. He hid them in a chest or behind books. That Saturday evening . . . he had got drunk. Arlette and I emptied the hiding places, I telephoned the young women asking them not to bring any more alcohol, and I scolded Sartre vehemently. . . . I could not understand the return of this passion for drinking. It did not square with his apparent mental balance. He put my questions aside, laughing. "But you're fond of drinking too," he said. (118)

Beauvoir appears here properly solicitous and protective, which under the circumstances was her defense mechanism. Her biographer Deirdre Bair tells of visiting Beauvoir when, having normalized her morning with vodka, Beauvoir demurely poured Scotch for the both of them. Five years later, Beauvoir was dead, of cirrhosis. Beauvoir said she learned many things from Sartre but, clearly, one of them was not how dangerous drinking can be.

Americans, the English, and the French each have their characteristic ways of handling and depicting heavy drinking, its inspirations, and its consequences, but when it comes to the archetypical cultural stereotype, the Celt reigns supreme, and none more so than the Welsh Dylan Thomas. His death was caused, in the poetic words of his autopsy report, by an alcohol-induced "[i]nsult to the brain" (FitzGibbon, 345–46), a description that is, in Thomas' biographer Constantine FitzGibbon's words, "equally meaningless in

British and in American medical parlance" (346). Just as poetically, Donald Hall called Thomas' end a "public suicide." Both phrases convey a mythic if not a clinical truth that has become an established part of literary folklore, and Thomas' flamboyant death caused a cultural commotion of the first magnitude. Indeed, I have my own memories—two of them.

The first was a reading Thomas gave at Northwestern University in the spring of 1952. A teacher of mine at Northwestern, the Joyce biographer Richard Ellmann, had the interesting responsibility of fetching Thomas from a New York-to-Chicago club car and, after numerous saloon stops, delivering him to the University in shape to perform. Ellmann told me that by a miracle he did so, and Thomas, only mildly drunk, held forth with such flair that I was instantly convinced that poetry and booze were one. A second memory is of an event at the 1953 Modern Language Association meeting shortly after Thomas died. I was in a hotel room with a group including the Chicago critic R. S. Crane, who was in a rage: "Those New York people killed Dylan, and Elder is writing a book about it!" (Elder Olson, another Chicago critic, did publish a critical work on Thomas the next year.) What stands out for me now in these recollections is the way the drinking was deflected by the melodrama so brilliantly on display: Dionysos in work and play.

We American scholars were, at that moment, so mesmerized by the arts of language and performance that we denied or ignored the terrible cost, or repeated, without much understanding, from *Lord Jim:* "In the destructive element immerse!" But we were not the only ones. Thomas' benefactor,

> Margaret Taylor, who saw him drunk and sober often enough insist[ed] that he was not an alcoholic; "he drank very heavily, but that is quite different. . . . Call him a drunk . . . but not an alcoholic." Caitlin [Thomas], asked on television in 1975 what effect drink had on her husband, seemed to be saying much the same thing when she replied, "It ruined him, of course. He'd have been a marvelous old man now if someone had snatched the booze

> away from him. I don't think he was even keen on the booze. It was just the company and the life and the weakness. (Ferris, 190)

To those for whom the defense of reputation is the ultimate mechanism, survival itself must give way: to be called an alcoholic is literally a fate worse than death.

In his tragedy, however, Dylan Thomas was not spared his farce. On the 40th anniversary of his death, the *New York Times* reported, "a retired Welsh clergyman, who had married Miss Piggy and Kermit the frog in one of the Muppet movies, and a waiter read the dead man's poems at his favorite table at the White Horse Tavern" (Kaufman, A15).

John Berryman was the only person present at Dylan Thomas' death bed, that final act of the "public suicide." Two decades later Berryman took his own life. At his death he left an unpublished essay on Thomas, written in 1959. Berryman writes that he had been invited by William Butler Yeats to the Athenaeum, but, having spent the afternoon beforehand drinking with Thomas, "I was too drunk to go to tea with the great man at his famous club" (13). It is a remarkably clearheaded essay, Berryman commenting that "[r]eminiscences of Dylan Thomas have centred grossly upon his boozing," (13) but

> [i]t must be remembered . . . that his weaknesses were often played on in order to get him into positions where he could be insulted with impunity; liquor was poured into him, and women not only threw themselves at him but were sometimes encouraged to do so by their academic husbands—I have myself seen this happen. (14)

Berryman could well have been writing about himself. Unlike Thomas, however, Berryman fought a heroic if losing battle against his alcoholism, a struggle that he related in his unfinished novel, *Recovery.*

Berryman had on occasion startling insight into his affliction. In the Berryman archives at the University of Minnesota is a manuscript titled *Third Alcoholic Treatment,* a "summary & deluded account of the beginning of my recovery." "Alcoholism," he wrote,

> produces inevitably what are known as "sincere delusions." A sincere delusion is a lie—an affective deformation of reality—which the liar does not know to be a lie. . . . His delusion is shared in some degree by that part of his society which is concerned with his welfare. (MSS 43, Box 1)

As Thomas B. Gilmore points out, there was a part of Berryman that never gave up the conviction that alcohol was a creative necessity (132–34), but his profound ambivalence suggests that his defense mechanisms, his "sincere delusions," were approaching dissolution.

Berryman's quest for serenity tragically failed, yet that failed quest raises the question: Was the attempt itself doomed? Is art after alcohol impossible? Or is there a Muse of Serenity? This is a subject for another inquiry, but the answers are starting to come in. In response to an interviewer's question, "Did you ever feel that alcohol was in any way an inspiration?" Raymond Carver said, "My God, no!" (Plimpton, 311). And Ivan Gold has written a wonderful novel, *Sams in a Dry Season,* about the addiction and recovery of a "shicker," a Jewish alcoholic—yes, they exist!—who has more defenses that the Maginot Line.

The alcoholic mechanism of "denial" has as many incarnations as Poseidon: it is the fifth master trope that Kenneth Burke forgot to mention. And as I discovered to my dismay, it appears in the most unexpected places. I recently published an article in which I declared that *Sams in a Dry Season* was emotionally complete at the point where Jason Sams admits his alcoholism and joins Alcoholics Anonymous. I added, "The final section of the novel, an account of this developing fellowship, is instructive but aesthetically unnecessary; we know where Jason's headed" (Forseth 24). Upon reading the essay, Ivan Gold wrote me, "I disagree somewhat with your thoughts about where my book should have ended, but understand why the Paradiso would seem (and be) less gripping than the Inferno." His comment set me to thinking: I haven't had a drink in twenty years, but it would seem some part of me would still prefer to dwell in chaos than in heaven. One more time, blindsided by booze!

BIBLIOGRAPHY

Anderson, Dwight. *The Other Side of the Bottle*. New York: A. A. Wyn, 1950.

Bair, Deirdre. *Simone de Beauvoir*. New York: Summit, 1990.

Barrows, Susanna and Robin Room, eds. *Drinking: Behavior and Belief in Modern History*. Berkeley: University of California Press, 1991.

Bayley, John. "The Black Wizard's Spell: Waugh's Self Justification through Art." *The Times Literary Supplement*. April 24, 1992. P. 3.

Beauvoir, Simone de. *Adieux: A Farewell to Sartre*. Tr. Patrick O'Brian. New York: Pantheon, 1984.

———. *Quiet Moments in a War: The Letters of Jean-Paul Sartre to Simone de Beauvoir, 1940–1963*. New York: Scribner, 1994.

Berryman, John. "After Many a Summer: Memories of Dylan Thomas." *The Times Literary Supplement*. September 3, 1993. P. 13.

———. MSS 43, Box 1, "Loose File." "Recovery Notes, Drafts, Reviews." John Berryman Papers, University of Minnesota Libraries Manuscript Division.

Brinnin, John Malcolm. *Dylan Thomas in America*. Boston: Little, Brown, 1955.

Burgess, Anthony. "The Writer as Drunk." *Urgent Copy: Literary Studies*. New York: Norton, 1968. Pp. 88–92.

Carver, Raymond. "Wine," *A New Path to the Waterfall*. New York: Atlantic Monthly Press, 1989. Pp. 32.

Cochrane, Hamilton E. "'Taking the Cure': Alcoholism and Recovery in the Fiction of Raymond Carver." *University of Dayton Review* 20.1 (Summer 1989). Pp. 79–88.

Crowley, John W. *The White Logic: Alcoholism and Gender in American Modernist Fiction*. Amherst: University of Massachusetts Press, 1994.

Ferris, Paul. *Dylan Thomas*. New York: Dial, 1977.

———. *The Life of Caitlin Thomas*. North Pomfret, VT: Pimlico/Trafalgar Square, 1995.

FitzGibbon, Constantine. *The Life of Dylan Thomas*. Boston: Atlantic Little Brown, 1965.

———. "Ye Olde Englishe Pubbe." *Drink*. Garden City, NY: Doubleday, 1979. Pp. 54–60.

Forseth, Roger. "Alcohol, Disease, and the Limitations of Artistic Representation." *Dionysos* 5.3 (Winter 1994). P. 24.

———. "Symposia as Ritual and Disease." *Dionysos* 4.2 (Fall 1992). Pp. 40–45.

Francis, Claude and Fernande Gontier. *Simone de Beauvoir.* New York: St. Martin's, 1987.

Freud, Anna. *The Ego and the Mechanisms of Defense, Vol. II, The Writings of Anna Freud.* Tr. Cecil Baines. Madison, CT: International Universities Press, 1966.

Gilmore, Thomas B. *Equivocal Spirits: Alcoholism and Drinking in Twentieth-Century Literature.* Chapel Hill: University of North Carolina Press, 1987.

Gold, Ivan. Personal letter to the author. November 10, 1991.

———. *Sams in a Dry Season.* Boston: Houghton Mifflin/Seymour Lawrence, 1990.

Goodwin, Donald W. *Alcohol and the Writer.* Kansas City, MO: Andrews and McMeel, 1988.

Hall, Donald. *Remembering Poets: Reminiscences and Opinions.* New York: Harper & Row, 1978.

Harman, Ronald. *Sartre.* New York: Simon & Schuster, 1987.

Heather, Nick and Ian Robertson. *Controlled Drinking.* London: Methuen, 1983.

Hurst, Daniel L. and Mary Jane Hurst. "Bromide Psychosis: A Literary Case Study." *Clinical Neuropharmacology* 7 (1984). P. 263.

Kaufman, Michael T. "The Light That Raged and Died." The *New York Times.* November 10, 1993. P. A15.

Kelly, Richard J. and Alan K. Lathrop, ed. *Recovering Berryman: Essays on a Poet.* Ann Arbor: University of Michigan Press, 1993.

King, Thomas R. and John Lippman. "Fatal Attraction," The *Wall Street Journal.* January 26, 1996. Pp. Al, A4.

O'Brien, John Maxwell. *Alexander the Great: The Invisible Enemy. A Biography.* London: Routledge, 1992.

Peschel, Enid, ed. *Yale French Studies: Intoxication and Literature* 50 (1974).

Plimpton, George and John Updike, eds. "Raymond Carver." *Writers at Work: The Paris Review Interviews. Seventh Series.* New York: Viking, 1986.

Rudgley, Richard. *Essential Substances: A Cultural History of Intoxicants in Society.* New York: Kodansha International, 1994.

Schierse Leonard, Linda. *Witness to the Fire: Creativity and the Veil of Addiction.* Boston: Shambala, 1990.

Shapiro, Karl. "Dylan Thomas." *In Defense of Ignorance.* New York: Vintage, 1960. Pp. 171–86.

Sournia, Jean-Charles. *A History of Alcoholism.* Tr. Nick Hindley and Gareth Stanton. Oxford: Blackwell, 1990.

Tremlett, George. *Dylan Thomas: In the Mercy of His Means*. New York: St. Martin's, 1991.

Vice, Sue, Matthew Campbell, and Tim Armstrong, eds. *Beyond the Pleasure Dome: Writing and Addiction from the Romantics*. Sheffield: Sheffield Academic Press, 1994.

Wakefield, Dan. *New York in the 50s*. Boston: Houghton Mifflin/Seymour Lawrence, 1992.

CHAPTER 2

ARISTOTLE AND THE LANGUAGE OF ADDICTION

Gregg Franzwa

THE LANGUAGE OF ADDICTION IN CONTEMPORARY North American culture has been popularly co-opted to a variety of ends. The medical industry has used the language to promote both chemical and behavioral treatments for a number of different sorts of behaviors labeled "addictive." The self-help industry, through both print and electronic media, has saturated the marketplace with a multitude of different applications of addiction language and nonprescription remedies, the newest entry I know of is "Internet Addiction." And finally, government officials have been using the language for decades promoting various "wars on drugs."

If we were to try to isolate the motives behind these sorts of uses of addiction language we would, I think, discover them to be primarily economic and political. There is, after all, a mind boggling amount of money involved in the various facets of drug addiction alone. But it is not the philosopher's central occupation to examine the motivations behind the actual uses to which various languages are put. Rather the philosopher's project is to reveal and critique the logic of the concepts purportedly expressed through language.

My central purpose will thus be to reveal and examine the deepest assumptions and implications of the language of addiction as it is currently used in North American culture. I will argue that there is a significant cleft in the concept of addiction that results in a systematic ambiguity in the language involved. Most broadly that cleft can be identified as a division between scientific and religious theories of human behavior. This division has been identified by many before in general terms; I will explore it in particular reference to addiction. In doing so I will appeal to Aristotle, the earliest Western thinker to speak to the topic. Using his *Nicomachean Ethics,* I will isolate four different plausible explanations for what we call addictive behavior and attempt to show that none is reducible to the others. And, thus, the apparent duality in contemporary addiction language in fact masks a pair of dualities that complicate these ambiguities further. Finally, I will conclude with a discussion of some of the obfuscating consequences of these ambiguities for the societal debate about addiction and the appropriate responses to it.

According to the *Oxford English Dictionary,* the history of the term "addiction" goes back to the sixteenth century. Originally it was a legal term, having to do with the surrender of something by order of a judge. This evolved into a more general notion of surrendering oneself to some pursuit or being a devotee or habitual practitioner of some activity. The 1971 edition of the *Oxford English Dictionary* does not, however, cite a meaning having to do with the physiological dimension that has come to be part of the term's current meaning.

The present cleft in the meaning of the term in the United States dates back to nineteenth-century medicine and the Temperance Movement. At that time a number of scientific models of behavior appeared that suggested a purely causal, physiological account of addiction. But at the same time the Temperance Movement relied on an older moral model of addiction, mainly to drink, as sin. Nineteenth-century revival meetings, prefiguring some aspects of AA, included drunkards standing to make public confessions and vows of abstinence before the Higher Power. These two historical forces provide the dualistic backdrop for the current uses of addiction language, most of which fall under either the "sin" or "sickness" models (Peele, 38–46).

As "addiction" is currently employed in North American culture I would suggest a definition in terms of two other words with a recently evolved meaning: "dysfunctional dependency." As this phrase is currently used, it refers to behavioral syndromes that act to fulfill needs at the cost of the overall functional success of the agent/patient. This definition, I will maintain, picks out the set of things we intuitively think of as addictive and is neutral with respect to the sin and sickness models. It does so by leaving ambiguous the connection between a need and its fulfilling behavior. If the need functions as a reason for choosing the behavior then the moral and related language of choice seem appropriate. But if the need simply causes the action then the scientific language of causal laws is primarily relevant. Under the first explanation the addict is an agent, with reason, will, and culpability. Under the second he or she is a patient, determined by forces independent of will and reason, a victim of disease. These explanations separate the sin and sickness models in both logic and semantics. Sin is simply not a relevant concept in the scientific account of behavior. Likewise, the notion of physiological sickness is not important to the religious account. Yet the concept of dysfunctional dependency can be defined in both terms, and can be used to refer to behaviors from the fully voluntary to the most physiologically compulsive. Using this concept thus allows for the discussion of various addictive behaviors free of the assumptions and connotations of either model.

The tension between the sin and sickness models has emerged full-blown in the twentieth century. But the conceptual roots of the distinction are in fact very old ones, dating to a time long before the advent of what we think of as science and even predating Christianity. The classical Greek thinkers discussed these ideas but without the theoretical assumptions of contemporary science or religion. Aristotle stands out among those thinkers in presenting a remarkably thorough treatment of the relevant concepts. Without scientific or religious axes to grind, he surveys the relevant patterns of human behavior from his rational, naturalist perspective.

In that survey he isolates four conceptually distinct explanations of behaviors we could call dysfunctional dependencies. He endorses none of them as the single "right" explanation, but recognizes the conceptual differences between them. I will express his distinctions in the language of the Ross translation of the *Nicomachean Ethics* as follows: the self-indulgent person, the incontinent person, the physically ill or damaged person, and the badly habituated person.

Aristotle defines the four types and compares them as to the appropriateness of blame and the possibility of change. He does so in the context of his account of the good life for humans. Broadly summarizing, the good life for Aristotle is one that is active, healthy, rational, and virtuous. It is happiness that all people seek, he believes, and the closest that people come to happiness is in rationally planned lives filled with activities, performed with skill and moderation. In his view physical, mental, and moral health are closely related, with none a prerequisite to the others. The four conceptions of "addictive" behavior thus represent several varieties of failure in achieving happiness.

Two of the core notions in Aristotle's view of human behavior are those of "moral virtue" (*ethikos*) and "habit" (*ethos*), the former having derived its meaning from the latter. The virtues and vices of civilized people do not arise by nature, but are rather the product of habituation. That Aristotle means to confine his generalizations to the civilized is obvious from his frequent references to their differences from the barbarians, as well as his assertion that the study of ethics is a subfield of politics. He states that:

> by doing the things that we do in our transactions with other men we become just or unjust, and by doing the acts that we do in the presence of danger, and by being habituated to feel fear or confidence, we become brave or cowardly. The same is true of appetites and feelings of anger; some men become temperate and good-tempered, others self-indulgent and irascible, by behaving one way or the other in appropriate circumstances. . . . It makes no small difference, then, whether we form habits of one kind or another from our very youth; it makes a very great difference, or rather, all the difference. (1103b, 15–26)

Humans are by nature neither morally good nor evil; they become so through habituation. The importance of this premise cannot be overestimated. It echoes through the text of *Nicomachean Ethics* with a parallel but opposite force of the contrary assumption that begins the Judeo-Christian scriptures. Save for the ill, the injured, and the mad, our natures are not prone to corruption. Rather our moral character is a product of practice, shaped both by the environment of our upbringing and our subsequent moral choices as adults. As such, Aristotle's account includes references to both causal and rational/moral sources of behavior. Our youthful environment has causal consequences for adult behavior, yet we can still talk of the latter as voluntary and properly subject to praise and blame. But unlike the later Christian notions of absolute goodness and evil, Aristotle takes praise and blame to be appropriate in degrees, corresponding to the distinction between more and less voluntary actions.

Thus Aristotle does not posit the dichotomy of the sin and sickness models of behavior that dominate the contemporary debate about addiction. To demand that either one of these models be able to account for every sort of dysfunctional dependency is more akin to embracing an ideology than it is to offering an explanation of actual human behavior. Aristotle's account is subtle where contemporary ones are crude. To say, for example, that heroin addiction is a sin and thus always voluntary is as far from the truth as saying it is an illness and thus always involuntary. But unlike adherents to the sin model, Aristotle is not seeking salvation. And unlike the partisans of the sickness model, he is not simply seeking correlation data. He is rather seeking wisdom, a state distinct from ideology, salvation, or mere empirical knowledge.

Aristotle defines a spectrum of what we would call addictive behaviors from the most to the least blameworthy. At the most blameworthy end is the vice of self-indulgence (*akolasia*), the opposite of the virtue of temperance (*sophrosune*). Self-indulgence is blameworthy because it is the result of deliberate choice.

> the man who pursues the excesses of things pleasant, or pursues to excess necessary objects, and does so by choice, for their own sake and not at all for the sake of any result distinct from them, is self-indulgent; for such a man is of necessity unlikely to repent, and

> therefore incurable, since a man who cannot repent cannot be cured. (1150a, 18–23)

Aristotle is here developing a point he has made earlier: "to the unjust and to the self-indulgent man it was open in the beginning not to become men of this kind, and so they are unjust and self-indulgent voluntarily, but now that they have become so it is not possible for them not to be so" (1114a, 20–23).

Here Aristotle has blended the language of the sin and sickness models to recognize the cases of repeated behaviors that begin as voluntary and become less so over time. When he states that "he who cannot repent cannot be cured" he recognizes a category of behavior that neither the sin nor sickness models can individually capture. Yet it is a category that we intuitively recognize to be real, and one which, incidentally, the AA program would seem to assume. The self-indulgent person is the worst sort of addict, and the most blameworthy. The self-indulgent person engages in harmful forms of behavior without thought as to the consequences. Like the "beasts," he or she is without reason, acting on impulse for immediate pleasure or the absence of pain, caught up in vice with no desire to become virtuous. This is as far from wisdom as a person can get.

The incontinent person (*akrates*), by contrast, is not vicious and possesses rationality. He or she is simply weak in the face of temptation, yet knows what is rationally and morally good. Incontinence is blameworthy, but not to the degree of self-indulgence. An incontinent person is one who is:

> carried away as a result of passion and contrary to the right rule—a man whom passion masters so that he does not act according to the right rule, but does not master to the extent of making him ready to believe that he ought to pursue such pleasures without reserve; this is the incontinent man, who is better than the self-indulgent man, and not bad without qualification; for the best thing in him, the first principle, is preserved. (1151a, 20–26)

The "first principle" here concerns the rational, moral sense. It informs the incontinent person correctly as to the rightness and wrongness of various kinds of actions, but weakness of the will subverts it. Passion clouds reason, resulting in error. Aristotle's analysis of this error reveals an intuitive understanding of this kind of behavior. Moral decisions in his view can be expressed in the form of the following practical syllogism: "actions of kind A are wrong; to do X would be an action of type A; thus one should refrain from X." The incontinent person knows the truth of the first premise, the general rule of conduct that is the "major premise" of the argument. But the force of passion distracts the person from the truth of the "minor premise," that to do this particular X would be to commit A. So to have the "first principle" is to believe the major premise of such an argument, as the incontinent person does. But weakness of will causes the person to ignore the truth of the minor premise, thus not acting on the conclusion of the major premise. Thus, for Aristotle, the incontinent person is only "half-wicked" since his or her general moral beliefs are correct. Such a person "is not a criminal, for he does not act of malice aforethought" (1152a, 18–19).

In this way the incontinent person represents a different sort of addict than the self-indulgent. Incontinence is not born of vice, but of weakness. The incontinent person is both more curable and less morally culpable in that, unlike the self-indulgent person, he or she recognizes the truth of the major premise of the moral argument in question. It is just that his or her passions are too strong. Aristotle melds the language of the two models, and, here once again, he is subtle where the contemporary models are crude. The sin model conflates viciousness and weakness, whereas the sickness model ignores the voluntary aspects of each. Aristotle recognizes how incontinence can involve passions that "actually alter our bodily condition, and in some men even produce fits of madness" (1147a, 17–18); he suggests that weakness of the will is an effect of physiological changes which cannot be eliminated from its explanation. What happens in our bodies directly influences the force of rational thought, sometimes even to the point of madness.

Madness is not blameworthy for Aristotle. It is an involuntary state. In this respect he treats it in the same way as illness and injury to the bodily system. These physical problems can give rise to behaviors which in a normal person would be seen as incontinent.

Aristotle describes these as incontinent in an "extended sense," citing the example of epilepsy as such a condition. His sense of pathology is thus similar to our own in that he recognizes no distinct line between mental and physical illness. The soul, in his view, is the form of a living body, not some ontologically distinct thing. Further there are no demons, spirits, or other supernatural forces affecting the human psyche. We are natural creatures in a natural environment. And as such we are subject to natural accidents of birth and development that have their effects on both our physical and mental lives.

Finally, the other form of incontinence in the "extended sense" is that which arises from unfortunate habituation from youth. Interestingly enough, the example he cites is of pederasty in the cases of "those who have been victims of lust from childhood" (1148b, 29–31). Bad habituation is possibly curable, he believes, but not blameworthy as vice or incontinence, as long as the habit does not arise from earlier adult choices themselves vicious in nature.

Aristotle's four kinds of addiction clearly reveal the superficialities of the sin/sickness dichotomy. His naturalistic grasp of the varieties of addiction provides a much richer basis for discussion than the bipolar classifications of our own day; this is further revealed in the interpretation of the terms of the definition suggested earlier. There are varieties of dysfunction as well as varieties of dependence. There are dysfunctional behaviors that do not involve dependencies, such as unsuccessfully attempting to beat a train through a crossing. And there are certainly dependencies that are not dysfunctional, such as our dependence on air. Dysfunctional behavior for humans is ultimately a cognitive-theoretic classification. That is, it cannot be defined solely in terms of behavior and/or physiological integrity. The same type of behavior may be functional in one intentional context and dysfunctional in another. Morphine addiction for the terminal cancer patient may well be a functional behavior given the rational goal of reducing pain in a situation where there is no long term. And whereas a diet of anything more interesting than roots and berries probably does not promote long-term physiological integrity, still only a fanatical few would want to call the occasional indulgence in French cuisine dysfunctional. The functionality of behavior must ultimately be assessed against the rational and moral goals of the agent. Heroic self-sacrifice for example, is often a bad thing physiologically, but it is not thought of as dysfunctional since it is in accord with personal moral goals that we consider praiseworthy.

Dependency, on the other hand, is at base a physiological category. There are two ways to talk about it: the first in terms of feelings and the second in the language of physiology, particularly neurophysiology. Consider the addiction to gambling: To what is the gambler addicted? Surely the answer does not include such behavioral categories as pulling handles or watching horses run in circles. Rather it involves the feelings that attend these behaviors in certain contexts; it is the particular form of excitement that the gambler seeks. Or to put it physiologically, the organism acts to reproduce particular kinds of brain states. This is why the notion of a merely psychological dependency makes no sense to the neurophysiologist. Whatever has psychological reality also has physiological reality. There are no changes of feeling unaccompanied by changes of brain states.

Thus the concept of addiction is hybrid—part intentional and part physiological. And for this reason it is obvious why neither the sin nor sickness models alone can capture it. The sin model focuses on the intentional factors and the sickness model on the physiological. Aristotle understood both, and the relations between them. His naturalistic conception of happiness made this understanding possible by incorporating both the intentional and physiological.

One example is nicotine addiction; the typical nicotine addict is the perfect example of incontinence. Currently one must be in deep denial not to recognize the threats posed by this substance to physiological integrity. But the dependency—the "passion" in Aristotle's terms—is a strong one for many. Smokers by and large are not vicious, merely weak. Most long-term smokers are addicted to nicotine. What this means is that they are dependent on it to produce pleasure and avoid pain in the short run. And all but the most fatalistic harbor the notion that they will somehow escape the long-term physiological consequences. In Aristotelian terms, they recognize the truth of the major premise that one ought not to cause oneself physical harm, but they convince themselves that their particular habit will not have such consequences, or at the very least, the next cigarette will not. Such weakness in the face of physiological/passionate compulsion is revealed in these self-deceptions, as well as the bouts of guilt that occur when the deceptions are revealed for what they are.

In contrast is the self-indulgent vice of anger. Aristotle is careful to distinguish the righteous from the vicious forms of angry behavior, and to the latter he attaches a higher level of moral culpability than to incontinence. The viciously angry engage in acts of gratuitous cruelty and refuse to accept the major premise that all such acts are morally evil. The man, for example, who beats his wife and children because of frustrations primarily unrelated to the home is surely acting in vicious anger. He is both more culpable and less curable than the merely incontinent; he does not even recognize that there is a moral principle at stake. Such behavior is morally distinct from that of the insane or diseased man. The latter's behavior may be seriously harmful to himself or others, but is not blameworthy since it is due to forces beyond his rational control. The epileptic may do serious harm, but is physiologically caused to do so by forces that transcend rational thought. Such persons are typically least culpable and least curable in Aristotle's view. In the latter respect, Aristotle must be excused for not anticipating the successes of modern medicine with such afflictions.

And finally, a fourth separate category of addictions are those arising from improper socialization. As I noted above, Aristotle's example is sexually abusive behavior toward children that arises out of similar abusive treatment of the agent as a child. Such behavior is more curable than madness or illness for Aristotle, but only marginally more blameworthy. Aristotle fully recognizes the force of early habituation. He takes it to be a central responsibility of the state, after all, to ensure the installation of virtuous habits in the young.

Contemporary North American culture, on the other hand, is profoundly divided over the degree of responsibility the state has for inculcating virtue. And, in a parallel way, it is divided over the sin and sickness models. Further, the adherents of each model are further divided amongst themselves. All this division results in a cacophony of conflicting claims that have been reduced virtually to the level of bumper stickers. In short, confusion reigns. Not surprisingly, political and economic forces have made use of the confusion to promote their own agendas.

Consider the interesting dichotomy between two high-profile women of influence, Betty Ford and Nancy Reagan. Each in her own way has become a cultural icon of the war on drugs. Betty Ford established a famous clinic to treat addicts, having recognized her own tendencies to addiction. Nancy Reagan, on the other hand, came to be identified with the slogan, "Just say no." The former represents the sickness model and the latter the sin model. After all, if a person has to go to a clinic he or she is generally thought to be sick. But if it is possible to "Just say no" then the behavior in question is voluntary and therefore not taken to be a sickness.

That North American culture has simultaneously assented to both icons reveals a confusion in adherence to one particular ideology; when one considers the economic divisions of the culture as they relate to the perception of addiction, the dichotomy dissolves. The addicts who turn up at the Betty Ford clinic are those with resources and social support systems typical of the most privileged segment of the population, while those who endure punishment for their addictions occupy the opposite end of the socioeconomic ladder. In short, wealthy addicts are considered sick while poor ones are seen as vicious. This political/economic division is in turn seemingly reinforced by the associated behaviors of the two groups. Wealthy addicts are not usually forced to commit violent criminal acts to support their habits. They can afford their addictions for a long while and are typically driven only to white-collar crime. Poor addicts, on the other hand, have daily or weekly difficulty maintaining their addictions and are thus driven to more personally threatening criminal acts. But from these differences in behavior we should not infer inherent differences in morality or physiology; poor heroin addicts are not necessarily more vicious or weaker of will than their richer counterparts. Indeed, according to Aristotle, the poor are often led to vicious excess through their attempts at emulating the rich (1095b, 20–22). Yet North American culture persists in the tendency to draw such moral distinctions between addictive behaviors of differently situated individuals.

This tendency is surely due in part to the influence of our collective historical denial of the class structure of American society. We are, as it were, in "cultural denial" regarding the patterns of class-generated inequities that have characterized our society for generations. Such denial is manifest, for instance, in various American myths, such as that of Horatio Alger. The moral of the myth is that in America anyone who works hard enough can be rich. From this it follows that if one is not rich, then one has not worked hard enough. But there is a further inference from the myth that many in the society have fallaciously drawn—that anyone who is wealthy must have worked hard. Even if the myth itself were true this latter conclusion would not follow from it. But a crucial moral premise is attached to this false conclusion, namely that hard work is morally virtuous. And, thus, if wealth is attained with hard work, it would seem to follow that the rich must be morally virtuous.

Given the latter conclusion it becomes clear how our cultural denial of class inequities can lead to moral distinctions between rich and poor addicts. The rich are, by the argument just given, naturally hard-working and virtuous; thus, they cannot be given to weakness of will and vice. The poor on the other hand are not assumed to be virtuous, and their failure to obtain wealth is taken to reveal an inherent lack of resolve associated with the weak-willed. Thus, wealthy persons who become addicted to something must be ill, since such behavior is inconsistent with their virtuous, hard-working natures. On the other hand, the poor addict is acting out of a characteristic weakness, and is easily led into sin. These perceived differences in character in turn are taken to require different social responses. The former deserve treatment for their illness; the latter deserve punishment for their sins.

The contemporary cultural mix of science and religion has resulted in a hybrid American ideology that recognizes only two possible explanations of addiction. But the hybrid nature of the concept of addiction itself renders each of those explanations inadequate unless we adopt the view that the rich are naturally more virtuous than the poor. If so, then it is appropriate for science to offer remedies to the rich while leaving the poor to be dealt with by religion and the penal system. But if we reject that premise and follow an Aristotelian line of reasoning then we must conclude that virtue and vice are not characteristics of socioeconomic classes but of individual natures and upbringing. Individuals of all social classes are vicious, weak-willed, badly habituated, and physiologically abnormal. The cause of an addiction and the nature of the possible cures, in the Aristotelian view, has nothing to do with social or economic status, but rather with moral training, rationality, and environmental/hereditary luck. It matters not what socioeconomic position one holds; if one is not habituated to virtuous deeds as a youth then vice will follow. If one is not schooled in the prudential logic of long-term self-interest then self-destructive behavior is more likely. If one is inordinately subject to passionate impulse, then even knowledge of moral truth may not prevail. And if one is a true victim of psychological or physiological disease then all the morality and reason in the world will not suffice. And, thus, in his naturalistic vision the vicious must be made to feel guilty; the weak-willed must be made strong; the badly habituated must be retrained, and the sick must be made comfortable, if not well. Aristotle's categories are in accord with common sense. The sin and sickness models are in accord with Judeo-Christian and scientific cultural ideologies, the first of which is grounded in the assumption that one and only one ancient text contains moral wisdom and the second in the assumption that there are no ancient truths at all, save perhaps the Oath of Hippocrates. At the very least, I hope I have raised genuine doubts about both assumptions.

BIBLIOGRAPHY

Aristotle. *Nicomachean Ethics*. Tr. Sir David Ross. London: Oxford University Press, 1925.

———. *The Basic Works of Aristotle*. Tr. Richard McKeon. New York: Random House, 1941.

Peele, Stanton. *Diseasing of America*. Lexington, MA: Lexington Books, 1989.

Sellars, Wilfrid. *Science, Perception, and Reality*. New York: The Humanities Press, 1963.

CHAPTER 3

HEAVY DRINKING AND THE AA MODEL

Ben Adams

IN THIS CENTURY AMERICANS HAVE SEEN a pendulum swing in the understanding of alcoholism from a view of abusive drinking as a moral weakness resulting from the individual's free choice to the view of alcoholism as a disease that can be alleviated by some form of treatment. Distinctions between drinking itself and alcoholism have never been easy to make, and much of the debate has been between temperance—the notion that all drinking is harmful—and a permissive view of drinking.

The concept of alcoholism as a disease was not unknown in the nineteenth century when physicians and mental hospital administrators connected with the American Association for the Cure of Inebriates proposed a disease model of alcoholism. They were subject to outspoken opposition from those who considered drinking a moral weakness. In spite of this, some alcoholics were treated in asylums and hospitals, including one in Boston, the Washingtonian, which continued in operation for more than a century until its closing in 1980. While a few leaders of the Temperance Movement also endorsed the disease concept, the vast majority were opposed to alcohol on moral grounds. More and more sections of the United States voted themselves alcohol-free until finally, in 1920, the entire nation outlawed alcohol.

During the Prohibition years the public debate about alcohol was not in terms of disease concept versus moral issue, but in political terms of the Wets versus the Drys. While Prohibition did result in considerable improvements in the overall rate of such alcohol-related problems as cirrhosis of the liver, drinking did persist, and there were additional problems such as the production of alcohol by criminals and the consumption of dangerously poor quality alcoholic beverages. Hospitals continued to see patients who had come to their doors for alcohol-related problems, but then, as now, alcoholics were the least sought-after patients.

The repeal of Prohibition in 1933 was a victory for the Wets, and that brought with it a certain discrediting of the Drys' moralistic attacks on drinking. Many prominent American writers had spent the Prohibition years in Europe from where they wrote very positive—"glowing" would certainly be the right word—accounts of drinking. And even in those works, such as the novels (and life) of F. Scott Fitzgerald, that illustrated some tragic consequences of alcohol abuse, the consequences had a romantic cast. Heavy drinking was tolerated or even approved of in many circles because to disapprove of it would appear to link oneself with the moralistic Drys.

It is significant that Alcoholics Anonymous was founded in 1935, just two years after the repeal of Prohibition. Even though published in 1988, Herbert Fingarette's book *Heavy Drinking: The Myth of Alcoholism as a Disease* recalls in tone the virulence of public debates about legal prohibition in the earliest years of the twentieth century and maintains a highly polemical tone in its opposition not only to the disease concept of alcoholism but also to Alcoholics Anonymous. Dr. Fingarette, who has been contributing scholarly articles on the field of alcoholism for almost as long as AA has been in existence, writes:

> The liquor industry is another player in this story of how and why the classic disease concept of alcoholism continues to be promoted and endorsed in the public arena. The classic disease concept admirably suits the interests of the liquor industry: by acknowledging that a small minority of the drinking population is susceptible to the

> disease of alcoholism, the industry can implicitly assure consumers that the vast majority of people who drink are *not* at risk. (27)

In an extremely curious passage Dr. Fingarette seems to reverse the likely historical antecedents of his position and that of AA in terms of wet and dry:

> Despite the repeal of Prohibition, the temperance creed lingered on in some quarters. In 1935 the old doctrine was given new life by the founders of Alcoholics Anonymous. Inspired by the teachings of a then popular religious sect, the Oxford Movement, two reformed heavy drinkers, a stockbroker and a physician, proposed a less extreme version of the temperance thesis . . . [which states that] most people can drink socially without any problem. (18)

Meanwhile, the Dry Movement continued to retain a good deal of life in the 1930s–1950s, even fielding presidential candidates. It hardly makes sense to equate AA's permissiveness of other people's drinking with the Temperance Movement; the founders of AA were drawn from the ranks of dyed-in-the-wool drinkers and not members of the Temperance Movement. Where the Wet-Dry controversy may have influenced AA is in the impetus it gave to Tradition 10, a central proposition in the Traditions that AA formalized in the 1950s: namely, that "AA has no opinion on outside issues; hence the AA name ought never to be drawn into public controversy." Tradition 10, one of many AA concepts that discourages divisive argument, is not done by enforcing conformity or agreement on issues but by permitting individuals to choose their own beliefs.

One of the founders of AA, Bill Wilson, was treated in 1934 by Dr. William Silkworth, a physician who did have a disease concept of alcoholism, at Towns Hospital in New York City. Dr. Silkworth believed that alcoholics had something like an allergy to alcohol whereby once they began drinking they were compelled to drink more of the very substance that would undermine their health. In other words, they did not choose to drink a lot just for the fun of it, but were constituted differently physiologically than other people. Their only hope—and until Bill Wilson, Dr. Silkworth had treated thousands of patients and seen very few recover—was to fully realize that they could not afford to have a single drink of alcohol. This became one of many concepts Bill Wilson and his associates incorporated into the AA program, and, as Fingarette argues, it is a disease concept of alcoholism.

The growth of AA and the growth of acceptance of the disease concept of alcoholism did go hand in hand. The startling success that AA was having in returning alcoholic drinkers to a normal way of life readily came to the attention of the Yale Institute of Alcohol Studies, founded in the late 1930s, and there was mutual collaboration between scholars at the Institute and AA members from the beginning. It was there that Dr. Jellinek did the studies for his major work *The Disease Concept of Alcoholism* (1960), which was the most thorough compendium of evidence for alcoholism being a disease that had been done to date. By the 1960s, when the American Medical Association voted to treat alcoholism as a disease, there were numerous treatment centers for alcoholism; industry had hired people to deal with alcohol problems among their personnel; and insurance companies were persuaded to cover alcohol treatment. By the 1970s, public drunkenness was decriminalized in many states, and public detoxification centers were established to treat those who had heretofore been imprisoned. While penalties for drunken driving were increased in the 1970s and 1980s, this was done in conjunction with and not in opposition to mandatory treatment components of sentences. By the 1970s and 1980s, many prominent Americans were acknowledging their need for substance abuse treatment, and there was even some evidence of a pendulum swing away from drinking in many circles (Kolata).

In the 1980s, however, some elements of the concept of alcoholism as a disease, which seemed to become widely accepted by the general public, were challenged. A key document in that challenge is Herbert Fingarette's aforementioned *Heavy Drinking: The Myth of Alcoholism as a Disease.* It was published in the spring of 1988 just as the Supreme Court ruled that the Veteran's Administration was entitled to refuse benefits to two veterans who claimed they had been disabled by alcoholism. The Veteran's Administration had defined abusive drinking as "wilful misconduct" and the Supreme

Court ruled that they were entitled to do so and need not endorse the concept of alcoholism as a disease. The Court specifically declined to endorse or oppose the theory of alcoholism as a disease, citing studies, including several articles by Fingarette, that showed that the disease concept did not enjoy a unanimity of acceptance in professional circles.

There has, since the ruling, been a substantial editorial response in columns and even cartoons welcoming an abandonment of a seemingly permissive understanding of abusive drinking as the result of a disease and a return to viewing it as a moral weakness under the individual's control for which he or she may be blamed. Such shifts in public opinion on whether to evaluate various forms of behavior in terms of good and bad or in terms of a morally neutral problem solving ethic are frequent in American life. We are accustomed to making adjustments between two of our central American values when they appear to conflict: that is, between our belief in individual responsibility and our belief in the fairness of taking mitigating circumstances into consideration in our judgements. The point here is that Fingarette's argument in *Heavy Drinking* is that a disease concept of alcoholism exempts heavy drinkers from their obligation to accept responsibility for their behavior, and much of the public response is to this argument.

I have referred above to the polemical tone of *Heavy Drinking.* It will be clear from the passages I cite that I have not exaggerated the intensity of the tone, which at least has the advantage that readers will be in no doubt as to where Dr. Fingarette stands. The short version of his thesis is as follows: the disease concept of alcoholism has been proven false, has been used to maintain an undesirable state of affairs, and Alcoholics Anonymous has been a major culprit in preventing this being made known to the public. In explanation of his tone, Dr. Fingarette writes:

> I wrote this book out of a sense of urgency, believing it was imperative to inform the general public of the latest research on heavy drinking and of the sea change that has occurred in professional scientific circles. Because I knew that outdated and often false ideas were firmly rooted in most people's minds, I felt that

> this was not an occasion for pussyfooting around the evidence nor for presenting a numbingly detailed analysis of every bit of evidence. But I have tried to use the sources responsibly and fairly, if somewhat confrontationally, to illuminate the central issue that ought to concern the general public. (144)

Surely there is a regular flow of news stories about alcohol research from the scientific community to the better newspapers. Why, then, is alcoholism still perceived as a disease? In response, Fingarette levels a very serious accusation.

> Why haven't we heard more from the scientists and researchers about this strife? Intimidation should not be discounted. The classical disease concept remains the cornerstone of traditional treatment and public opinion, the central premise of media coverage and social debate, such that anyone who publicly doubts or challenges the disease concept is likely to be ignored, dismissed or ostracized. In this version of the emperor's new clothes, truthfulness can threaten, block, or ruin the truth teller's career. (24)

The strife to which he refers is that between professionals and paraprofessionals working in the alcoholism field, with the paraprofessionals largely drawn from the ranks of AA:

> How can it be that the treatment programs themselves are working from the scientifically untenable disease concept? One key factor is the widespread presence in the treatment and lobbying communities of paraprofessional staff members who define themselves as "recovering alcoholics." Indeed, the largest single category of direct service staff in programs specifically concerned with alcohol consists of counselors without professional degrees, many of whom were once heavy drinkers and now claim special qualification to help others by reason of their own experience. Since their own treatment was effected at a time when the classic disease concept of alcoholism was dominant, they tend to have faith in the old dogma and tend to perceive any challenge to the disease concept as a challenge to the validity of their own emotional ordeal and conversion to sobriety. (23)

The picture Fingarette is painting here is credible enough for those who are not versed in the history of alcoholism research. Some readers could believe that once upon a time, say in the 1930s and 1940s, some scientists joined AA members in endorsing the theory that alcoholism was a disease. As scientists continued to research, they came to the conclusion that in fact alcoholism is not a disease. However, by then vast numbers of uneducated AA members had a lock on alcoholism treatment and lobbying outfits, and they imposed an embargo on any news of this getting out to the general public, that is until Dr. Fingarette managed to find a publisher for *Heavy Drinking.*

The reader who has stayed with me thus far will note that I have not engaged the issue of whether or not alcoholism is a disease; there is a reason for this. Much of Fingarette's case rests on the assumption that settling a debate between those who hold that alcoholism is a disease and those who oppose this concept is of paramount importance. He has portrayed AA as fanatically and ignorantly wedded to the disease concept and the scientific and professional community as nearly unanimously opposed. With these claims he has erred on both accounts, in his portrayal of AA and of the consensus in the professional world. How the disease concept stands in both AA and the professional alcoholism community could hardly be more distanced from the highly charged polemical cast attached to it by Fingarette. Surely it is safe to say that there would be a minority of individuals in AA and in the professional community for whom a position on the disease concept, pro or con, is a matter of serious contention. And the idea that most members of AA and most professionals in the field are highly partisan and locked in controversy on this issue seriously misrepresents the breadth and sophistication of viewpoints in both camps and the cooperative and tolerant style more characteristic of both. While there are indeed various areas of controversy, they are usually, although not always, fairly genial, and dedication to a faction appears rare. Most current anthologies of recent works in alcoholism note that their contributors espouse varying theories. For instance, Bean and Zinberg note in their preface to *Dynamic Approaches to the Understanding and Treatment of Alcoholism* that:

> All of the contributors use a psychodynamic model to direct patient care and for teaching. Yet when it came to a discussion of alcohol use, it became clear that there were important and consistent divergences of views and, further, that the divergences of views in the group seemed representative of the field. George E. Vaillant presents a direct view of the disease model of alcoholism and an A.A. position essentially negative to ordinary psychiatric treatment for alcoholism and suggests a minimal focus on individual problems. Margaret M. Bean is less concerned with the overall philosophy of alcoholism than with the mechanics by which alcoholics and those around them are able to deny the condition. Norman E. Zinberg finds it of crucial importance to put alcohol use and alcoholism within their social perspective, while John E. Mack presents a coherent effort to understand the problems and effects of alcoholism as they are centered within the "self," also in its social context.

All the researchers cited are psychiatrists at the Harvard Medical School who have been working together and in collaboration with paraprofessionals at the Cambridge Hospital alcoholism program for the past 20 years. Rather than being locked in strife over the disease concept, they seem able to work with others of differing views and to place their emphasis in many other areas besides whether or not alcoholism is a disease.

The same eclectic spirit exists in the Milkman and Shaffer anthology, *The Addictions*. The dust jacket notes:

> The authors link theory to practice by then presenting perspectives on treatment that respond directly to each theoretical position. The authors examine methods of diagnosis and assessment, traditional and innovative approaches to treatment and varying dependency disorders. These explorations uncover the intensifying debate between practitioners who view addiction as a disease and those who place more emphasis on personal and social responsibility for addictive behavior.

This hardly reflects a professional climate in which various points of views, specifically those that do not endorse the disease concept, are being kept out of print by intimidation. I will demonstrate subsequently that Dr. Fingarette's view of alcoholism as a result of choices and not a disease is responsive to a behavioral treatment that also has a philosophical commitment to individual responsibility. Consequently, to inform the general public that his views and those of the behaviorists regarding alcoholism are the dominant ones in scientific circles and that until the publication of his book these views could not reach the public because recovering alcoholic paraprofessionals were using intimidation to prevent it is simply a compound of untruths designed to give his own views unearned sympathy and attention.

But even if Fingarette has underestimated the support for the disease concept of alcoholism in scientific circles, and even if he has exaggerated the degree to which others are engaged in strife over the issue, could he not be correct in his description of AA as demanding assent to a monolithic disease concept? If AA holds that alcoholism is a disease and insists that its members agree to this, and if the bulk of the paraprofessionals working in alcoholism treatment are members of AA, would this not constitute a formidable obstacle to objective scientific discussion? Despite what Fingarette has said about how his point of view has been kept out of the public media by the intimidation of the paraprofessional, the above charges have been maliciously made against AA before.

In the February, 1963, *Harpers* and the September 19, 1965, *Saturday Evening Post* a Columbia-trained psychologist named Arthur Cain wrote articles attacking Alcoholics Anonymous as a cult, saying, "AA has become a dogmatic cult whose chapters too often turn sobriety into slavery to AA. Because of its narrow outlook, Alcoholics Anonymous prevents thousands from ever being cured. Moreover AA has retarded scientific research into one of America's most serious health problems" (Kurz, 144). I referred earlier to the history of the Wet-Dry controversy and how AA adopted a nondebating position partly in response to that. A good example of the spirit of AA in wishing to avoid taking a position in any controversy, even one involving alcoholism, is in AA founder Bill Wilson's response to the Cain Articles:

> probably the Cain article kept some people away from A.A. Maybe some will stay sick longer, and maybe a few will die because of it. But so far as we folks who are in the fold are concerned, I think it is a rather good experience. In all the years this is the first thorough-going criticism our fellowship ever had. So the practice of absorbing stuff like that in good humor should be of value. Despite its petulant and biased nature, the piece did contain some half-truths. It certainly applied to some AAs at some places at some times. Therefore it should help us take heed of these natural tendencies. (Kurz, 143)

The charge of dogmatism against AA is particularly strange because an antidogmatic and action-oriented thread has been part of AA from the very beginning. AA's success in being able to attract to the Fellowship alcoholics who hold quite varied opinions has been partly due to this suspension of debate. Could it be that AA is flexible in many areas but dogmatic on the point of alcoholism as a disease? For if AA is not dogmatic on that point then Fingarette's thesis collapses.

Here is the discussion of this question presented by AA in its 1952 pamphlet *40 Questions.* "Not too long ago, alcoholism was viewed as a moral problem. Today, many regard it as primarily a health problem. To each problem drinker, it will always remain an intensely personal matter" (4). This recognition of the element of personal feeling in the forming of opinion—an awareness of which can be life-saving in some barrooms should one be tempted to bring up politics or religion for discussion—permeates AA and is part of its policy not to impose a doctrine on anyone that would offend against their own views. Readers can see that such a policy applies to beliefs about the nature of alcoholism as well. The pamphlet goes on:

> There are many different ideas about what alcoholism really is. The explanation that seems to make sense to most AA members is that alcoholism is an illness, a progressive illness, which can never be cured but which, like some other illnesses, can be arrested. Going one step further, many AAs feel that the illness represents the combination of physical sensitivity to alcohol and a mental ob-

> session with drinking, which, regardless of consequences, cannot be broken by will power alone. (4)

Although the wording talks of illness rather than disease, this is the concept to which Fingarette objects. But the point is that it is a concept offered to help people recover from alcoholism and not one imposed on all members of AA. The founder of AA, Bill Wilson, wrote:

> We have never called alcoholism a disease because, technically speaking, it is not a disease entity. For example, there is no such thing as heart disease. Instead there are many separate heart ailments, or combinations of them. It is something like that with alcoholism. Therefore we did not wish to get in wrong with the medical profession by pronouncing alcoholism a disease entity. Therefore we always called it an illness, or a malady—a far safer term for us to use. (Kurz 22)

Here is Fingarette's version of Alcoholics Anonymous, one which, in my view, would be virtually unrecognizable by anyone who has participated in AA. "AA groups provide individual members with powerful emotional and moral support, as well as practical aid and advice—provided the member conforms to key expectations of the group" (Fingarette 88). That "provided" is simply untrue; great pains have been taken in AA to prevent any withdrawal of support from others because of differences. The stress is on "the only requirement for membership is a desire to stop drinking." Fingarette goes on to write that AA members are "expected to gradually discover therein a personal history that by and large conforms to the AA picture of the course of alcoholism. Members whose memories or understanding of their experiences are inconsistent with AA doctrine may be confronted and charged with denial" (Kurz 88). That would actually be inconceivable at an AA meeting. There is thorough freedom in AA for people to tell their own stories as they understand them, and there is no tradition of critiquing the stories, much less of confronting.

Other than to discredit AA, why does the focus of attack on it so often take the form of accusing it of a dogmatism that a little investigation would easily refute? Nan Robertson in her account of AA, *Getting Better: Inside Alcoholics Anonymous,* quotes Robert J. Pandina, a neuropsychologist at Rutgers:

> Some scientists and psychotherapists wrongly perceive AA as a kind of magic. They are baffled by AAs success because the first thing you have to accept in AA is the notion that you're powerless—helpless—over a drug. And that's anti-science, anti-reason, anti-logic. My belief is that AA principles—applied not just to alcoholism but to addiction in general—hold up very well. It's also my opinion that AA principles are not antithetical to the basic principles of psychology. But there's another problem. I don't know of a more emotion-laden field than the field of alcoholism. People come to it with baggage and that baggage gets in the way. (193)

The ostensible subject of *Heavy Drinking* is a refutation of the disease concept, or to be more accurate, an account to the public of evidence that the disease concept has already been refuted. I have tried to show that Fingarette's central premise of the significance of the disease concept—that it is a dogmatic AA principle that is imposed on the scientific community—is incorrect, and therefore will now turn my attention to the real subject of the book.

The real subject is a critique of Alcoholics Anonymous. The professional literature on the disease concept is extremely varied and, as I have shown, is rarely directed to any particular controversy. I have chosen not to focus on the details of the research on the disease concept because of my contention that Fingarette has both misrepresented it and used it as a red herring to launch an attack on AA. What I have tried to do in this response to Fingarette is to indicate what distortions and misconceptions would have to be cleared away before the useful issues that Fingarette brings up could be fruitfully discussed.

The issues are useful, and Fingarette has certainly done the readers a service in presenting them despite the disservice of the distortions. Hundreds of thousands of Americans, not to mention the worldwide population affected by the scope of the problem, are suffering from and seeking recovery for conditions involving drinking.

Something like a million people have been recovering in Alcoholics Anonymous, including a quarter of a million in Mexico alone. As the late Bill Wilson would doubtless have been the first to agree, there is always room for improvement in AA, and even the harshest criticisms may have truths that people in AA should consider.

Fingarette cannot, in all fairness, be accused of merely attacking without offering any suggestions of his own on how to help alcoholics and heavy drinkers recover. However, what he suggests to replace treatment related to the disease concept turns out to be a return to what is fundamentally a moral approach to heavy drinking. Where I would feel confident referring a person with a drinking problem to Alcoholics Anonymous and a person whose loved one has a drinking problem to Al-Anon, Fingarette has ruled them out. Here is his suggestion:

> In sum, any efforts that heavy drinkers take to change their drinking activities must be predicated on an acceptance of personal responsibility. This resolve, in turn, must be followed by actions intended to achieve a reshaping of their way of life that fosters change and precludes situations that frustrate the will to change. And because heavy drinking as a central activity has many meanings for the drinker, the reconstructions of life must go well beyond eliminating the drinking activity to building new and satisfying ways of meeting life's challenges. (111)

Although the reader would certainly not know it from Fingarette's account, the recovery work in Alcoholics Anonymous goes well beyond eliminating drinking, and that is doubtless one of the reasons for its success. Fingarette's approach offers absolutely no evidence for his contention that successful recovery must be preceded by an acceptance of personal responsibility. I am sure alcoholics are not the only ones who have been on the receiving end of criticism that exhorts them to get a hold on themselves, shape up, and take responsibility. The advantages of that approach lie mostly with the sense of righteous satisfaction on the part of the one exhorting. Fingarette would be absolutely correct in noting that this plays no part in the way AA members actually approach and help new people; nor is this an oversight on their part. By approaching the fellow alcoholic as an equal, by telling of oneself to him or her rather than prescribing for him or her, by delivering help instead of requiring compliance, the AA members have been able to start hundreds of thousands of people on lifetimes of recovery.

My response to Fingarette can only touch the surface of a discussion of varied approaches to alcoholism that go far beyond a simple debating issue of whether or not it is a disease. My aim is not to convince the reader to take one side or another in such a debate but to appreciate how much more sophisticated as well as deep-rooted the issues are. Even if one is among those who have never been touched by alcoholism, the issues of what this behavior means, how it may be judged, or how to respond to it are surely universal. Those who choose to pursue the subject further will find, to either their pleasure or their dismay, that they are soon thrust in the midst of central philosophical issues that they cannot be expected to resolve alone.

BIBLIOGRAPHY

Bean, Margaret H. and Norman E. Zinberg, eds. *Dynamic Approaches to the Understanding and Treatment of Alcoholism.* New York: Free Press, 1957.

Fingarette, Herbert. *Heavy Drinking: The Myth of Alcoholism as a Disease.* Berkeley: University of California Press, 1988.

Forty-Four Questions. New York: Alcoholics Anonymous World Services, 1982.

Jellinek, E. M. *The Disease Concept of Alcohol.* New Haven: Hillhouse Press, 1960.

Kolata, Gina. "Temperance: An Old Cycle Repeats Itself." *New York Times.* January 1, 1991. Sec. 1: 15.

Kurz, Ernest. *A. A. The Story.* New York: Harper and Row, 1979, 1980.

Milkman, Harvey and Howard Shaffer, eds. *The Addictions: Multidisciplinary Perspectives and Treatments.* Lexington, MA: Lexington Books, 1985.

Robertson, Nan. *Getting Better: Inside A.A.* New York: Morrow & Company, 1988.

CHAPTER 4

SELF-REGULATION AND SELF-MEDICATION FACTORS IN ALCOHOLISM AND THE ADDICTIONS

Similarities and Differences

Edward J. Khantzian, M.D.

INTRODUCTION

IT IS PROBABLY NOT INSIGNIFICANT THAT the widespread misuse and abuse of addictive drugs in our society emerged approximately one decade after the introduction of modern psychopharmacological agents. When these drugs were first introduced in the 1950s, they were called "major" (for major mental illness, for example, psychosis) or "minor" (for minor mental illness, for example, neurosis) tranquilizers, and, as the terms imply, it was believed they worked simply by tranquilizing or attenuating emotional distress. However, with the subsequent advent of antidepressants in the early 1960s and the identification and clarification of the role of neuroreceptors and neurotransmitters, researchers and clinicians began to appreciate that psychoactive drugs had different sites and modes of action. Consequently, this appreciation modified our designation of these drugs to more precisely describe their action—for example, antipsychotic, antianxiety, antidepressant, and antimanic agents.

As the original and subsequent names of these drugs implied, these agents promised to reduce or counter emotional suffering associated with mental illness. It should not be surprising, then, that some of these drugs, especially antianxiety drugs, and other illicit substances were adopted and used increasingly in the 1960s and 1970s by individuals, who were not necessarily patients, to relieve and remove emotional distress.

However, for the most part, and until recently, few investigators, clinicians, or theoreticians have considered drugs of abuse to have appeal or addictive potential because of their ability to reduce emotional pain or suffering. Instead, motives of stimulus seeking, pleasure drive, or self-destructiveness are and have been invoked on the psychological side, or biogenetic addictive mechanisms on the physiological side, to account for why individuals become so dependent on substances of abuse. Notwithstanding the scientific advances that have allowed the measurement of genetic and physiological factors, clinical work with and diagnostic studies of addicts, guided by a modern psychodynamic perspective, offer a basis to conclude that the need to control or reduce emotional suffering is an important motivating factor in addictive disorders. Pleasure- or stimulus-seeking and self-destructive motives are indeed apparent in addictions, but in my opinion they are more often byproducts of or are secondary to problems in self-regulation in which the capacities for managing feelings, self-esteem, relationships, and self-care loom large (Khantzian, "Ego"; "Self-Regulation").

In this essay I explore how self-medication factors play an important role in individuals becoming dependent on alcohol and drugs, with an emphasis on alcoholism. The self-medication hypothesis implies that individuals prefer or depend on different drugs because each class of drugs, much like the classes of drugs legitimately used in psychiatry, have a distinctive action and effect that interact with specific painful feeling states and related psychiatric disorders. I use clinical examples to demonstrate that self-medication factors are as important with alcohol dependence as they are with other addictive drugs. I will compare and contrast the appeal of alcohol with other classes of drugs that are misused and abused, for example, narcotics and stimulants.

THE CHALLENGE OF SELF-REGULATION

Because humans are governed less by instincts and more by coping skills and capacities acquired from the care-taking environment, requirements for human survival and adaptation place a lifelong challenge on humans for self-regulation. Regulating emotion or feeling-life is one of the most central of these challenges. I believe self-medication factors in addictive disorders are intimately related to human self-regulation problems and, in particular, to the regulation of affects or feeling life. Accordingly, in this essay I shall place and discuss self-medication factors and substance abuse in a broader context of the human need for self-regulation.

Clinical investigators working with alcoholics and addicts over the past three decades have accumulated observations and findings suggesting a self-medication hypothesis of addictive disorders (Weider and Kaplan; Krystal and Raskin; Milkman and Frosch; Wurmser; Khantzian, "Opiate"; Khantzian, "Self-Medication"). Many of these reports stressed major developmental impairments and severe psychopathology and associated painful affect states that made reliance on drugs likely and compelling. Subsequent diagnostic and treatment studies provided supporting and empirical evidence that addicts suffer with coexisting psychiatric disorders and structural psychopathology (Woody, O'Brien, and Rickels; McLellan, Woody, and O'Brien; Dorus and Senay; Weissman, Slobetz, Prusoff, Merritz, and Howard; Rounsaville, Weissman, Kleber, and Wilber; Rounsaville, Weissman, Crits-Cristoph, Wilber, and Kleber; Treece and Nicholson; Nicholson and Treece; Khantzian and Treece, "DSM-III"; Blatt, Berman, Bloom-Feshback, Sugarman, Wilber, and Kelber; Woody, Luborsky, McLellan, O'Brien, Beck, Blaine, Herman, and Hole).

Despite the documented association between substance abuse and psychopathology, I have more recently become convinced that there is a wide range of emotional vulnerability or susceptibility to addictive and alcoholic disorders. Admittedly, the cases of severe psychopathology represent an extreme, but they and the less severely or minimally affected individuals with psychopathology are all more or less subject to human experiences and processes involving distress and suffering. It is distress and suffering that is at the heart of alcoholism and addiction, and cases of individuals with more extreme psychopathology are examples of where the emotional pain is greater as a consequence of their psychopathology.

The self-medication hypothesis takes into consideration how the effects or actions of the different classes of drugs—for example, stimulants, opiates, and sedative-hypnotics—interact with states of distress to make them appealing and to cause certain individuals to become dependent on them. The self-medication perspective of drug and alcohol dependence places heavy emphasis on painful affects, but other self-regulating factors involving self-esteem, self-other relationships, and self-care also interact with affect states in substance use and misuse. I will expand on these other factors subsequently,

As we have indicated, our emphasis in exploring self-medication factors in alcoholism and addictions is on suffering and its psychological determinants. There are clearly other determinants, however, in addition to the psychological factors that cause or contribute to the development of dependency on alcohol and drugs. These include genetic, environmental, and cultural factors that may either protect against or heighten a person's vulnerability to substance use disorders. Exploration of these factors goes beyond the scope of this essay, and we limit ourselves to the psychological factors. However, a comprehensive explanation or theory of substance dependence must ultimately attempt to integrate and account for how all these factors interact.

OLD AND NEW THEORIES OF HUMAN DISTRESS

Drives and Conflict

Early psychoanalytic theory of the mind advanced by Sigmund Freud emphasized instinctual factors—for example, pleasure and aggressive drives—and a topographic view of the mind in which much of mental life and psychic process was considered to be unconscious. Freud and his followers later placed greater emphasis on internal processes and states involving wishes and needs and a more detailed appreciation of structural factors and functions involved in regulating psychic life and adjustment to reality. In these earlier psychodynamic formulations, psychic suffering and human distress were viewed for the most part in terms of conflict psychology. Distress was felt to be the result of human drives or wishes pressing for discharge but opposed by inhibitions or repression.

Early psychoanalytic approaches to relieving conflict and distress emphasized making unconscious mental life—for example, fantasies, wishes, and desires—conscious, and verbalizing and working through pent-up sexual and aggressive drives. Employing free association and cathartic techniques, the objective was to reduce or minimize tensions, conflict, and distress that resulted from excessive control or repression of drives and related impulses.

Affects and Structure

There has been a decided shift from these early psychodynamic theories, which stressed drives and conflict, and reducing or keeping drives at a minimum as a means to avoid distress and conflict. Contemporary psychodynamic theory has placed affects and feeling life center stage and more systematically considers the ways ego and self-structures develop and unfold to optimally regulate affects, such as feeling-life, self-esteem, relationships, and adaptation to external reality.

Although modern psychodynamic clinicians still employ free association to access the nature and source of emotional distress, greater efforts are placed on actively building empathic connections and contact with patients to help them identify their feelings and needs, to derive a better sense of self and others, and to develop a sense of safety and comfort. Emphasis in contemporary clinical approaches focuses more on fostering improved capacities for containment of feelings and self-regulation. Rather than releasing or reducing drive tensions to minimal levels, modern approaches stress the maintenance of optimal, versus maximum or minimal, affects and helping individuals grow in their capacity to control and transform distress.

Development and Adaptation

The degree to which individuals can tolerate distress and find relief from human suffering is proportional to the degree they have been able to develop and internalize capacities to regulate feelings, to establish and maintain a healthy regard for self and others, and to take care of themselves. These capacities are incorporated as mental structures and functions in our personality organization and reflect our ego capacities and sense of self.

The development of ego and sense of self begins in infancy and continues over a lifetime. The attitudes and functions that are internalized derive primarily from our parents and, subsequently, from association with other significant individuals and groups. If the growing-up environment is optimally constant, nurturing, and relatively free of major trauma or neglect, ego functions and the sense of self coalesce to give us a mature and adaptable character structure. In contrast, major developmental flaws, defects, and distortions occur in a person's character structure as a function of environmental inconstancy, trauma, and neglect (Khantzian and Mack, "A.A."). Our focus on problems in self-regulation and the use of substances for the purpose of self-medication is based on this appreciation of these developmental processes and disabilities. These developmental flaws and deficits in the character structure of substance abusers are responsible for the difficulties they experience in adapting to their internal emotional life and external world of reality. It is on this basis that addicts and alcoholics attempt to correct these flaws through the use of substances, a "correction" they feel they cannot achieve on their own.

COMMON FACTORS IN ALCOHOLISM AND THE ADDICTIONS

The common factors in alcoholism and the addictions center around the use of substances as a means to achieve and maintain self-regulation. However, considering how disregulated, disorganized, and out of control addicts and alcoholics appear, it is hard to believe that they could be using these substances for purposes of regulating themselves. In fact, it is on the basis of this latter observation that many argue that substances cause distress and disregulation rather than the other way around (Vaillant). Such accounts, in my estimation, focus excessively on the admitted regression in psychological function associated with long-term use of drugs, some drugs—such as stimulants and sedative-hypnotics—causing more regression than others (McLellan, Woody, and O'Brien). They fail to take into account sufficiently the more enduring and relatively immutable personality structures of such individuals that reveal long-standing difficulties in managing their inner psychological life and their external behaviors. Systematic study of such factors reveals that many of the protracted states of dysphoria, or "hypophoria," associated with drug withdrawal are some of the same states that coexisted with other determining personality traits and features predating the substance dependence (Martin, Hewett, Baker, and Haertzen; Martin, Haertzen, and Hewett).

I would argue that the regular reliance on any drug causes a "disuse" atrophy in a person's capacity to achieve a subjective or behavioral end in more ordinary ways. That is, the more individuals depend on a drug or alcohol to calm, activate, relate to others, play, and so forth, the less they develop capacities to achieve them normally, and more often and tragically they undermine any existing capacities they might have developed. But as we gain an appreciation of substance abusers' lifelong difficulties in coping with distress, their initial and subsequent reliance on drugs becomes more understandable. In this section I review how sectors of vulnerability in personality organization common to alcoholics and addicts, involving feeling-life (affects), self-esteem, self-other relations, and self-care, can predispose individuals to use and become dependent on substances.

Affects

The nature of the distress or suffering associated with alcoholism and addiction, I feel, is closely linked with the complex ways in which individuals with these problems experience, tolerate, and express their feelings, or affects. They seem to suffer in extremes, either feeling too much or feeling too little. Some seem to be more chronically "disaffected" (McDougall) or unable to name their feelings (Krystal, "Alexithymia") and seem more pervasively devoid of feelings; others seem, more often than not, overwhelmed with intense affects, such as rage, shame, loneliness, and depression, and yet others "flip-flop" between the extremes of emotional flooding and emptiness (Khantzian, "Ego," "Self-Regulation"; Weider and Kaplan; Krystal and Raskin; Milkman and Frosch; Wurmser).

Individuals who suffer in these ways use drugs and alcohol to help them cope with emotions. Depending on one's state and the doses of drugs used, drug and alcohol effects may, in some instances, attenuate or allow feelings. When individuals feel a need to repeatedly resort to drugs or alcohol to achieve such effects, it is usually a sign that they suffer with developmental deficits and handicaps and thus need drug and alcohol effects to achieve and maintain states of feeling that they cannot achieve on their own. That is, drugs and alcohol are used as a "prosthetic" (Weider and Kaplan) to compensate for deficits in regulating affect life.

We will elaborate subsequently on the differences in the effects of the various classes of drugs, including alcohol, and how they interact with specific affect states to make them compelling. However, there is one more general aspect of drug and alcohol use involved in controlling feelings that I believe is important to review. I am referring to a paradoxical aspect of drug and alcohol dependency, namely, that as much as substances may be used to relieve distress and painful affect states, such a reliance also perpetuates and often worsens such states. Although at first this result might seem to be a case of enduring some distress in exchange for even momentary relief, more recently I have realized that substance abusers employ this negative effect in the service of controlling their suffering. In this instance, at least part of the "tradeoff" in accepting the pain of drug use involves converting the passive experience of not knowing or being able to access feelings, to an experience where one actively controls feelings, even if the feelings they produce are painful. This seems to apply especially to those patients I have described who more often are devoid of feelings. Rather than just relieving painful affects when they are overwhelming, drugs and alcohol, and the distress they entail, may also be adopted as a way of being in control, especially when people feel out of control because affects are vague, elusive, and nameless (Khantzian, "Clinical").

Well-Being and Self-Esteem

Basic states of well-being and positive self-regard derive from earliest stages of development. Addicts and alcoholics suffer with developmental deficits involving a failure to internalize the comforting, soothing, validating, and mobilizing aspects of their parenting or care-taking environment (Khantzian, "Ego").

I have been repeatedly impressed that drug- and alcohol-dependent individuals are vulnerable to problems involving soothing and calming themselves, especially when they are stressed and overwrought. While conversely, they may also suffer with initiative and activation problems when their safety or well-being depends on taking action. Deriving from these basic states, but related to subsequent developmental challenges and need for mastery, substance abusers also suffer because they have not developed a sufficient capacity for self-esteem or self-love where they enjoy a confidence in themselves and their potential, and a balanced valuation of their importance in relation to self and others (Khantzian and Mack, "A.A."; Mack).

Drug and alcohol effects interact with affect states and characterological or characteristic defenses related to states of disharmony, immobilization, and self-esteem in ways that relieve or alter the suffering entailed with these states. I discuss these interactions more specifically below. When substance abusers speak of the "high" or euphoria that they experience with drugs or alcohol, they are probably referring to the self-soothing, comfort, repair, and sense of well-being and power they cannot obtain or sustain within themselves or from others unless they resort to drugs or alcohol (Khantzian, Mack, and Schatzberg; Krystal, "Self-Representation").

Relationships

The problems addicts and alcoholics have in relation to regulating their feelings and maintaining their self-esteem make relating to and depending on others a precarious, if not an erratic, experience. As much as they need others to know how they feel, they often fear and distrust their dependency, disavow their need, and act in counterdependent ways. Their defenses of self-sufficiency and disavowal leave them isolated and cut off, and they disguise from themselves and others their need for nurturance and validation, which is often excessive given their developmental deficits. Consequently, there is a tendency to be inconsistent in satisfying their own and others' needs in relationships. They alternate between being selfless and demanding, but are more chronically dissatisfied and cut off, and thus more susceptible to using drugs and alcohol to process emotions around their needs and wants (Khantzian, "Ego").

Self-Care

Because of the obvious dangers associated with acute and chronic use of drugs and alcohol, substance abusers are often accused, and they also accuse themselves, of harboring self-destructive motives. Some have suggested that addictive behavior is a form of "suicide on the installment plan." This kind of cynical, negative, destructive motive attributed to addicts derives from early drive psychology (Khantzian and Treece, "Psychodynamics") and detracts from an empathic understanding of addicts' vulnerabilities. Addictive behavior is governed less by self-destructive motives but is more the result of developmental failures and deficits that leave certain individuals ill-equipped to protect and take care of themselves. Along these lines we have proposed that addicts and alcoholics suffer with deficits or deficiencies in a capacity for self-care (Khantzian and Mack; "A.A.," "Self-Preservation). Although we first identified and described self-care deficits in opiate addicts, we have continued to observe this vulnerability to varying degrees in all substance abusers, including alcoholics and cocaine addicts.

The capacity for self-care or self-protection involves certain ego functions that serve and ensure survival. These functions include signal anxiety, judgments, reality testing, control, and the ability to make cause-consequence connections. The capacity for self-care is acquired and internalized from early and subsequent phases of childhood development, and it derives from the nurturing and protective roles and function of the child's parents. If adequately developed, the capacity for self-care assures appropriate planning, action, and anticipation of events to avoid mishaps or danger. Healthy self-care is apparent in adults who demonstrate appropriate degrees of anticipatory affects, including embarrassment, shame, fear, worry, and so forth, when facing hazardous or harmful situations (Khantzian, "Self-Regulation"; Khantzian and Mack, "A.A.," "Self-Preservation").

As I have indicated, deficits or vulnerabilities in the capacity for self-care cut across all substance abusers. However, the degree of deficiency or disability in self-care may vary over time in any one individual, but it is more global and pervasive in some types of addictions than others, for example, in certain polydrug addicts and more so in intravenous drug abusers. Self-care functions may be better established in some individuals, but they may lapse or deteriorate under conditions of major stress, depression, or as a consequence of prolonged drug and alcohol use. These functions may also be overridden because for certain individuals survival concerns become subordinate to needs for relief from painful affect states or a drive to achieve or perform, which drug effects may enhance (Khantzian, "Self-Regulation"). Whether this involves a lapse or is the result of more severe impairment, self-care problems in substance abusers are apparent in addicts and alcoholics in their failure or inability to adequately worry about, fear, or consider the long- and short-term complications and dangers associated with drugs and alcohol.

DRUGS AND SELF-MEDICATION

Most individuals who become and remain dependent on drugs and alcohol have experimented with or tried many drugs and even continue to use more than one drug. However, if asked, most addicts will indicate they prefer a particular drug. Exploring psychological characteristics of such individuals reveals that the drug they select or prefer is a function of characteristic defenses, organization in personality style or structure, and related affect states that dominate their inner emotional life and their relationships with others. Addicts and alcoholics have a special "discovery" that specific painful feeling states may be relieved or that pleasant, special states of well-being may be achieved through a particular drug.

If an analogy for personality structure and affects can be made to a container and its contents, respectively, one could then say that drugs exercise their effects in the way they alter or modify the container and its contents, the two main factors with which drugs interact. For some individuals, the container is too porous and the contents—such as rage and anger—pour out too readily, causing self and others much distress and disharmony. For others, the container is overly restrictive and sealed and thus constricts the experience and communication of a range of contained emotions. And for yet others, certain emotions or energy are depleted and diminished. Drugs and alcohol can modify or act on either the container (structure) or the contents (affects). There may be some duplication and overlap in effects from drugs, and depending on dose and setting, two different drugs might produce similar effects but based on different mechanisms of action. For example, both alcohol, in low to moderate doses, and cocaine enhance socialization. Alcohol dissolves the container and lets feelings out, whereas cocaine mobilizes the contents and produces increased energy and euphoric feeling. Both effects enhance social interaction. On the other hand, alcohol in heavy doses, like opiates, may have a containing or muting effect on intense, painful emotions. Notwithstanding some of these similarities, the self-medication hypothesis rests on the assumption that the three main classes of drugs of abuse—that is, stimulants, opiate-analgesics, and sedative-hypnotics—have distinctly different actions and effects.

The process whereby substance abusers discover that the particular action of a drug suits them best has been variously described as the "drug-of-choice" (Weider and Kaplan), "the preferential use of drugs" (Milkman and Frosch), "the self-selection process" (Khantzian, "Self-Selection"), and "the drug of commitment." In this section, I discussed the appeal of stimulants and opiates, and in the next section, I will discuss the appeal of the sedative-hypnotics, in particular, alcohol.

Stimulants

Within one decade cocaine has gone from being a relatively low-profile, elite, exclusive drug of glamorous, fast-living, and famous people, to a drug that pervades all strata of our society. Because it is the most widespread and prevalent stimulant of abuse, I will consider it the representative drug of the stimulant class of drugs.

The main desired effects of cocaine derive from its activating and energizing properties. It probably has wide appeal because its stimulating effects allure both low-energy- and high-energy-type individuals. For the former, cocaine helps to overcome fatigue and depletion states associated with depression (Khantzian, "Self-Medication," "Self-Selection") or relieves feelings of boredom and emptiness (Wurmser); for high-energy individuals, cocaine provides increased feelings of assertiveness, self-esteem, and frustration tolerance (Weider and Kaplan) or "augments a hyperactive, restless lifestyle and an exaggerated need for self sufficiency" (Khantzian, "Impulse," 100).

The affect states that respond to the stimulating action of cocaine are more often than not related to an individual's personality organization and defensive style, which probably predispose the individual to characteristic-associated states of depression, boredom, emptiness, and hyperactivity and make drug-seeking behavior and involvement more likely. Although an extensive review of these personality factors is not possible, the following are examples of factors that can contribute to cocaine use: (1) states of boredom and emptiness with which certain cocaine addicts suffer could be the basis on which they are described as "sensation" or "stimulus-seeking" personalities; (2) other individuals who are overcompensating, ambitious, and driven in their character style use stimulants to augment their drive to achieve, or to compensate for their not infrequent collapse in self-esteem and depression when their ambitions fail; and (3) cocaine may act paradoxically to calm certain restless, emotionally labile individuals with attention deficit disorder (Khantzian, "Self-Regulation," "Self-Medication").

Case Vignette. Sam, a 39-year-old, successful businessman, one year into recovery, poignantly demonstrated many of these features of distress and lifelong character flaws that set him up to "love" cocaine. Despite being very personable, handsome, and successful in his businesses, he complained of always being afraid of people, "out of touch with his desires and needs and pleasing people." Despite many sexual liaisons, he said until recently he never felt close to anyone, and more recently when he did, he "lost" himself in the relationship. He described how minor or major external events could rapidly flip his self-esteem. At these times he would fuel an insatiable need for love and admiration with cocaine. Action and activity, he said, was his main mode of coping, and cocaine provided the means to get started and continue moving. The drug would help him to overcome his overbearing depression and to feel empowered and attractive enough to literally cruise around and find a woman to satisfy his needs.

Opiate-Analgesics

In contrast to the stimulants, opiates principally have a muting and containing action. Although opiates mute and relieve physical pain—and on this basis we might surmise that they generally alleviate emotional pain, and they do—I have been impressed that they have a much more specific effect and appeal. Working more exclusively with narcotic addicts in the early 1970s in a methadone treatment program, I became impressed with how many of the narcotic addicts conveyed and demonstrated the muting and containing action of opiates on aggression and violent feelings (Khantzian, "Opiate," "Preliminary"). A subsequent series of reports (Wurmser; Khantzian, "Psychological"; Vereby) described how individuals who prefer and have become dependent on opiates have had longstanding histories as victims of physical abuse and violence and in many cases often turned into the perpetrators of violence. Such people, whether victims or perpetrators, suffer with acute and chronic states of associated aggressive and rageful feelings. Individuals predisposed to opiate use discover that these intense, disorganizing affects are significantly contained or attenuated when they first use opiates, and on this basis they described this action as "calming—feeling mellow—safe—[or]—normal for the first time."

In my experience, the problem with aggression in such individuals is a function of an excess of this intense affect—partly constitutional and partly environmental in origin—that interacts with ego and self structures that are underdeveloped or deficient and thus fail to contain this affect. Opiates are compelling because their anti-aggression/rage action mutes uncontrolled aggression and reverses internal psychological disorganization and the external threat of counter aggression with which these intense emotions are associated (Khantzian, "Self-Medication," "Psychological").

> *Case Vignette.* A 47-year-old psychologist described graphically how her preference for the containing and soothing effects of opiates compensated for her inability to process emotional distress. Although she was more subdued at the time she offered the following complaints and concerns, early in treatment she had powerfully displayed an intensely angry and intemperate self when frustrated.
>
> Anticipating a stressful, overseas flight that day, she complained, "There's no place in my brain for [dealing with] discomfort." She was expecting to experience a "cranky sleeplessness" on the flight and worried that she would target her husband with her feelings. She was anticipating that her only alternative would be to use drugs. She pointed to a print portraying a mother comfortably and comfortingly holding a child and lamented that she could not calm or sooth herself. Not insignificantly she contrasted her lot to that of two other patients in group therapy who used alcohol to overcome inhibitions and to socialize.

ALCOHOL AND SELF-MEDICATION

The patient in the last vignette perceptively and intuitively grasped how alcohol affects individuals who prefer it differently from the way alcohol affects those who prefer opiates. Whereas opiate addicts brim with intense and most often angry feelings, alcoholics suffer because they more often are restricted and overcontained in the ways they experience and express emotion. Sedative-hypnotics including alcohol have appeal because these drugs relieve tense, anxious states associated with rigid, overdrawn defenses. The psychoanalyst Fenichel quotes an unknown source that "the superego is that part of the mind that is soluble in alcohol." This quote corresponds better to the dynamics that are emphasized in early psychoanalytic formulations. These early views stressed that an overdrawn conscience could leave individuals conflicted and tense about sexual and aggressive drives and impulses and that alcohol acted on releasing individuals from their restrictive superego defenses. More recent formulations focus on ego defenses and the subjective aspects of self and self-other experiences.

In this section, I chiefly use alcohol as the main and representative drug for the sedative-hypnotic class of substances. Beyond alcohol, the main types of drugs abused in this class are the barbiturates, such as secobarbital, and the barbiturate-like drugs, such as glutethimide. More recently, these drugs have been replaced by benzodiazepines. The abuse potential of the benzodiazepines is variable and to some degree seems to be a function of pharmacokinetics. On the other hand, a recent report suggested that states of distress, "probably . . . discomfort with people and one's surroundings, discontentment and dysphoria," (Ciraulo, Barnhill, and Greenblatt, 336) are greater in alcoholics and are probably the main determinants as well in the abuse of benzodiazepines. In this report, Ciraulo and associates provided empirical support for self-medication factors in alcoholism. They showed that alcoholics react with a more positive change to the benzodiazepine alprazolam than controls do and are therefore more likely to abuse this drug. Notwithstanding the differences in form—that is, a pill versus a drink—and meaning, there are enough similarities to use alcohol as the representative drug of this class of drugs to explore their appeal as self-medication agents.

Affects and Alcohol

Whereas early psychodynamic formulations stressed the dissolving or disinhibiting effect of alcohol on rigid superego mechanisms of defense, more contemporary formulations have placed greater emphasis on alcohol's effect on constricted ego defenses and subjective feelings involving the sense of self and self in relationships with other people. A modern song by Jimmy Buffet captures how alcohol releases feelings and allows him, and most likely others, to enjoy a better sense of well-being within himself:

> I drink a lot of whiskey
> It gives me such a glow
> It makes me quite immobile
> But it lets my feelings show.
> "Brahma Fear"

As I have suggested, some substance abusers, like this artist and others, suffer because they cannot feel their feelings. Our current understanding of why it is that certain individuals cannot feel and need substances to do so is not entirely clear. Some argue that certain patients who are totally out of touch with feelings are "disaffected" and use drugs and activity to ameliorate feelingless, lifeless states related to primitive defenses against anxieties associated with rage and terror (McDougall). This formulation is reminiscent of conflict psychology, but on a more archaic level. Others (Krystal and Raskin) have proposed that feeling-life is underdeveloped in alcoholics and that affects, when underdeveloped, tend to remain somatized, not differentiated—for example, alcoholics cannot distinguish anxiety from depression—and not verbalized. Whether deriving from conflict or developmental deficits, sedative-hypnotic abusers' descriptions of their experience may better convey how their preferred drugs alter their feelings, as the following example demonstrates:

> *Case Vignette.* A 30-year-old divorcée, brought up by a restricted and restricting mother and an alcoholic father, withdrew from her family and engaged in much promiscuous activity while a teenager to avoid, in particular, her mother's harsh and critical attitudes. She married in her early twenties and almost totally reversed her behavior and attitudes, adopting strict measures of propriety. By her late twenties, dissatisfaction with her unhappy marriage ultimately left her with a chronic sense of dysphoria and disabling migraine headaches. She dramatically discovered that

the barbiturates in a commonly prescribed drug for headaches relieved more than her physical distress. Describing the drug effects, she said, "It's wonderful—[it] relieves the boredom and fills the void."

Well-Being, Self-Esteem, and Alcohol

For some, the principal reason for using alcohol or related drugs is to just feel, as the previous case example and Jimmy Buffet's song suggests. For others, it is to feel better inside oneself or to feel better about oneself. Much of this had to do with splits in personality organization that wall-off comforting, soothing, and validating parts of self and do not allow a person to provide these functions for self. Krystal ("Self-Representation") and Krystal and Raskin have proposed that this class of drugs has appeal because the drugs dissolve exaggerated defenses of denial and splitting. For some, alcohol allows the brief and therefore safe experience of loving and aggressive feelings that are otherwise "walled-off" and leave such individuals feeling cut off and empty. Others discover that the soothing effect of alcohol calms internal clamor and emotional "noise," as the following example shows:

Case Vignette. A 40-year-old psychiatrist described her nightly dependence on a bottle of wine as a means of achieving a sense of "bliss, harmony, and oneness." She emphasized that it was the only time she felt "all right," and that she drank "to maintain a blissful oneness with the world." Although in her recovery she was discovering that Alcoholics Anonymous, jogging, and music could get her outside of the "inner [emotional] noise," she described how she still had to fight the other alternative that would immediately "quiet the noise," namely, the alcohol.

Relationships and Alcohol

The notion of alcohol as a superego solvent partly explains why certain tense, neurotically inhibited individuals "enjoy" alcohol as a social lubricant and why this effect is enjoyed by many more in Western cultures for purposes of socializing and partying. Its main attraction, however, is more likely related to deeply seated defenses related to discomfort and fears about human closeness, dependency, and intimacy. Both superego and ego defenses may, nevertheless, rigidly coalesce in such individuals to leave them feeling chronically distant, cut off, and cold in relationships with significant others. It is often under these conditions that certain predisposed people have a powerful and often dramatic realization as to what alcohol and sedative-hypnotics can do. A popular author and lecturer describes how a child rigidly internalizes harsh parental controls, and subsequently, how the resultant strictures in personality yield to the discovery of drug and alcohol effects:

> So you couldn't be mad, you couldn't be sad, you couldn't be glad. You became a walking uptight. Then when you put the chemical in your body—pow! You could relax for the very first time. You were functional! You could feel your feelings, dance, talk to girls. I'm alive! Alive! (Bradshaw, 89).

CONCLUSION

Self-medication factors play an important role in the development of a reliance on drugs and alcohol. Each class of drugs-of-abuse interacts with painful affect states and related personality factors to make an individual's preferred drug appealing and compelling. Drug addicts and alcoholics share in common general problems in self-regulation involving difficulties with affect life, self-esteem, relationships, and self-care. These self-regulation problems combine to make people more desperate, driven, isolated, and impulsive and more likely to assume the risks of drug and alcohol seeking and using. Addiction-prone individuals discover which drug suits them best through the unique qualities of their affect experience, and these choices are what distinguish drug addicts and alcoholics from each other.

Given that all humans more or less struggle with self-regulation issues, what probably distinguishes substance abusers in general from non-substance abusers is the way capacities to experience and regulate feeling interact with the capacity to manage and contain behavior or impulses. We need to study further how, for example, basic states of well-being, a healthy regard for self and others, and mature self-care protect against addictive and alcoholic dependence. Considerable clinical and empirical evidence has accumulated over the past two decades indicating that it is probably the malignant combination of defects in regulating affects and self-care, or problems in managing feelings and impulses, that are the necessary and sufficient deficiencies that produce addiction and alcoholism. Addictive and alcoholic solutions, then, are a way of compensating for self-regulation problems that individuals cannot otherwise correct on their own (Khantzian, "Contemporary"; Donovan). Unfortunately, such solutions are short-lived and the attempts at self-correction backfire and fail.

BIBLIOGRAPHY

Blatt, S. J., W. Berman, S. Bloom-Feshback, A. Sugarman, C. Wilber, and H. Kleber. "Psychological Assessment of Psychopathology in Opiate Addicts." *Journal of Nervous and Mental Disease* 172 (1984). Pp. 156–65.

Bradshaw, J. "Our Families, Ourselves." *Self Center* September/October 1988.

Ciraulo, D. A., J. C. Barnhill, and D. J. Greenblatt. "Abuse Liability and Clinical Pharmacokinetics of Alprazolam in Alcoholic Men." *The Journal of Clinical Psychiatry* 49 (1988). Pp. 333–37.

Donovan, J. M. "An Etiologic Model of Alcoholism." *American Journal of Psychiatry* 143 (1986). Pp. 1–11.

Dorus, W. and E. C. Senay. "Depression, Demographic Dimension, and Drug Abuse." *American Journal of Psychiatry* 137 (1980). Pp. 699–704.

Fenichel, O. *The Psychoanalytic Theory of Neurosis.* New York: Norton, 1945.

Khantzian, E. J. "A Clinical Perspective of the Cause-Consequence Controversy in Alcoholic and Addictive Suffering." *Journal of the American Academy of Psychoanalysis.* 15.4 (1987). Pp. 521–37.

———. "A Contemporary Psychodynamic Approach to Drug Abuse Treatment." *American Journal of Drug and Alcohol Abuse* 12.3 (1986). Pp. 213–222.

———. "An Ego-Self Theory of Substance Dependence." *Theories of Addiction. NIDA Monograph #30.* Eds. E. J. Lettieri, M. Sayers, and H. W. Wallenstein. Rockville, MD: National Institute on Drug Abuse, 1980. Pp. 29–33

———. "Impulse Problems in Addiction: Cause and Effect Relationships." *Working with the Impulsive Person.* Ed. H. Wishnie. New York: Plenum Press, 1979. Pp. 97–112.

———. "Opiate Addiction: A Critique of Theory and Some Implications for Treatment." *American Journal of Psychotherapy* 28 (1974). Pp. 59–70.

———. "Preliminary Dynamic Formulation of the Psychopharmacologic Action of Methadone." *Proceedings of the Fourth National Methadone Conference, San Francisco. 1972.* New York: National Association for the Prevention of Addiction to Narcotics, 1972.

———. "Psychological (Structural) Vulnerabilities and the Specific Appeal of Narcotics." *Annals of the New York Academy of Science* 398 (1982). Pp. 24–32.

———. "Psychopathological Causes and Consequences of Drug Dependence." *Etiological Aspects of Alcohol and Drug Abuse.* Eds. E. Gottheil, K. A. Druley, T. E. Skoloda, and H. Waxman. Springfield, IL: Charles Thomas, 1983. Pp. 89–97.

———. "The Self-Medication Hypothesis of Addictive Disorders: Focus on Heroin and Cocaine Dependence." *American Journal of Psychiatry* 142.11 (1985). Pp. 1259–64.

———. "Self-Regulation Factors in Cocaine Dependence: A Clinical Perspective." *The Epidemiology of Cocaine Use and Abuse.* Rockville, MD: National Institute on Drug Abuse, 1988.

———. "Self-Selection and Progression in Drug Dependence." *Psychiatry Digest* 10 (1975). Pp. 19–22.

Khantzian, E. J. and J. E. Mack. "A.A. and Contemporary Psychodynamic Theory." *Recent Developments in Alcoholism, Volume 7.* Ed. M. Galanter. New York: Plenum Press, 1989. Pp. 67–89.

———. "Self-Preservation and the Care of the Self-Ego Instincts Reconsidered." *Psychoanalytic Study of the Child* 38 (1983). Pp. 209–32.

Khantzian, E. J., J. E. Mack, and A. F. Schatzberg. "Heroin Use As an Attempt to Cope: Clinical Observations." *American Journal of Psychiatry* 131 (1974). Pp. 160–64.

Khantzian, E. J. and C. Treece. "DSM-III Psychiatric Diagnosis of Narcotic Addicts: Recent Findings." *Archives of General Psychiatry* 42 (1985). Pp. 1067–71.

———. "Psychodynamics of Drug Dependence: An Overview." *Psychodynamics of Drug Dependence. NIDA Monograph #12.* Ed. J. D. Blaine, and D. A. Julius. Rockville, MD: National Institute on Drug Abuse, 1977. Pp. 11–25.

Krystal, H. "Alexithymia and the Effectiveness of Psychoanalytic Treatment." *International Journal of Psychoanalytic Psychotherapy* 9 (1982). Pp. 353–88.

———. "Self-Representation and the Capacity for Self-Care." *The Annual of Psychoanalysis* 6 (1977). Pp. 209–46.

Krystal, H. and H. A. Raskin. *Drug Dependence: Aspects of Ego Functions.* Detroit: Wayne State University Press, 1970.

Mack, J. E. "Alcoholism, A.A., and the Governance of the Self." *Dynamic Approaches to the Understanding and Treatment of Alcoholism.* Eds. M. H. Bean, and N. E. Zinberg. New York: Free Press, 1981. Pp. 125–62.

Martin, W. R., C. A. Haertzen, and B. B. Hewett. "Psychopathology and Pathophysiology of Narcotic Addicts, Alcoholics, and Drug Abusers." *Psychopharmacology: A Generation of Progress.* Eds. V. A. Lipton, A. DiMascio, and K. F. Killam. New York: Raven Press, 1978.

Martin, W. R., B. B. Hewett, A. J. Baker, and C. A. Haertzen. "Aspects of the Psychopathology and Pathophysiology of Addiction." *Drug Alcohol Dependence* 2 (1977). Pp. 185–202.

McDougall, J. "The 'Dis-Affected' Patient: Reflection on Affect Pathology." *Psychoanalytic Quarterly* 53 (1984). Pp. 386–409.

McLellan, A. T., G. E. Woody, and C. P. O'Brien. "Development of Psychiatric Illness in Drug Abusers." *New England Journal of Medicine* 201 (1979). Pp. 1310–14.

Milkman, H., and W. A. Frosch. "On the Preferential Abuse of Heroin and Emphetamine." *Journal of Nervous and Mental Disease* 156 (1973). Pp. 242–48.

Nicholson, B., and C. Treece. "Object Relations and Differential Treatment Response to Methadone Maintenance." *Journal of Nervous and Mental Disease* 169 (1981). Pp. 424–29.

Rounsaville, B. J., M. M. Weissman, H. Kleber, and C. Wilber. "Heterogeneity of Psychiatric Diagnosis in Treated Opiate Addicts." *Archives of General Psychiatry* 39 (1982). Pp. 161–66.

Rounsaville, B. J., M. M. Weissman, K. Crits-Cristoph, C. Wilber, and H. Kleber. "Diagnosis and Symptoms of Depression in Opiate Addicts: Course and Relationship to Treatment Outcome." *Archives of General Psychiatry* 39 (1982). Pp. 151–56.

Treece, C., and B. Nicholson." DSM-III Personality Type and Dose Levels in Methadone Maintenance Patients." *Journal of Nervous and Mental Disease* 168 (1980). Pp. 621–28.

Vaillant, G. E. "National History of Male Psychological Health. VIII: Antecedents of Alcoholism and 'orality.'" *American Journal of Psychiatry* 137 (1980). Pp. 181–86.

Vereby, K., ed. "Opiods in Mental Illness: Theories, Clinical Observations, and Treatment Possibilities." *Annals of the New York Academy of Science* 168 (1982). Pp. 621–28.

Weider, H., and E. H. Kaplan. "Drug Use in Adolescents: Psychodynamic Meaning and Pharmacogenic Effect." *Psychoanalytical Study of Children* 24 (1969). Pp. 399–431.

Weissman, M. M., F. Slobetz, B. Prusoff, M. Merritz, and P. Howard. "Clinical Depression among Narcotic Addicts Maintained on Methadone in the Community." *American Journal of Psychiatry* 133 (1976). Pp. 1434–38.

Woody, G. E., L. Luborsky, A. T. McLellen, C. P. O'Brien, A. T. Beck, J. Blaine, I. Herman, and A. Hole. "Psychotherapy for Opiate Addicts." *Archives of General Psychiatry* 40 (1983). Pp. 639–45.

Woody, G. E., C. P. O'Brien, and K. Rickels. "Depression and Anxiety in Heroin Addicts: A Placebo-Controlled Study of Doxepin in Combination with Methadone." *American Journal of Psychiatry* 132 (1975). Pp. 447–50.

Wurmser, L. "Psychoanalytic Considerations of the Etiology of Compulsive Drug Use." *Journal of the American Psychoanalytic Association* 22 (1974). Pp. 820–43.

Part II

Theoretical Literary Interventions

CHAPTER 5

"SOMETHING STRANGE BUT NOT UNPLEASANT"

Freud on Cocaine

Lawrence Driscoll

> *Something strange but not unpleasant has happened to me. I put a noticeable end to the last horrible attack with cocaine; since then things have been fine and a great amount of pus is coming out.*
>
> —*Freud in a letter to Fleiss, April 26, 1895*

> *To average bourgeois common sense I have been lost long ago.*
>
> —*Freud (Cocaine, 41)*

ONE MONTH BEFORE ROBERT LOUIS STEVENSON wrote *Jekyll and Hyde* in September 1885, an article appeared in the *Lancet* that described a technique whereby a solution of cocaine could be applied to the larynx. The article was an abstract of the lectures on cocaine that Freud had delivered to the Psychiatrische Verien on March 5, 1885 (*Cocaine,* 154). Freud was not alone in his suggestions that cocaine could be a panacea for the medical community. As Schultz points out, by 1884, "[a]n avalanche of papers appeared in the world's medical literature describing the use of cocaine, not only for local and regional anesthesia, but also as a cure for acute coryza, gonorrhea, vomiting of pregnancy, seasickness, hay fever, opium addiction, sore nipples, vaginismus, whooping cough, neuralgia, dysentery, asthma, syphilis, and angina pectoris" (92).

It is my intention to suggest that when reading Freud's comments on cocaine it is possible to see someone who is anxious to ensure that the meaning of cocaine remains open. The conventional ways of reading Freud's work on cocaine fall into two camps that usually meet at various points. The first way is to treat the work as juvenilia, engaged in by an eager young student whose genius was not yet mature. This disables the text while enabling the commentator to humor Freud's fanciful statements, skipping over them so as to spend more time on Freud's "real," mature work. The second way, which is really an angry magnification of the first position, is to treat the work not as innocent juvenilia from someone who as yet knew no better, but to read it as a highly conscious, dangerous, and irresponsible endorsement of a drug that is "obviously" dangerous. E. M. Thornton's *Freud and Cocaine: The Freudian Fallacy* is a good example of the second approach and his statements also nicely summarize the first position as well, which, for reasons which will become clear, he opposes: "The behavioral eccentricities displayed by Freud in the nineties and dismissed by Jones [Freud's biographer] as the harmless peccadilloes of a man of genius, *must now be given a more sinister interpretations*" (2, my emphasis). Why must they? What is gained by giving the events of the cocaine episode a sinister interpretation? More importantly what is lost by doing this?

What I wish to suggest in this essay, however, is that neither of these positions is very useful in understanding what Freud was trying to say about cocaine. The first position prevents taking what Freud said seriously. The second intimates taking it so seriously that the statements on cocaine may appear to be the mere rantings of an addict, and so once again, they can be dismissed, as Thornton notes, because it is "obvious" from what Freud says about cocaine that these writings are "not the preoccupations of a normal mind" (253). By approaching the work in this way, Freud's contemporaries essentially succeeded in pushing aside Freud's desire to keep the meaning of the drug open, and cocaine now is denotatively linked to addiction and death. This essay hopes to suggest that re-opening Freud's initial line of inquiry and essentially re-opening the range of meanings that Freud was trying to ensure remained in circulation is of vital importance.

In retrospect, Freud said that the cocaine episode was an "allotrion" (*Cocaine,* 35)—from the Greek: *allos,* meaning "other" or "a turning away from the norm"—and that like a perversion, it was a side-path, and not the main route. But more importantly the episode was quite literally, and still is, an allotrion: a turning away from the norm regarding how the "meaning" of cocaine can and should be constructed. Moreover, Freud realized that the only way to get around the deadening weight of common sense was to take a side-route that would enable him to sidestep conventional "wisdom." He also suggests that it was "a side interest, though it was [also] a deep one" (*Cocaine,* 255). I feel that while it has been assumed by Jones and his associates that this remark permits the dismissal of the work, and that Freud is encouraging his readers to do so, the reference to an allotrion actually is a clue to what Freud thought he was doing, which was going against the norm in order to keep the meaning of cocaine from being locked into a pernicious chain of significations. Freud, in this sense, is following Nietzsche, in that the allotrion, which can also mean a "hobby," allows him to come closer to locating a new terrain in which cocaine could run and be free. As Nietzsche says "I know of no other way of dealing with great tasks than that of play" (*Ecce Homo,* 67). I think that Freud was aware that very often a perverse thought is often the best way to get around rigid constructions or "problems," and, although he almost wrecked his career by doing so, he has left behind a trace of scientific knowledge that should hopefully resist any easy positioning of the meaning of the drug.

In opposition to his contemporaries who wanted to condemn him, Freud wanted the meaning of cocaine to stay free from criticism and to remain endlessly open to revision. Obviously, I think this is why the cocaine papers have been so very hard to hear with any degree of accuracy. Freud offers today's reader a cultural reading of cocaine that is quite simply no longer available, and so cannot be heard for what it is: a seriously perverted and pervertedly serious attempt to protect the drug from any of the charges leveled against it, not because Freud was prodrug, but simply because as a concerned doctor he wished the jury to remain out on the subject of cocaine so that we could constantly reinvent our position and remain, healthily, *anti*-antidrug.

Two of Freud's main sources that stirred his interest in cocaine are the works of Theodor Aschenbrandt and W. E. Bentley. In the September 1880 issue of *The Therapeutic Gazette,* Bentley outlined how in 1878 he had written an article that suggested that "if the victim of either opium or alcohol could find a preparation that would produce his accustomed stimulus without leaving a feeling of depression, he could, with the aid of very little exercise of his will, abandon his vice and regain his normal condition. In the erythoxylon coca we find that very article" (*Cocaine,* 16). From the beginning cocaine is framed as a cure, not as a poison.

Bentley's work outlines the story of a man in 1879 who had had an opium habit for five years: "I put him on coca . . . In the October following, I met him and he assured me that he was entirely relieved of the habit" (*Cocaine,* 18). *The Therapeutic Gazette* also outlined in June 1880 the work of Dr. Palmer who had also conducted research on curing opium addiction with cocaine, and the *Gazette* cannot understand why "it was not sooner recommended" (20). The June 1880 article goes on to suggest that although many drugs have not been widely experimented with it is the duty of the "educated practitioner" to "interest themselves in investigation into the possibilities of the newer remedies" (*Cocaine,* 20). *The Therapeutic Gazette* concludes with a reference to the *Louisville Medical News,* which says, in referring to Dr. Palmer's paper, "One feels like trying coca, with or without the opium habit. A harmless remedy for the blues is imperial." (21).

Aschenbrandt had conducted many experiments using cocaine, which again resulted in very favorable results. He cites the work of scientists Schildbach and Mantegazza who suggested that "even if coca were nothing more than a stimulant . . . it still seems to surpass all usual stimulants in harmlessness and agreeability" (*Cocaine,* 22). Aschenbrandt then details how he administered the drug to the battalion that he was working with the result that several soldiers who had been sick or tired would become "cheerful and strong" (25) and, rather than relapsing to their former condition, "maintained the best state of health in the division" (26). If these comments are not quite strange enough for contemporary ears, he adds that "the influence of cocaine on the body is *more benign* than that of the alcohols or cold coffee" (*Cocaine,* 26, my emphasis). These "professional" positions may sound irresponsible and dangerous to some today; yet, why were they not heard this way at the time? The odds are that if these ideas sounds strange to today's reader, I'm sure that today's antidrug position, while it appears quite "sensible" and "true" to many, would also seem dangerous and irresponsible to Freud's contemporaries.

When it actually comes to Freud's *Uber Coca* (1884) the first difficulty the reader will encounter is that the text is not easy to locate. Gay suggests that "the best German edition of Freud's psychoanalytical writings is *Gesammelte Werke, Chronologisch Geordnet*" (*Bourgeois,* 741). Unfortunately *Uber Coca* is not found in the *Gesammelte Werke.* For those texts that are not included in the *Gesammelte Werke,* Gay suggests that the reader may turn to the "handy Studienausgabe"; unfortunately this "omits some *minor* papers" (Gay, 741, my emphasis). The *Standard Edition of the Complete Psychological Works,* a work of "international authority" according to Gay (741), includes a collection that "introduces each work, even the slightest paper, with indispensable bibliographical and historical information" (Gay, 741). Yet, again, the cocaine papers are not included. While these telling absences are not Gay's fault, it is frustrating to discover that *Uber Coca* is also excluded from Gay's *The Freud Reader.* Moreover, the Robert Byck edition of the *Cocaine Papers* that I use for my research has been out of print since 1974. The cocaine episode does not appear in *The Standard Collected Works* and was only published in English in 1963 in Vienna by the obscure Dunquin Press. Robert Byck points out how the historical library of the Yale University School of Medicine did not list the Dunquin Press edition in its catalogue (xvii). Moreover, by comparing the standard edition of Freud's letters to Fleiss edited by Anna Freud with more recent editions, it is possible to see how many of the references to cocaine were removed. For example, in the

June 12, 1895, letters one notices that Freud's remark "I need a lot of cocaine" has been deleted from recent editions. The standard edition of the letters, mistakenly entitled "The Origins of Psychoanalysis," begins in 1887, whereas Freud's major letters detailing his work with cocaine were written in 1884–1886. The letters to Martha Bernays would also be a crucial source of information surrounding this episode. Unfortunately Ernst Jones has published "only an alluring selection of some ninety-three" (Gay, *Bourgeois,* 743). What is it about Freud's work with cocaine that makes it so uniformly absent? Is there some fear that this text, if allowed to escape from obscurity, will somehow poison the entire Freudian canon?

If Freud had openly said that the work with cocaine was an allotrion, Ernest Jones suggests that the cocaine episode was nothing more than a "surreptitious shortcut" (Freud, *Cocaine,* 11), which, by framing the allotrion as secretive and artificial, as well as lazy, suggests that it is not the "real" way of achieving something. In the same way that Jekyll refers to Hyde as "a thick cloak" (Stevenson, 86) that can be discarded at will, Jones desires that the cocaine episode be perceived as merely an ornament, and not the essence of Freud's career. Ernest Jones also wishes to reinforce the sense that the cocaine project was perverse: "To achieve virility and enjoy the bliss of union with the beloved he had forsaken the straight and narrow path of sober 'scientific' work on brain anatomy and seized a surreptitious shortcut: one that was to bring him suffering in the place of success" (*Cocaine,* 11). So, sobriety is on the side of virility and success, while cocaine occupies the space of impotence, suffering, and failure. Jones' interpretation of this part of Freud's oeuvre has been accepted in so far as the cocaine project has not been allowed to come into contact with, or enter into, the Freudian canon.

Before writing *Uber Coca* (1884), Freud felt that Martha Bernays was weak and pale so Freud sent her cocaine "to make her strong and give her cheeks a red colour" (*Cocaine,* 7). Looking forward to visiting her he states: "Woe to you, my Princess, when I am come. I will kiss you quite red and feed you till you are plump. And if you are froward [sic] you shall see who is the stronger, a gentle little girl who doesn't eat enough or a big wild man who has cocaine in his body" (*Cocaine,* 10). The economic significance of cocaine for Freud emerges in a letter to Bernays in 1884, in which he says that they only need one "lucky hit" to be able to "think of setting up home" (*Cocaine,* 6). Freud hopes that his interest in cocaine will turn out like the gold chloride method he invented: "less than [he] imagined, but still something quite respectable" (*Cocaine,* 6). This focus on Freud's economic position is also another way of dismissing the work as lacking real value insofar as he was simply in a rush to find anything that would make him rich. In short, many critics take the Freud's material concerns at this stage of his life as a way of undermining the validity of his statements about cocaine. As Gay points out, Freud is simply hoping that cocaine will assist him in what he referred to as "the chase after money, position, and reputation" (Gay, 43).

In his work on cocaine up to and including *Uber Coca* (1884), Freud, as does Aschenbrandt, presents the drug as a potent source of strength, and as a natural and unharmful substance. Freud suggests that cocaine is a "potent" stimulant (*Cocaine,* 6–4) that can enable one "to hold strength in reserve to meet further demands" (63). Linking cocaine with hard work, he sees it as generating a healthy body, one conducive to the growth of the Victorian family. Blurring the line between Sherlock Holmes and Dr. Livingstone, Freud describes himself in *Uber Coca* as both an "investigator" of cocaine (6) and an "explorer" (40). Cocaine is a "magical substance" (10); it can make him "strong as a lion, gay and cheerful" (41). Not only can Freud feel "quite calm with a small dose of cocaine" (162), the drug is not debilitating and in fact enhances bodily strength: "I won't be tired . . . I shall be traveling under the influence of coca" (42).

To "understand" cocaine, Freud decided to measure its effects on the strength of muscles, and reaction times. For the purposes of the former he used a dynamometer and found that with cocaine he noticed "a marked increase in the motor power of the arm" (99); moreover, "results achieved under the influence of cocaine even exceed the maximum under normal conditions" (104). Freud also concluded that "under cocaine my reaction times were shorter and more uniform than before taking the drug" (104). This parallel between cocaine and its relation to health and work/creativity is developed when Freud offers examples of men who find themselves able to write after taking cocaine. One male patient was able, after treatment, "to write a long letter" (67) and awoke the next morning "ready for work" (61) whilst a "young writer . . . was enabled by treatment with coca to resume his work after a longish illness" (73). Another example tells of a writer, "who for weeks before had been incapable of any literary production and who was able to work for 14 hours without interruption after taking 0.1g of cocaine" (114–5).

Uber Coca opens by establishing the geographical and historical origins of cocaine. The background that Freud offers serves to place the drug firmly within the realm of nature in that cocaine begins life as a "plant" in South America. Not only is it seen as "an indispensable stimulant" to some ten million people, but it also contributes to the economy of the region: "The large-scale production (allegedly 30 million pounds annually) makes coca leaves an important item of trade, and taxation" (*Cocaine,* 50). Freud outlines how, amongst the Peruvians, the "divine plant . . . satiates the hungry, strengthens the weak, and causes them to forget their misfortune" (50). While Freud is writing this article in the hope that the drug that he is (re)discovering will win him his reputation, and will thus erase his current economic "misfortune," it is not surprising that he tells how coca leaves were "offered in sacrifice to the gods . . . and were placed in the mouths of the dead to ensure them a favourable reception in the beyond" (50). The only difference being that Freud hopes that his pronouncements on cocaine will earn him a favourable reception from his colleagues.

These attempts include separating cocaine from the devil and magic and placing it firmly into the category of a natural drug conducive to the work ethic. He relates how the council of Lima changed its policy when it became clear that "the Indians could not perform the heavy labour imposed upon them in the mines if they were forbidden to partake of coca" (50). Possibly looking forward to his own fame and the generalized acceptance of the drug amongst the medical profession, Freud concludes proudly that "the coca plant has maintained its position among the natives to the present day; there even remain traces of the religious veneration which was once accorded to it" (50). By inserting his (re)discovery of the drug into the initial discovery of Peru and the coca plant, Freud the "explorer" hopes that he has found his "treasure." One thing that is interesting about these parts of the narrative is that Freud opens up many contradictory positions for himself: he can be a detective, a defender of the indigenous Peruvian population, a defender of the drug, *and* an explorer. Only through a proliferation of positions can the meaning of cocaine be prized open. In contrast, today there is one position: that of the soldier constantly fighting an invasion by an evil drug that threatens to overwhelm all at every turn. Freud's position seems to me preferable, for it grants the strength to explore even further and locate even more positions.

All of Freud's later pronouncements on cocaine are basically variations on these original themes. The drug is pastoral in origin; "it thrives best in the warm valleys on the slopes of the Andes" (*Cocaine,* 49); it has religious associations; it is conducive to the economy both as a product and in its contribution to labor power in that it can restore strength while eliminating the need for food. Freud does note that Weddell and Mantegazza suggest that an "immoderate use of coca leads to a cachexia characterized physically by digestive complaints, emaciation, etc., and mentally by moral depravity and a complete apathy toward everything not connected with the enjoyment of the stimulant" (52), but he dismisses these problems as being caused by a weakness in the individual user.

In order to represent the drug, and himself, as "respectable," Freud minimizes the extent to which the drug could be interpreted as possessing weakening qualities. Freud attempts to suggest that cocaine is not a "narcotic," pointing out that most of the contemporary evidence is in agreement with his categorization: "only the elder Schroff refers to cocaine as a narcotic and classes it with opium and cannabis, while almost everyone else ranks it with caffeine, etc." (*Cocaine,* 57–58).

Another striking difference between Freud's understanding of cocaine and the contemporary view can be found in Freud's experiments with cocaine. In every case Freud asserts that the drug produces no artificial effects: on the contrary, the drug brings forth a self more natural than nature. The drug produces natural results that, according to Freud, will not interfere with the workings of the body or the body politic. The natural plant provides "a lasting gain in strength" (62) and "one . . . feels more vigorous and more capable of work . . . One is simply normal, and soon finds it difficult to believe that one is under the influence of a drug at all" (60). The drug and the body have now collapsed into each other to the point that one cannot distinguish where the "natural" body ends and the "artificial" drug begins. Cocaine becomes the body's supplement, without which it is unfinished and incomplete: for Freud, the body can only be natural *with* drugs.

Freud hoped that the cocaine project would be acceptable to his colleagues insofar as it is encased in an economy that leads back to the good path, rechannelling desire away from the pathology of narcissism and addiction into respectability and work. Possibly aware that his flirtation with cocaine would be seen as a perverse activity, Freud was careful to ensure that his interest in cocaine was in no way linked to iatrogenic auto-affection, or unnatural desires, going to great lengths to assure the reader not only of the naturalness of the drug but also to convince them of the naturalness of his desire for cocaine. For Freud, the "euphoria" that cocaine produces is not unnatural: "the mood induced by coca in such doses is due not so much to direct stimulation as to the disappearance of elements in one's general state of well-being which cause depression" (60). In Freud's framework cocaine does not artificially stimulate the body, introducing something alien into it, but on the contrary the drug actually removes bad things from the body leaving behind a normal self. Far from bringing forth some horrendous monster, Freud suggests that the effects of cocaine are *so minor* that one might fail to recognize the benefits of this alkaloid: "[the] absence of signs that could distinguish the state from the normal euphoria of good health makes it even more likely that we will underestimate it" (114). Moreover, far from cocaine producing an altered state, the alteration is barely perceptible; Freud defines this as "the absence of any feeling of alteration" (114) and declares that when on cocaine "it is difficult to believe that one is under the influence of a foreign agent" (114).

In a letter to Bernays, written under the influence of cocaine, Freud tells her of how Bruer told him that "hidden under the surface of timidity there lay in [himself] an extremely daring and fearless human being" to which Freud responds that he "had always felt so, but never dared tell anyone . . . I always felt so helpless and incapable of expressing these ardent passions even by a word or a poem. So I have always restrained myself, and it is this, I think, which people must see in me" (165). In the same cocaine-inspired letter, Freud writes that he feels he may also have unleashed "something alien in [himself]" (165) and dismisses ideas about things in his personality that are "hidden under the surface" claiming that he is merely "making silly confessions to [Martha], my sweet darling, and really without any reason whatever *unless it is the cocaine that makes me talk so much*" (165). Freud is unwilling to carry on writing if the work has no reason to be written, but this letter also implies that what Freud is writing, because it is a drugged confession given without his conscious consent, is somehow lacking in rationality and logical reason and can be discounted. He almost fears his own position in that he is making a case for cocaine that the "alien" part of himself knows must be permissible; yet the powerful drug of common sense asks him to question himself. It is as if he almost cannot quite believe what he is saying about cocaine, and, even though he is dismissive in this letter, he stands by his alien idea throughout his life and never retracts any of his major pronouncements on cocaine. In a sense he is right: the stance that he is making on cocaine is "extremely daring."

Having positioned the drug as natural, he goes on to reveal how it is not destructive of natural willpower, but actually increases willpower: "One senses an increase of self-control . . . During this stage of the cocaine condition, which is not otherwise distinguished, appear those symptoms which have been described as the wonderful stimulating effect of coca. Long-lasting, intensive mental or physical work can be performed without fatigue" (60). Although Freud discovers that cocaine displaces the natural desire to eat and sleep, he dismisses this point in so far as the needs of the body can be overridden, allowing the mind to operate with greater, not lesser, degrees of productivity:

> While the effects of cocaine last one can, if urged to do so, eat copiously and without revulsion; but one has the clear feeling that

> the meal was superfluous. Similarly, as the effect of coca declines it is possible to sleep on going to bed, but sleep can just as easily be omitted with no unpleasant consequences. During the first hours of the coca effect one cannot sleep, but this sleeplessness is in no way distressing.
>
> I have tested this effect of coca, which wards off hunger, sleep and fatigue and steels one to intellectual effort, some dozen times on myself" (60)

In positioning cocaine as natural, Freud asserts that the drug does not undermine self-control and is therefore *not addictive:*

> It seems to me noteworthy—and I discovered this in myself and in other observers who were capable of judging such things—that a first dose or even repeated doses of coca produce no compulsive desire to use the stimulant further; on the contrary, one feels a certain unmotivated aversion to the substance. (62)

Freud even cites the drugs' nonaddictive properties as the reason why cocaine has not "established itself in Europe" in spite of "some warm recommendations" (62). Moreover, cocaine is recommended by Freud because it actually cleans up after itself, leaving the body exactly as it found it, leaving no "trace" of itself behind: "[the drug] left no sign whatsoever that the experimenter had passed through a period of intoxication" nor does it leave any trace of "depression" (62).

At this point Freud points out how "[i]t was inevitable that a plant which had achieved such a reputation for marvelous effects in its country of origin should have been used to treat the most varied disorders and illnesses of the body" (63). Unlike in *Jekyll and Hyde* where we think that the powder caused Jekyll to become hysterical, Freud claims that "according to Caldwell [cocaine] is *the best tonic* for hysteria" (65). Readers may tend to imagine that cocaine upsets the natural balance of the body yet Freud suggests that it can actually return the body to a natural harmony, returning one "to a normal desire to eat" in the case of "gastronomic excesses" (66). Bulimia is an example of a case of a natural desire that becomes unnatural, but could be returned to a natural state through the intervention of cocaine. The drug offers a "permanent cure" for "dyspeptic complaints" (65), and where there is a "chronic lack of appetite the use of coca restored the patient to health" (68).

Whereas today readers assume that the use of cocaine leads to emaciation and the degeneration of the body, Freud believed that cocaine actually assists in "limiting degeneration of the body" (68). As an example Freud cites the case of a Dr. Hole who had a patient suffering from "chronic lack of appetite [and] an advanced condition of emaciation and exhaustion," this person was soon "restored . . . to health" by administering cocaine (67). Freud also presents cocaine in a favorable light by revealing that not only is cocaine a friend to the body, it is also a friend to other medicines. As an example Freud shows how cocaine is extremely useful in treating syphilis because the drug can protect the patient from the side effects of mercury. Although Freud does admit in *Uber Coca* that the model of cocaine as a source of healing has been "disproven" (69), he goes on to argue that the case of the starvation in La Paz, which for Freud has the authority of an experiment "carried out by history itself," seems "to contradict this conclusion" (69) because only the inhabitants who had "partaken of coca are said to have escaped death by starvation" (69). Once again the implication is that cocaine is so natural that it can imperceptibly supplement food, working for, not against human survival.

Concerned that cocaine will be connected to addiction, sensitivity, and "weakness," Freud outlines how the drug can in fact be used as a cure for morphine addiction.

> In America the important discovery has recently been made that coca preparations possess the power to suppress the craving for morphine in habitual addicts, and also to reduce to negligible proportions the serious symptoms of collapse which appear while the patient is being weaned away from the morphine habit. (70)

Freud also asserts that "the treatment of morphine addiction with coca does not, therefore, result merely in the exchange of one kind of addiction for another . . . the use of coca is only temporary" (71). Not only does the drug strengthen the body, it also actively fights the morphine on behalf of the body: "coca has a directly antagonistic effect on morphine" (71). So while it can work together with the curative effects of mercury, it can also work *against* the negative effects of morphine.

Freud suggests that cocaine could also be used to cure people of addiction to alcohol. In *Uber Coca* he states that in North America cocaine has been used to treat "chronic alcoholism" with a degree of "undoubted success" (72). Freud goes on to discuss several other case studies, conducted by W. E. Bentley, in which "coca was responsible for the cure" (73). Having suggested earlier that coca can be a cure for syphilis, Freud also suggests that cocaine functions as an aphrodisiac, re-inscribing cocaine into the realm of familial desire by asserting that it can be of use in cases of "functional weaknesses," that is, impotence (73). Cocaine is seen here as a cure for the failing heterosexual family, facilitating procreation and the repetition of "natural" desire.

Once *Uber Coca* was written, Freud continually added to it, either to offer improved suggestions or to revise certain aspects. In effect, he persisted, much to the annoyance of his contemporaries, in constantly keeping the meaning of the drug open. In February 1885, Freud republished *Uber Coca* with an addenda in which he confirmed some of the points made in the 1884 text. For Freud there is a "diversity of individual reactions to cocaine" (107) and while some people "showed signs of coca euphoria" there are "others who experienced absolutely no effect" (107). Obviously these statements point accusingly to the holes in the rhetoric whereby drugs operate in a uniform and constant way. He also continues to remind his contemporaries of cocaine's efficacy in cases of "morphine collapse" and states that "subcutaneous injections" of cocaine are "quite harmless" (109).

By 1886, reports of cocaine "addiction" were appearing, and Freud's metaphors of self control and health were brought into contact with late-nineteenth-century philosophies that actively portrayed addiction as a loss of self-control, passivity, and weak morals. Freud then had to deal with the fact that many reports "of the toxic effects of cocaine were received . . . from eye and throat specialists [in which] cocaine began to get the reputation of a highly dangerous drug whose use over a long period of time produces a 'habit' or 'condition similar to morphinism'" (172).

In response to these criticisms Freud defended himself in *Craving for and Fear of Cocaine* (July 1887). In this paper Freud never confesses that he ever made any errors in judgment but, conversely, continues to defend the drug. In the paper he cites the case of Dr. Hammond who, like Freud, was also eager to "test the truth of reports appearing recently in the journals that have aroused a great deal of fear" (176). Hammond's work makes it clear that "the first authors who reported on the use of coca among South American natives had greatly exaggerated its noxiousness" (176). What bothers Freud is that these reports "were repeatedly warmed over and served anew, without reference as to source, and thus inspired the currently prevailing bias" (176). Dr. Hammond was injecting cocaine "repeatedly" and Freud draws our attention to the fact that he could "give up the drug whenever he wished" (176). Dr. Hammond was also using cocaine to treat a woman who was suffering from Graves' Disease; similarly, Freud notes that "she was able to discontinue its use without any difficulty" (176). Freud states that in spite of all the criticisms, his "original statements had in no way been invalidated" (172) and suggests that this "agitation against the new alkaloid . . . has gone much too far" (173):

> *All reports of addiction to cocaine and deterioration resulting from it refer to morphine addicts,* persons who, already in the grip of one demon are so weak in will power, so susceptible, that they would misuse, and indeed have misused, any stimulant held out to them. *Cocaine has claimed no other, no victim on its own.* (173, italics in the original)

Unfortunately, many physical disorders begin to emerge that Freud could not dismiss and so he concedes that "another set of observations must, however, be characterized unequivocally as cocaine poisoning because of their similarity to symptoms which can be produced experimentally by an overdose of cocaine: stupor, dizziness, increase of pulse rate, irregular respiration, anorexia, insomnia and eventually delirium and muscular weakness" (*Cocaine,* 173), but he feels that these are "rare occurrences" (174). While he acknowledged that cocaine poisoning is possible, Freud still attempted to keep cocaine separate from the question of addiction. The same kind of logic is applied that was used with morphine addicts, because while there are varying effects that can occur with cocaine, whereby "one does not know when a toxic effect will appear" (174), these are dependent finally not upon the chemistry of the drug, but of the person, and of "the sensitivity of certain individuals to cocaine" (174). Freud concludes that "the reason for the irregularity of the cocaine effect lies in the individual variations in excitability and in the variation of the condition of the vasomotor nerves on which cocaine acts" (175). In *Craving for and Fear of Cocaine,* Freud states that although individual reactions to the drug may occur, it is clear that "the possibility of toxic effects need not preclude the application of cocaine to attain a desirable end" (174). Freud knew, then, that in order to reach a "cure" for the drug addiction one had to endure a period of toxicity. If one reads Ernest Jones' comments on *Craving for and Fear of Cocaine,* it is apparent that Jones is intent on minimizing Freud's statements. For example, Jones states that "[m]any must have at least have regarded him as a man of reckless judgment" and Jones feels that Freud's "sensitive conscience passed the same sentence" (198). Peter Gay states that "[w]hen Fritz Wittels declared in his biography that Freud, concerning the 'mistakes' of the cocaine episode, had 'thought long and painfully just how this could have happened to him,' Freud denied it: 'False!' he wrote in the margin" (*Freud,* 45). It is tempting to think that Freud would respond in the same way to Jones' remark.

Craving for and Fear of Cocaine (July 1887) was the last piece that Freud wrote on the topic until the cocaine dreams of 1895 and 1898. Freud felt that his first year in practice was his "least successful and darkest year" (*Cocaine,* 343) as a result of simultaneously trying to ensure his own "material existence as well as that of a rapidly increasing family" (343). As the critic Bernfield points out, "[i]n this situation he found himself simultaneously rejected by the leaders of the Vienna Medical School as the propagandist of the foreigner Charcot, and on the national scene accused of the greatest irresponsibility and recklessness [due to the cocaine episode]" (*Cocaine,* 343). In 1898, Freud discusses *The Dream of the Botanical Monograph.* The text of the dream is very brief: "I had written a monograph on a certain plant. The book lay before me and I was at the moment turning over a folded coloured plate. Bound up in each copy there was a dried specimen of the plant, as though it had been taken from a herbarium" (*Cocaine,* 224). Contrary to the universal blame to which he had been subjected, Freud interprets the dream as essentially exonerating him from the blame that was directed at him in the 1880s:

> What it meant was: "After all, I'm the man who wrote the valuable and memorable paper (on cocaine)," just as in the earlier dream I had said on my behalf, "I'm a conscientious and hard-working student." In both cases what I was insisting was: "I may allow myself to do this." (229)

As with Stevenson's Dr. Jekyll who asked Lanyon to ensure that Hyde gets his "rights" after his death, Freud sees the dream as "a plea on behalf of [his] own rights" (229). The dream of Irma's injection also operates in the same way for Freud. This dream, which was to become the first specimen dream in the *1900 Interpretation of Dreams,* concerns a patient who is suffering after receiving an unclean injection from Freud. Freud asserts that the meaning of the dream is that "Irma's pains had been caused by Otto giving her an incautious injection of an unsuitable drug . . . a thing I should never have done; I never did any harm with my injections" (*Cocaine,* 219). While he is desirous to make himself free of the blame for Irma's sufferings, Freud's reading of the dream can also be read as his attempt to separate his "cure" (cocaine) from the poison that it has become. It would appear then that in spite of the general sense that Freud had behaved irresponsibly, Freud himself never believed that his opinions or his statements on cocaine were irresponsible. Like Hyde, who has no interest in confessing, Freud could not satisfy his detractors and confess he made a professional mistake because as far as he was concerned no mistake had been made. This very refusal to confess appeared to infuriate Freud's contemporaries, seeming to prove to their minds that he was, after all, guilty, irresponsible, and perhaps mad. This may be the reason for excluding *Uber Coca* from the Freudian canon, because it resists being made into part of the story that many now want to tell about cocaine. As the Freudian scholar David Musto reminds us, "Freud never publicly retracted his broad endorsement of cocaine" (*Cocaine,* 368).

Avital Ronell feels that Freud became involved with cocaine "for the sake of some unplumbable purpose" (52) and in *Crack Wars* states that "[t]his is not the place to analyze that fatal encounter" (53). In his recent biography of Freud, Peter Gay suggests that "cocaine held some uncomfortable, not wholly acknowledged meaning for [Freud]" (43), who was at the same time "intent on minimizing the effects of the affair upon him" (45). Although it only occupies one page in Gay's eight hundred page text, this "misadventure remained one of the most troubling episodes in Freud's life" (45). Notice too that like Jones, Gay almost imperceptibly assumes that Freud's work with cocaine must be framed as a "misadventure," or in Ronell's perhaps ironical remark, a *fatal* encounter. Writing from within an historical moment in which the meaning of cocaine has been both fixed as well as substantially altered from what Freud was hoping for, Ernest Jones is retrospectively empowered to present a picture of Freud as a dangerous drug pusher: "he pressed it on his friends and colleagues, both for themselves and their patients; he gave it to his sisters. In short, looked at from the vantage point of our present knowledge, he was rapidly becoming a public menace" (*Cocaine,* 7).

Jones also dismisses *Uber Coca* suggesting that "it might well be ranked higher as a literary production than as an original scientific contribution" (*Cocaine,* 8). Moreover, what bothers Jones, and what prevents the work from being taken seriously, is the degree of closeness that exists between Freud and his subject. What makes Jones anxious is that Freud is speaking with a "personal warmth as if he were in love with the content itself" (8). Jones also insists on framing the work as something less than normal or correct. For Jones the cocaine episode was a "foolhardy episode" that Freud apparently exacerbated by his constant "evasion and confusion of the issue" (xxxiv). Recently E. M. Thornton has taken this dismissal of the work even further, suggesting that *all* of Freud's theories should be discarded for they are "not the preoccupations of a normal mind" (253) but instead are the product of a paranoid coke fiend with "poisoned brain cells" (3). Thornton even suggests that on the subject of the cocaine episode Freud engaged in "deliberate mendacity," which is conveniently located as "simply another symptom of his addiction" to cocaine (3). His conclusion is that Freud's entire oeuvre is the product "of his cocaine usage and had no basis in fact" (5), and is merely the sad product of his "drugged brain" (6). In his bibliographical essay, Gay notes the existence of some critical works on Freud and cocaine, but divides them up into those that are "dependable," including the Byck edition, and those like E. M. Thornton's *Freud and Cocaine: The Freudian Fallacy*, which, in accusing Freud of being a drugged charlatan, is no more than a model of "the literature of denigration" (749). While Gay may be disturbed by Thornton's sweeping conclusions, they essentially share the same opinion on the cocaine episode as Jones: it was a mistake, a foolhardy episode, an error, an obsession, irresponsible behavior, deception, mendacity, a perversion of science, and something not worthy of attention, but instead of condemnation.

My view, however, is that Freud wanted to keep the book open on cocaine. Jones says that he can easily see that from his "current vantage point" Freud was becoming a public menace, but Jones can see this not because he has a vantage point but because that is all that he is being allowed to see. In a sense his vantage point, like that of today's, is nothing more than a "disadvantage point" from which one can actually see very little. What would it mean to read against today's "vantage point" and *with* Freud? While the book was shut and the narrative was closed off, perhaps from Freud's vantage today's readers might (re)gain a different view of the history of cocaine in order to construct a better relationship with the drug.

BIBLIOGRAPHY

Adams, J. W. *Psychoanalysis of Drug Dependence: The Understanding and Treatment of a Particular Form of Pathological Narcissism.* New York: Grune and Stratton, 1978.

Allen, David F. and James F. Jekel. *Crack: The Broken Promise.* St. Martin's Press: New York, 1991.

Berridge, V. and G. Edwards. *Opium and the People: Opiate Use in Nineteenth-Century England.* London, New York: Allen Lane/St. Martin's Press, 1981.

Blane, H. T. and T. R. Kosten, eds. *Addiction and the Vulnerable Self: Modified Dynamic Group Therapy for Substance Abusers.* New York: The Guildford Press, 1990.

Brennan, Teresa. *The Interpretation of the Flesh: Freud and Femininity.* New York: Routledge, 1992.

Canguilhem, Georges. *The Normal and the Pathological.* New York: Zone Books, 1991.

Clèment, Catherine. *The Weary Sons of Freud.* Tr. Nicole Ball. London, New York: Verso, 1987.

Cocteau, Jean. *Opium: Journal of a Cure.* London: Peter Owen, 1990.

Crowley, Aleister. *The Diary of a Drug Fiend.* Maine: Samuel Weiser, 1970.

David-Mènard, Monique. *Hysteria from Freud to Lacan.* Tr. Catherine Porter. Ithaca, NY: Cornell University Press, 1989.

Decker, Hannah S. *Freud, Dora, and Vienna 1900.* New York: The Free Press, 1991.

Ehrenreich, Barbara and Deirdre English. *Complaints and Disorders: The Sexual Politics of Sickness.* New York: The Feminist Press, 1973.

Ettorre, Elizabeth. *Women and Substance Use.* New Brunswick, NJ, Rutgers University Press, 1992.

Freud, Sigmund. *An Autobiographical Study.* Tr. James Strachey. London: Hogarth, 1935.

———. *Civilization and Its Discontents.* Tr. James Strachey. New York: Norton, 1989.

———. *Cocaine Papers.* Ed. Robert Byck, New York: Stonehill, 1974.

———. *Collected Papers: Volume Five.* Ed. James Strachey. New York: Basic Books, 1959.

———. *Dora: An Analysis of a Case of Hysteria.* Ed. Phillip Reiff. New York: Collier Books, 1963.

———. *The Origins of Psychoanalysis: Letters to Wilhel Fleiss. Drafts and Notes: 1887–1902.* Ed. Anna Freud. New York: Basic Books, 1954.

———. "On Narcissism: An Introduction." *The Standard Edition of the Complete Psychological Works of Sigmund Freud.* Tr. J. Strachey. London: Hogarth Press, 1957.

———. *Standard Edition of the Complete Psychological Works.* London: Hogarth Press, 1962.

———. *Three Essays on the Theory of Sexuality.* Tr. James Strachey. New York: Basic Books, 1975.

Gay, Peter. *The Bourgeois Experience, Victorian to Freud. Vol.1. Education of the Senses.* New York and Oxford: Oxford University Press, 1984.

———. *Freud, A Life for Our Time.* New York: Norton, 1988.

Gill, Kerry. "Princess Speaks Up for Addicts." *The Times* (London) August 18, 1992. Pp. 1–2.

Gomberg, E. "Historical and Political Perspectives: Women and Drug Use." *Social Issues* 38.2 (1982). Pp. 9–23.

Gossop, Michael. *Living with Drugs.* Cambridge, UK: Cambridge University Press, 1993.

Haley, Bruce. *The Healthy Body and Victorian Culture.* Cambridge, MA: Harvard University Press, 1978.

Hollender, Marc H. "Conversion Hysteria: A Post-Freudian Reinterpretation of 19th Century Psychosocial Data." *Archives of General Psychiatry* 26 (1972). Pp. 311–14.

Jordavana, Ludmilla. *Sexual Visions: Images of Gender in Science and Medicine between the Eighteenth and Twentieth Centuries.* Madison: University of Wisconsin Press, 1989.

Kincaid, James R. *Child-Loving: The Erotic Child and Victorian Culture.* New York and London: Routledge, 1992.

Kofman, Sarah. *The Enigma of Woman: Women in Freud's Writing.* Tr. Catherine Porter. Ithaca, NY: Cornell University Press, 1985.

———. *Freud and Fiction.* Tr. Sarah Wykes. Boston: Northeastern University Press, 1991.

Koller, Karl. "Personal Reminiscences of the First Use of Cocaine as a Local Anaesthetic in Eye Surgery." *Anesthesia and Analgesia* January-February, 1928. Pp. 10–11.

Levenstein, Edward. *Morbid Craving for Morphia* (1878). Tr. C. Harrer. New York: Arno Press, 1981.

Mehlman, Jeffrey. "Trimethylamin: Notes on Freud's Specimen Dream." *Diacritics* Spring 1976. Pp. 42–45.

Mitchell, Juliet. *Psychoanalysis and Feminism: Freud. Reich, Laing and Women.* New York: Vintage, 1974.

Moreau, Jacques-Joseph. *Hashish and Mental Illness.* New York: Raven Press, 1973.

Nietzsche, Friedrich. *Ecce Homo: How One Becomes What One Is.* London: Penguin, 1988.

Riceour, Paul. *Freud and Philosophy: An Essay in Interpretation.* Tr. Dennis Savage. New Haven, CT: Yale University Press, 1970.

Ronell, Avital. *Crack Wars: Literature, Addiction, Mania.* Lincoln: University of Nebraska Press, 1992.

Schultz, Myron. "The 'Strange Case' of Robert Louis Stevenson." *Journal of the American Medical Association* 216.1 (April 5, 1971). Pp. 90–94.

Sedgwick, Eve Kosofsky. *Between Men, English Literature, and Male Homosocial Desire.* New York: University of Columbia Press, 1985.

———. *Epistemology of the Closet.* Berkeley: University of California Press, 1990.

———. *Tendencies.* Durham, NC: Duke University Press, 1993.

Showalter, Elaine. *Sexual Anarchy: Gender and Culture at the Fin de Siecle.* New York: Viking, 1990.

Silverman, Kaja. *Male Subjectivity at the Margins.* New York and London: Routledge, 1992.

Thornton, E. M. *The Freudian Fallacy: An Alternative View of Freudian Theory.* Garden City, NY: Dial Press, 1984.

———. *The Freudian Fallacy: Freud and Cocaine.* London, Paladin, 1986.

Woodwards, J. and Richards, D. eds. *Health Care and Popular Medicine in Nineteenth Century England: Essays in the Social History of Medicine.* New York: Holmes and Meier, 1977.

CHAPTER 6

FEMALE ADDICTION AND SACRIFICE

Literary Tradition or User's Manual?

Stephen C. Infantino

AS CULTURAL MYTHOLOGY, LITERATURE CAN both reflect and prescribe. Recurrent dynamic structure in narrative reveals certain habits and truths about the social history that produced and conserved it. In his book *Violence and Difference,* Andrew McKenna constructs a summary dialogue among the creative and analytical voices of Western culture, compounded with considerations of literary myth and its relation to cultural history. The author's rereading of Plato, Descartes, Derrida, Girard, and others reveals the basic tenets of sacrifice and communion that, when projected against the textual history of our culture, make visible the dynamic of the victim as inherent to narrative or even philosophical integrity. McKenna demonstrates clearly that the indivisible radical of violence and difference combines inextricably as a cultural mainstay underlying the mythical dynamic of sacrifice.

The designation of the sin-bearing—that is an excluded, different individual—lends unity and definition to the greater community. This designation may assume a number of forms, but the function remains the same. In her study *Crack Wars,* Avital Ronell considers the combined elements of desire, addiction, and (self-)exclusion as defining aspects of the textual victim. Addiction represents the sacrifice of the will, and consequently the individual. Often voluntary at the outset only to become involuntary in the long-term, such an attachment makes the substance a mitigating agent, compromising the will of the individual while creating a framework of clearly definable difference for all others. Both McKenna and Ronell compile a selected series of literary and philosophical texts in the course of their respective dialogues. Their positions call for a rereading of certain traditions in literature as disseminated philosophy and cultural mythology.

Both women and drug users may easily identify with notions of alterity and exclusion. Their combined status bears investigation. This retrospective overview places in relief the recurrent sacrifice of female central characters as a textual premise for intrigue and development in a popular literary tradition as viewed through a selected series of stories. A rereading of popular literary history in light of recent critical perspectives yields dramatic examples of a particular mode of representation of female characters. Although not always literally murdered, the female characters in representation are made to undergo spiritual and corporeal effacement, trials and treatment by one or more others reducing them to a debased and somewhat dehumanized status by virtue of a process of addictive dependency. The term "addiction" is intended here in its largest sense: a subject's induced physical and/or psychological attachment to the influence of an external agent. As an individual female's will and existence are compromised and gradually effaced, the textual figures become victims assuming the role of privileged object and the object of privileges, occupying the center of a narrative structure that revolves around that debilitation.

This textual device finds its basis in early, seminal works. The subjugation of the female by controlled substance for purposes of perpetuating other characters and unifying their story line echos a recurrent authorial posture that requires sacrifice as central to the interactive community. Indeed, the very element of the victim becomes necessary to the composition of a narrative that would otherwise lose its integrity. From the Tristan legend and fairy tales to the abductions and infidelities of European classical theater, from eighteenth-century epistolaries of compromised women through Emma Bovary to the twentieth century, readers of Western literature find a morass of yarns whose pretextual given is the sacrifice of a female enacted by or through her contact with controlled substance and dictated circumstance. As Andrew McKenna demonstrates, the act of writing is itself bound by elements of exclusion and sacrifice (27). Given that such a textual dynamic is still present in popular culture, it should come as no surprise that the same elements, with a focus on the double alterity of drugs and female being, has been present all along.

The most widespread, commonplace domain of the sacrificial dynamic is found in the brutal domain of the fairy tale. Snow White, Sleeping Beauty, and their ilk share the common role of victims of spells. Their salvation may occur only with the help of an exceptional male hero. The violently victimizing structure of many fairy tales often bears upon the beautiful—and therefore apparently helpless—unwitting female figure who must experience death or its analogies before attaining the ultimate freedom of relinquishing herself to yet another role assigned by her savior and his community. However, as cultural indices, fairy tales follow more dominant stereotypes before prescribing them; the most pointed and defining mechanisms of female sacrifice as a pretextual condition are manifest in earlier, canonical works.

Tristan and Isolde (Beroul, c. 1100 AD) is one of the oldest romances in existence. Nine hundred years ago began the inscription of female addiction by a binding substance wherein love, sex, and romantic adventure have as their motor source the loss of will and self-abandonment to the chemically induced agent of necessity. The story's initial premise contains the elements of my thesis: Isolde, a beautiful woman, is designated by king and prince as the elected source of bliss; she is given a love potion (*philtre*) by her mother the witch, to ensure permanent attachment to the lover and the impossibility of separation—an undifferentiating substitute for natural emotive impulse: the potion will work for anybody who drinks it; the potion is taken in concert with Tristan, the king's nephew and messenger, condemning the couple to a lifetime of secrecy and adultery. The marriage between Isolde and the king takes place as arranged, giving rise to a situation where Isolde is bound to King Marc by law and to Tristan by drug-induced dictum. Hence the groundwork is laid for a lifetime of deceit, ruse, and flight that in time gave rise to hundreds of years of episodes, versions, and various interpretations of this seminal myth wherein the dynamics of fatal love originate from a bottle of drink. Beroul, Thomas, Marie de France, Chrétien de Troies, and others will find cause for endless elaboration in the hiding places, itinerations of flight, and frustrated passion of two people whose common destiny results from a chemically induced loss of will. It is equally noteworthy that most of the adventures recounted represent the exploits of the male hero Tristan, while the hooked female remains comparatively passive.

Such scenarios recall the entire medieval view of love as an illness that prevents sleeping, eating, or other normal human functions. The Tristan and Isolde myth gives literal body and substance—through the *philtre* and its effects—to the normally intangible virtue of courtly love thus imbuing it with the status of material vice. The *philtre* comes from outside. It is introduced to the body and the body is then introduced to an inextricable relationship to the other and to the world. In his 1946 edition of Beroul's version of the Tristan legend, Joseph Bedier explains the author's fascination with the "beverage" as symbolic of the "fatal and mysterious" character of the lovers' union (vii). Yet, in the telling, that radical signifier capable of indiscriminately binding any couple causes endless and profound compromise of those addicted in body and soul. Meanwhile the alchemically conceived "symbolic representation" of lovers bound by a drink should not be overlooked. In the realm of chemical control, the figurative function of the addicting/binding agent is no longer distinguishable from its literal function as an addicting substance.

The potion, as do all addictive substances, represents a quintessential binder and acts as such in its physical capacity as the synthetic agent of irreversible effects. In the discursive plane described by the intersection of drugs, sex, and text, the free-floating gramm, or radical signifier of involuntary attachment, becomes the drinkable dram, and the dram becomes the drama of dreamlike trauma. The administration of the radical agent of controlling substance becomes the pretextual given for a lifetime bound to tumultuous flight from the law into the marginal caves and dungeons of society's excluded.

The ties that bind are not always as immediately dispensable as the Beroulian beverage. The surreptitious transactions of love's addiction find a more sadistic narrative host in the epistolary novel of the eighteenth century. *Les Liaisons dangereuses* (Laclos, 1782) posits the other and his attraction as the substance of dependency through progressive psychological and emotional addiction. Not all drugs come in a bottle. In a power play where endorphins summoned from within manifest effects much like those of morphine, with gradually increased administration of artifice, the Vicomte de Valmont has it that Cecile, his virgin prey and eventual dependent, compromises her body, safety, and will in her growing attachment to his medicine. For this victim, sexual intimacy, its pleasure and taboo, represents the drug, the substance of control whose absence never posed a problem prior to its habitual enjoyment. Insofar as a drug may be defined as that which is introduced to a pre-existent totality, the transition from first taste to regular solicitation to the abandonment of will describes the stages of Cecile's addiction. Her habitual sacrifice will bring her close to death as her eventual pregnancy requires the abortion of her unborn child and of her future while the convent vault closes behind her in an irreversible series of induced events. In the equation between the other and artificial stimulus, Cecile's newfound attachment to Valmont constitutes a type of habit-forming behavior: the subject is no longer the same as before the introduction of a controlled/controlling substance ingested with immoderate frequency whereby the subject continues to experience the effects of that attachment even when use is curtailed. As her doses of sex are meted out with increasing intensity, Cecile lives increasingly for those moments of immediate physical gratification until such time when she experiences the full impact of seduction, abandonment and sacrifice of self to an externally impersonal agent.

Avital Ronell compiles texts and assembles dialogues all related to her book's subtitle "literature/addiction/mania" as the drug issue continues its cultural and textual resurfacing both in and out of literature. A literary prologomena to elective anesthesia, *Crack Wars* pays attention to the force of habit and its effects and the role of drugs in a reading of these elements as literary and cultural signifiers. Although hers is a study in representational narrative forms, literature, the immediate cultural implications, past and present, are clearly visible, addiction/mania. Sacrifice within the community reassigns identities, even when it is a sacrifice of the self. Ronell's reading is a discourse of desire and consumption in an economy of excess. Ronell makes the important distinction between being and "being-on-drugs" (11). Indeed, "being-on-drugs" assumes the nature of a residual existence of recuperative desire in synthetic form, a mode of existence where neither the substance, drug, nor the subject, user, are "really themselves" but are instead transformed into the third entity. In an analogy between external agents and writing itself, Andrew McKenna cites the identification of any predisposed radical as a *pharamakon,* strong medicine that acts as either poison or cure. He cites further Platonic text, establishing "lexical ties, that writing as *pharmakon* has structural and functional affinities with the *pharmakos* in Greek culture: the scapegoat, the sacrificial victim whose violent expulsion purifies the community" (28). In *Les Liaisons dangereuses* and *Tristan and Isolde,* we see that the other assumes the quality of altering enhanced by the quality and quantity of exposure to the addicted subject who, in turn, reduces to an incomplete habitually needy, not-quite-individual individual.

Both sacrifice and addiction occur within a greater textual economy of narrative and share that common space. As integral to ongoing narrative, recurrent sacrifice points backward to its mythically ritual counterpart of communion. The undoing of the one is cause for a gathering of the many. What was intended to make King Marc happy but makes Tristan a hero, what unites viscount and marquise, what conjures up Prince Charming and continues to hold an audience requires a venomous administration to a central figure and the mitigation of her will. The transactions that together make up this tradition in popular narrative have this prerequisite. Thus the introduction of substances that are themselves subject to laws of excess and scarcity plays so well into the textual formula of sacrifice by addiction. The addictive-romantic esthetic would have it that the present/absent dynamic of the beloved finds echos in the availability/scarcity of the binding agent. Even ancient societies practicing human sacrifice used some sort of a sedative agent intended to ease the impact and terror of death on the chosen victim. However, in the case of Isolde, Cecile and others, it is the addicting agent itself and the ensuing consequences that result in the loss of will and bring death closer to the user.

Potions, alcohol, sex, endorphins, and pricks that put the subject under all come into a play that displays a victim essential to the tale's integrity and without whom there would be no story to tell. As Ronell has elaborated in *Crack Wars,* the evolved subject engages in more than one substance, entertaining the element of serial substitution in the course of her downfall. Consider the evolution of this theme well into the nineteenth century.

In Flaubert's *Madame Bovary* (1857), Emma Bovary's first contact with the doctor who will be her husband occurs over a drink. Throughout her marriage, Emma runs the full deck of substance abuse, including a variety of drugs and two love affairs. When Leon Dupuis moves in over the pharmacy, Emma begins her designs on him and on gaining access to his medicine chest, or "shelter." When Monsieur Lheureux hawks his catalogue of goods for sale, Emma will buy. When Homais the apothecary suggests a remedy, Emma will take it. All dressed up with nowhere to go, Emma's series of transactions will take her from indecent thought to forbidden act—her own *liaison dangereuse*—to the economic ruin of overextended credit, controlling merchandise and controlled substance. Emma's progressive acquisition of suicidal poison stems from the economy of her imposed status: surrounded by men, merchandise, money, and drugs and all alone. Self-gratified obsessive compulsion has it that Emma feels that she is owed by the world and writes checks she cannot pay. Emma smokes, drinks, gambles, borrows, has sex, and forever spends what she does not have. The victim of progressive sacrificial transaction, Emma finds a use for those around her as they use her but no one to save her. The scarcity of love incurs the excesses of overcompensation and, reduced to a body with no recognizably independent will, she receives allotted treatment, but of pharmaceutical help rather than medical.

Ronell reminds us that Emma experiments with a variety of stimuli that begins with literature, religion, and the search for love only to end in the domain of physical hallucinogenics and poison (74). In a victimizing *pharmakon* of self-medication, Emma forever shifts her dependency from substance to person to ideal back to substance in a series of substitutions that attempt to replace the initial absence for which the first replacement failed (Ronell, 24–25). Emma, like Isolde and Cecile, loses her self in chemically prosthetic transactions of recuperation (Ronell, 71) where aggravated frustration testifies to the fact that this is no longer the same subject as was first exposed to the foreign agents and that the agent is less and less effective. Textually conceived sacrifice via addiction involves the object taking possession of the subject to a point beyond her will while others observe (Ronell, 55).

The illumination of Ronell's reading of *Madame Bovary* is its ability to pierce the veil of convention and of conventional reading. Contemporary notions of addiction ascribe to models of group behavior and, at the unsupervised extreme, to stereotypes. The addictive transactions of an individual are usually viewed in terms of belonging to a group as designated by common practice that easily translates to stereotypes. Apparent exceptions to stereotypical groups can go unobserved, especially in a canonical context of cultural convention. Many readers of *Madame Bovary* undoubtedly share the view held by her fellow characters, that she is incomprehensibly upset about something but they don't know what. Clearly, Emma did not begin as a poverty stricken, love starved, relief seeking, outcast beggar woman. In fact, her transition and fall *are* the novel's basis. At the outset, Emma is an attractive, upper-class, white woman who won scholastic prizes in school and married *comme il faut*. Her sacrifice and death come about as the story develops; the making of the tale entails her undoing in the grip of drugs and subordination. The resistance of her character to the addicted stereotype requires the reading guidance of a sometimes oblique Ronell: "To gain access to the question of 'being-on-drugs' we have had to go the way of literature. We have chosen a work that exemplarily treats the persecutory object of an addiction. It does so within a fictional space, according to the fanatical exigency of realism" (11).

Emma's role as victim vis-à-vis the literary device imposed by the authors of her fate, both inside and outside the text, cements her lonely romantic character in a realistic setting. Making little distinction between characters and authors, Ronell places Emma in good company: Proust (cortisone), Dickens and Browning (laudanum), Voltaire and Balzac (coffee), and a host of others, including Poe and Baudelaire who did whatever they could find. She demonstrates that literature illustrates "the history of our culture as a problem in *narcossism*" (23), the repeated presentation of an overexposed individual as defined by her dependencies and others' collective view of those dependencies.

Authors aside, the trauma of the female figure entails her victimization by exposure to the intoxicating drives of others, or to the other as a toxic drive. Isolde, Cecile, and Emma discover through their situations the pharmakonical, ambivalent structure of modern medicine/drug use where poison and cure share the combined characteristics of short-term stimulant and long-term depressant (Ronell, 5). The mystical dimension of drug-induced states coupled with the mythical value of the story draws the subject out of the profane, immediate time frame into ritualistic or mythically conceived time. In the tradition under scrutiny here, the sacred dimensions of altered reality and sacrifice translate to an individual existence in dramatic time as persona. Isolde's character is contingent upon her mystically/chemically altered state: who is she if not the woman stuck to Tristan until death do them part? Who is Emma if not the relief seeking wife of the doctor? And who is Valmont if not the cream in Cecile's short-term stimulant/long-term depressant coffee? Their substance of addiction integrates their character, and their addicted character furnishes the substance for a story. The women's mythically *dramatis personae* stems in great part from the implicit forever of their irreversible position: they've had it all and now can't get enough, at the core of a story for which they have been "altered."

The discourse of addiction is the discourse of exclusion or of inclusion for the sole purpose of sacrifice. These female protagonists are written into the center of the narrative only to be "written off" in the course of their development. As "sin bearer," the addicted subject experiences social abuse that then reinforces her identity as sacrificial, a subjugated consumer destined to become the consumed. The will is lost or so affected that it constitutes a change in subject as the designated personages fall to the unshakeable *dictum* of addiction. They obey a governing substance within an entire scheme of domination that eliminates free will and sends them on a course toward death, that cuts off the head to eat the body. But these are not Salem witches found out and done in for the betterment of the community, are they? It is worth noting that even in the happy endings of *Snow White* and *Sleeping Beauty,* another woman must be undone to emancipate the central figure from her sedated state. In a universe where females fall into trances, toads become princes, and women's only hope is to be rescued from under a spell, children learn to perpetuate a narrative tradition that teaches that all women are potentially vulnerable to the inducement of substance and that every man is actually a prince, if some woman can be made to "kiss his lizard."

In light of the late twentieth century's widely expressed "politically correct" mandate, J. F. Garner, in his *Politically Correct Bedtime Stories* (1994), retouches various fairytales into p.c. versions of victimization. These rewrites reveal the undoing of both the tradition and the story lines with a consequential reflective and comical effects. In one instance, Snow White has just fallen asleep in a strange house with seven small beds:

> When she awoke several hours later, she saw the faces of seven bearded, vertically challenged men surrounding the bed. She sat up with a start and gasped. One of the men said, "You see that? Just like a flighty woman: resting peacefully one minute, up and screaming the next."
>
> "I agree," said another. "She'll disrupt our strong bond of brotherhood and create competition among us for her affections. I say we throw her in the river in a sack full of rocks." . . .
>
> "Please no!" she cried . . .
>
> "Don't try and play the victim with us kid!" (46–47)

In *Violence and Difference,* McKenna marks an equivalence between René Girard's reading of culture and Jacques Derrida's reading of scripture in their common consideration of sacrificial signification. Be it a christ, a woman, or the gramm, the signifier of communion and convention cannot be so without inherent expendability:

> When René Girad interrogates mythical texts, he uncovers a scapegoat mechanism that he argues lies at the foundation of human culture. When Jacques Derrida interrogates philosophical texts he uncovers a systematic exclusion of writing, of the gramm or the signifier, and he argues that this exclusion is necessary to the generation and stabilization of concepts. Notwithstanding the substantial difference between a discourse concerned with signifiers and one concerned with victims, there is a *formal* or *structural* resemblance in the process of expulsion and mystification analyzed by these two writers. (27)

Called into being to be discarded, these female figures' inextricable situations do not entail a purification in the conventionally ritualistic sense of sacrifice. They are instead progressively "soiled" for purposes of the promotion of others, while their status as the marginalized victim lays groundwork for the unity of the community. In the light of a European literary tradition embedded in its religious culture, Girard's sacrificial inquiry and Derrida's reified pharmacy have sprouted from fertile ground. In a long tradition of narrative, men and authors commune around a sacrificial body within a literary body. Or, as Ronell sums it up, author Flaubert wins recognition and pharmacist Homais wins an apothecary prize while Emma dies of poisoning (95). Flaubert has equated the worth of a book with its "punch plus recovery time" (Ronell, 58). This drug user's description of a good time seems appropriate here. While tradition has it that Isolde, Cecile, or Emma will never recover, much of contemporary culture still reels as well, recuperating from a narrative structure that silences and sacrifices in the course of establishing its unity. The parallel economies of addiction and sacrifice compose a series of checks and balances that favor the pusher over the user and maintain the succumbed subject in a particular posture in preparation for a fall. From Garner's politically correct *Cinderella:*

Suddenly there was a flash of light, and in front of Cinderella stood a man dressed in loose-fitting, all-cotton clothes and wearing a wide-brimmed hat. At first Cinderella thought he was a Southern lawyer or a band leader, but he soon put her straight.

"Hello Cinderella, I am your fairy godperson, or individual deity proxy, if you prefer. So you want to go to the ball, eh? And bind yourself into the male concept of beauty? Squeeze into some tight-fitting dress that will cut off your circulation? Jam your feet into high-heeled shoes that will ruin your bone structure? Paint your face with chemicals and make-up that have been tested on non-human animals?"

"Oh yes, definitely," she said in an instant. Her fairy godperson heaved a great sigh and decided to put off her political education to another day. (33)

BIBLIOGRAPHY

Beroul. *Le Roman de Tristan et Iseut*. Ed. Joseph Bedier. Paris: Éditions Piazza, 1946.

Flaubert, Gustave. *Madame Bovary*. Paris: Gallimard, 1972.

Garner, James F. *Politically Correct Bedtime Stories*. New York: Macmillan, 1994.

Laclos, Choderlos de. *Les Liaisons dangereuses*. Paris: Gallimard, 1958.

McKenna, Andrew. *Violence and Difference*. Urbana and Chicago: University of Illinois Press, 1992.

Marie de France. *Les Lais de Marie de France*. Paris: Éditions Champion, 1973.

Ronell, Avital. *Crack Wars: Lierature, Addiction, Mania*. Lincoln and London: University of Nebraska Press, 1992.

Part III

Teaching Interventions

CHAPTER 7

A RHETORIC OF CLASSROOM DENIAL

Resisting Resistance to Alcohol Questions While Teaching Louise Erdrich's *Love Medicine*

Krista Ratcliffe

IN PEDAGOGY SCHOLARSHIP, THE TERM "resistance" functions as an antanaclasis; that is, the term has two very different definitions that emerge from competing theories. In post-Freudian psychoanalytic theory, "resistance" describes "a subject's *refusal* to admit the hidden meaning of his symptom" (Grigg, 102). This usage has entered pedagogical lore, referring to students' refusals to critique their own commonplace assumptions about race, gender, class, and other cultural categories (Aronowitz and Giroux; Chappell; Freire; hooks; Luke). In neo-Marxist theory however, "resistance" describes "a personal 'space,' . . . [of] subjective agency" from which students may "subvert the process of socialization" by contesting our cultural commonplaces (Giroux, *Teachers*, 162). This critical pedagogy usage most often refers to teachers' helping students identify and then employ their own agencies in order to interrupt their cultural socialization (Bauer and Jarratt; Bizzell; Giroux; Graff; hooks;

Lewis). Despite the differences between these two uses of "resistance," they both posit teachers as those-who-know and students as those-who-do-not-know.

But what happens when teachers occupy the position of those-who-do-not-know? More specifically, what happens when teachers refuse to critique the (un)conscious strategies, assumptions, and effects of their own pedagogies? Such post-Freudian teacher resistance may merge with post-Freudian student resistance to construct what I am calling classroom denial. Classroom denial occurs in those moments when teachers and students (un)knowingly refuse to address a topic, shutting down all possible conversations about it; as such, classroom denial exposes that students and teachers are more fearful that their beliefs may be transformed than hopeful that these beliefs may be affirmed. If such post-Freudian resistance is to be challenged, the classroom must become a space for neo-Marxist resistance.

The antanaclatic uses of student resistance are much debated in pedagogy scholarship. But the particular synergy of student/teacher resistance, which I am calling classroom denial, is rarely discussed. The reasons are obvious. As teachers we can detect our students' post-Freudian resistance, theorize about it, and attempt to interrupt it with neo-Marxist resistance. We have a harder time, however, recognizing how our own post-Freudian resistance merges with students' to construct classroom denial. But one place where classroom denial may be seen and heard is in our classroom discourses, that is, in the ways we talk to and with our students and in the ways we encourage them to talk to and with us and each other. Such classroom discourses may be read as rhetorical maps of classroom denial. By reading these discourses, we may conceptualize, critique, and negotiate our rhetorics of classroom denial in order to re-vise them.

To demonstrate how rhetorics of classroom denial may be conceptualized, critiqued, and negotiated, I will examine the following three teaching moments that have haunted me, three moments that occurred in an introductory women's literature course when my students and I were studying Louise Erdrich's *Love Medicine:*

Moment #1: Kathy Whitson, who wrote a fine dissertation on Erdrich, came to my Women's Literature class to talk with students about Erdrich and *Love Medicine.* During this discussion, she asked students who they considered the main character of the novel to be, if indeed such a character existed. A student, "Bev," hesitantly replied, "June?" Another student, "Susan," confidently countered, "But she was only in the first chapter."

Moment #2: At the next class meeting, "Kim" named an alcohol question in the novel. She established her authority to speak on such matters by first claiming that her grandfather was full-blooded Cherokee and then conspiratorially confiding, "*They* drink a lot, you know."

Moment #3: "Jane" came to my office for a paper conference and confided that: one, she viewed June's family as an addictive, dysfunctional family much like her own and, two, she thought this interpretive schema explained behaviors and dialogues of Erdrich's characters—behaviors and dialogues that seen from another schema might seem confusing or, worse yet, just poorly written. But she questioned whether this topic was appropriate for the essay assignment.

These three moments haunted me because I did not handle them particularly well. I did not explore the presence of June, the absent alcoholic mother in the novel, because other discussion topics had been planned for the day. I shut down Kim's claim about Native Americans and alcoholism by shifting into my best teacher voice and suggesting that perhaps we should not make such sweeping generalizations about any group of people. And I inadvertently reinforced Jane's suspicion that addiction was not an appropriate topic by saying something like, "That sounds interesting," and then immediately asking for other possible topics. These three moments haunted me until I named them; they are, in fact, moments of classroom denial. They are moments when the alcohol questions in the novel could have been explored but were not.

In this chapter I want to reopen these alcohol questions in *Love Medicine* and, in the process, consider the possibilities of resisting resistance, that is, resisting classroom denial. To do so, I will make two moves. First, I will articulate the rhetoric of classroom denial that emerges in my students' comments and in my responses, exposing how this rhetoric is structured. Because particular rhetorics of classroom denial may emerge differently, my goal is to model a reflective pedagogical praxis that other teachers can adapt for their particular situations. Second, beginning from the context of my students' alcohol questions, I will explore not only how we might have read *Love Medicine* differently in terms of addiction, but also what these differences might mean pedagogically.

Rhetorics of classroom denial are manifested in discursive structures that possess their own strategies, assumptions, and effects. Such rhetorics are neither static, a/historical, developmental, unified, or universal; nor do they assure that every moment of classroom denial will emerge identically. Instead, the components of these rhetorics are constantly in flux, emerging in many different forms, in many different combinations, in many different situations—all of which depend upon the teacher, the students, the institution, the historical moment, and the cultural conditions in which they all intersect. The importance of these rhetorics is that they may be critiqued to expose functions of classroom denial and then revised to confront this denial. But recognizing moments of classroom denial is not an easy task; such recognitions usually occur after the fact—as teachers walk back to their offices, fight traffic on the freeway, reflect on their courses a year later. The problem with such delayed recognitions is that, once the moments have passed, so too have the pedagogical opportunities. Although the teacher can sometimes reconstruct these moments the next day or the next week in class, the passage of time usually dulls the interest in as well as the urgency of such discussions; in the case of a year's passage, the moments are lost forever.

If teachers could only recognize such moments as they occur, classroom denial could be transformed into classroom possibility. For such recognitions to occur, teachers must be alert to the existence of classroom denial and also be willing and able to note its rhetorical structure. In this section, I will model how to conceptualize the rhetorical structure of classroom denial. Grounding my claims in the three classroom moments described earlier, I will articulate the strategies, assumptions, and effects of this rhetoric in hopes that, once identified, this rhetoric may be used as a model by other teachers who want to identify and revise their own rhetorics of classroom denial.

The strategies employed in a class's rhetoric of classroom denial may be read through the trope of (not) speaking. For example, a popular strategy is silence or the absence of speaking about a topic either in class, in conferences, or in writing. Silence allows students and teachers to avoid focusing on subjects such as June's alcoholism in *Love Medicine;* it also allows them to avoid responding to such topics when they are voiced by someone else. The reasons for silence are varied. Both students and teachers may be silent because they want to remain in the same place and do not want uncomfortable topics to lead to other areas of discussion, which is probably the reason I did not follow up on the alcohol questions posed by my students. People may be silent because they are formulating responses, which are not yet conceptualized fully enough for public consumption. Or they may use silence as a form of (un)conscious "lying," for example, students' letting the teacher believe they agree or vice versa in order to avoid real or imagined consequences, which is probably the reason my students did not challenge my silencing their questions. Whatever its cause, silence serves as a powerful socializing tool. It pressures those who want to bring up uncomfortable topics not to do so, and it also pressures those who do bring up these subjects never to do so again. Within a rhetoric of classroom denial, silence can speak loudly.

A second strategy of classroom denial is changing the subject. If, for whatever reason, silence has become impossible, an uncomfortable subject may be introduced into classroom discussions, conferences, student papers, and/or teacher responses. Although Bev, Kim, and Jane introduced alcohol questions, I sidestepped the issue by changing the subject, and because of the power differentials of the classroom the students did not challenge my move. The motivations for this strategy are similar to those for silence. Changing the subject allows us to avoid addressing our discomfort. The difference, however, lies in the effects. Once a topic has been voiced, its presence hangs heavily in the air; that is, the entire class consciously recognizes that the topic is taboo whether or not it is aware of the reason why.

A third strategy, using tone of voice to imply a form/content split, is employed when people want to emphasize attitudes more than claims. Bev, Kim, and Jane all employed tentative or hushed tones when introducing alcohol questions. In such situations, students often employ a conspiratorial tone as if to say, "I'm not sure we should talk about this." This tone seems to ask someone else for either the permission to speak or a reason not to speak. It implies that the students know that classroom boundaries are being transgressed and that they also know the listeners know. Students hope that the tone of their delivery, which implies a form/content split, will enable listeners to forgive the transgression of their words. Ironically, their tone also reveals that they do not really believe this forgiveness will be forthcoming. Likewise, my invoking a teacherly voice in response to Kim's claim and Jane's essay topic begs a form/content split. My words acknowledge their questions; my tone forces closure on these same questions. In all these cases, tones contradict claims. Teachers must be aware that a form/content split is not possible; such awareness will help confront the doubled "truths" of discourses.

A fourth strategy of classroom denial is the introduction of uncomfortable topics by students and teachers not to critique them but to reaffirm their opinions about them. The appeals used in such discussions reaffirm not only the "truth" of the uncomfortable topics but also the logics that deem the topics uncomfortable. Two such appeals occurred in my class: an appeal to common sense and an appeal to unambiguous boundaries. Although appeals to common sense often make communication easier, they can also perpetuate unthinking stereotypes. For example, Kim's use of "you know" implies that everyone else will agree with her claim that Native Americans "drink a lot." This use further implies that the subject is not even open for discussion. Although appeals to clear boundaries can challenge dysfunction, they are often unknowingly invoked in the classroom to promote a compartmentalized view of the world. For example, Kim's claim that Native Americans "drink a lot" implies that the problem lies with *them,* not *me.* Thus, the *they* are branded as failures, and the *me* is relieved of any responsibility for this failing. In the process of reaffirming these claims, both appeals reinforce a "pull-yourself-up-by-your-bootstrap" logic. Each individual becomes solely responsible for his or her actions. The structural forces that might encourage drinking in Native Americans or stereotyping in Anglo-Americans are rendered invisible. So too is the intersubjectivity of people, which might redefine the problems of drinking and stereotyping as individual *and* cultural issues.

Undergirding all these strategies of classroom denial are certain assumptions. First, students often strongly defend their belief in *the* right answer. Truth is assumed to be a static, discoverable entity instead of a fluid, constructed process. This is exemplified in Susan's confident refutation of Bev's claim that June might be the main character of the novel. Second, and closely related to the first assumption, is that students frequently assume a common logic exists. The possibility of multiple logics are perceived not only as illogical—for example, Susan's inability to imagine a character who dies on page six as the main character—but also as dangerous—Jane's asking my permission to employ a different logic with which to interpret *Love Medicine.*

Third, students narrowly define the presence and absence of identification. If an experience is present in their lives, then it can be present in anyone's life. Conversely, if an experience is absent in theirs, it need not be a problem for others. If an experience is a problem, such as alcoholism within Native American communities, then some cultural, psychological, and/or biological inferiority in others must be at fault. Fourth, students oftentimes assume that identity is essentially located in DNA, not in a person's ever-changing life experiences. Kim's *they/me* logic exemplifies this belief: *they* cannot change, and *me* is not subject to their problem. Fifth, students invoke appropriateness as the primary criterion of classroom etiquette. This major metaphor of classical rhetoric is exemplified when Jane asks if alcoholism is an appropriate paper topic. What is said, how it is said, to whom it is said—students know that there are definite rules for these procedures. Yet these rules are hardly ever articulated by the teacher. Students must become proficient at reading each teacher's "etiquette handbook" which is written in a teacher's verbal responses, facial expressions, syllabi, assignment sheets, and so on.

Finally, perhaps the most powerful assumption undergirding classroom denial is fear, and fear takes many forms: fear of being wrong, fear of offending, fear of exposing oneself, fear of upsetting one's beliefs, fear of losing control. Fear may explain my students' silences, changing of subjects, hushed tones, and so on. On a more personal note, fear explains my avoidance of alcohol questions in the classroom: for example, fear of what topics and behaviors will surface in the class, fear of how students will be affected both inside and outside the classroom, fear of how students will react to one another and to me, fear of how I will or will not react, fear of possible administrative repercussions, and fear of losing control of the class. A decade or more of teaching has taught me that when alcohol questions are introduced, students' outside lives quickly become visible inside the classroom. A few years ago I would have defended my avoidance as a refusal to play psychologist to my students' patient, a practice that too often degenerates into a teacher's constructing students as "sick" so that the teacher can play doctor and use the class experience to heal them all. I still consider this practice dangerous and my former stance valid, given that teachers are not trained psychologists and that they have no right to make psychological assumptions about particular students while planning a syllabus a semester before ever meeting these students. Today, however, I realize that my avoidance of alcohol questions is more complex than this ethical stance. For, in actuality, teachers have been playing psychologist for as long as teaching has existed as a profession: they anticipate student anxiety about talking in class, write student-centered assignments or constructive comments on students' papers, chat with students during conferences and after class about issues that effect the students' private lives, and in feminist classrooms pride themselves on foregrounding issues from private life as a valid response to the assigned texts. Consequently, teachers must be prepared to provide support options for students when troubles in their private lives become visible.

The effects of classroom denial are tremendously important. When classroom denial is not challenged, no productive discourse emerges; hence, no minds are changed, and no actions are taken. Each participant in classroom denial places the burden for changing attitudes and actions upon others. In my class, Kim puts the burden on Native Americans to change their patterns of alcoholism, and I put the burden on Jane to come up with a more acceptable paper topic. While putting the burden on others to do their own cultural work is not necessarily bad, giving oneself permission to stand outside this work as the-one-who-already-knows may be a counterproductive move. Such a privileged stance may be a way of ignoring what one does not know. When this occurs, old patterns of thought and behavior continue, and education becomes a means of mindlessly reinforcing the status quo rather than a means of critically reinforcing or revising it.

With the aforementioned rhetorical components of classroom denial identified, I am compelled to confront the following questions that teachers all need to ask themselves on occasion:

1. What do I consider "proper" topics for classroom discussions, and why am I thinking in terms of "proper"?
2. What *are* the possibilities of a literary text in a literature classroom?
3. Why do I sometimes dismiss students who seemingly spout clichés—like Kim's claim that "They drink a lot, you know"—when such "clichés" can actually open up spaces for productive discussions about cultural stereotypes, such as Native Americans and addiction?
4. What do I really mean when I tell students that they should assert their right to speak in class?
5. Why is "control" a dominant pedagogical metaphor for me?
6. Why have I so narrowly construed the psychology metaphor?
7. What are my criteria for deciding when to confront students and when to let their comments slide?

My response to this last question evokes two other questions: How could I have approached Erdrich's text differently if I had refused to let students' comments about addiction slide? And what might these differences mean pedagogically?

What if I had used the three classroom moments that haunt me as prompts for discussing Erdrich's novel? That is, what if my class and I had followed Bev's lead and read the text with June, an alcoholic, as the main character? What if we had not dismissed Kim's claim and instead explored the alcohol question in June's family as well as in the Chippewa community? And what if we had encouraged Jane to use alcoholism as a dominant metaphor for writing about the text? Such moves obviously will not provide a unified vision of the text nor *the* one right reading, but they just may provide possibilities for using *Love Medicine* to explore alcohol questions in composition and literature classrooms.

First, could a case be made for June Kashpaw's being the main character of the novel, even though she dies on page six? The answer is yes. June is the first character the narrator introduces; readers encounter her in the first sentence "walking down the clogged main street of oil boomtown Williston, North Dakota, killing time before the noon bus arrived that would take her home" (1). Subsequently, she can be seen as a thread that weaves the families in the novel together, linking the Lazarres, the Kashpaws, the Lamartines, and their interwoven blood lines through her birth and adoption, her marriage and affairs, and her legitimate and illegitimate sons, King and Lipsha. June's niece Albertine Johnson provides perhaps the most balanced vision of June: not only was she someone who was pretty, who gave gum as presents, and who talked to children as if they were adults, but she was also someone who was frequently drunk, who lost jobs as a result, and who left her sons to be raised by other family members (8). Yet by the end of the novel June has created a space for Lipsha to have the last words as he drives the car his legitimate brother purchased with June's life insurance money: "So there was nothing to do but cross the water, and bring *her* home" (272, emphasis mine). As the frame of the novel and as an influence in the lives of most other characters in the novel, June could easily be read as the main character of *Love Medicine.*

Simply making this case is not enough; teachers should use it as a premise to ask other questions about the implications of June's status as a main character. What narrative events do June and her alcoholism set in motion? What is the affect of her drinking on her own character? What do readers find out about other characters in the novel when they read the work in light of June as an absent alcoholic mother, daughter, niece, wife, lover? Such questions allow the discussion of narrative concerns such as narrator, plot, and character as well as cultural concerns such as death and addiction. These questions also ask us to interweave the material dimensions of narrative and cultural concerns, that is, to view alcoholism as a literary trope and as a physical addiction of the body.

Also, could a case be made that an alcohol problem exists within June's family and within the novel's Chippewa community? Here the answer is most definitely yes. June's family history of alcoholism emerges in the scene where her maternal grandparents and her father turn her over to Marie Kashpaw to rear. June's maternal grandparents, who at this point the reader also believes to be Marie's parents, are drunk; June's father, "the whining no-good" Morrissey, is drunk; and June herself is drunk, even though she is only nine years old (63–64). June's adoptive family, the Kashpaws, also have their own troubles with alcoholism: Nestor drinks to escape his reality until his wife Made demands he stop and he chooses to put his "nose against the wheel" (93); their son Gordie, who eventually marries June, begins drinking after June dies, for "then the need was upon him" (172); June and Gordie's son King physically abuses his wife Lynette and his cousin Albertine in a drunken frenzy (38); and June's other son Lipsha drinks too much after finding out that June is his mother but stops after meeting his father, Gerry Lamartine, who has "been on the wagon for thirteen years" (155). And Gerry's family, the Lamartines, obviously have their share of alcohol-related troubles: Henry Lamartine Sr., who is not the biological father of any of the sons who bear his name, gets drunk in a bar and then sits on a railroad track waiting for a train to hit him (75); Henry Lamartine Jr., picks up a young Albertine after returning from Vietnam and proceeds to get drunk to escape his Vietnam flashbacks (134–41); later he gets drunk with his brother Lyman and drowns himself in a fast-flowing river (154).

I could continue citing examples, but the point is obvious. The alcoholism in the characters' families and communities—whether genetically or culturally induced—influences all aspects of the novel. Yet once this alcoholism question is established, questions emerge. For example, how could information about addictive personalities and dysfunctional families enrich our reading of the characters, their families, and their communities? What particular cultural forces in the Chippewa community promote and/or condemn drinking? And how can the teacher address the alcohol question so as to complicate students' understanding of alcoholism in Chippewa and other Native American nations, and not just reinforce their opinions that "*They* drink a lot, you know"? Such questions invite addiction research into the classroom; they also invite questions about the tension between universal and culturally specific claims; and they invite students's responses and stereotypical assumptions to be material for class discussion.

Further, could alcoholism be used as a dominant metaphor with which to construct a reading of *Love Medicine?* Again the answer is yes. One reading would juxtapose alcoholism with the breaking apart phenomenon that haunts Erdrich's novel. Lipsha defines this phenomenon, in terms of his grandpa Nestor, as a person's mind becoming so full that it explodes. And Lipsha cites the result of this phenomenon: "I always used to say that's why Indians drink" (190). Thus, Lipsha implies that this breaking apart is both an individual and a cultural phenomenon: individual characters are in the process of being shattered because so too is the Chippewa nation to which they belong.

In the first six pages, June breaks apart twice. In the bar restroom, after she has picked up the mud engineer Andy, she seems "to drift out of her clothes and skin with no help from anyone" and feels "that underneath it all her body was pure and naked—only the skins were stiff and old" (4). Yet, she pulls herself together and goes back into the bar. Later after having sex in Andy's truck, her "skin felt smooth and strange. And then she knew that if she lay there any longer she would crack wide open, not in one place but in many pieces" (5). And once broken apart and either not willing or not able to pull herself back together, she walks into a snowy death on the North Dakota plains. Later Albertine describes June as someone who "broke, little by little, into someone whose shoulders sagged when she thought no one was looking" (8). But it is Marie Kashpaw who identifies the source of June's breaking apart. After she saves a young June from being hanged by the other children at June's instigation, she notes:

> I turned her head toward me and looked into her sorrowful black eyes. I looked a long time, as if I was falling down a hill. She blinked gravely and returned my stare. There was a sadness I couldn't touch there. It was a hurt place; it was deep; it was with her all the time like a broke rib that stabbed when she breathed. (68)

But June is not the only character who possesses "a hurt place," who threatens to break apart, and who uses alcohol to ward off pain and sadness. June's abusive ex-husband Gordie does the same. When he is so drunk that he believes a deer he has just killed is June, the narrator describes him as "cracking, giving way" (181). June and Gordie's son King also experiences this phenomenon. Although readers never get inside his head as with some of the other characters, readers do see the breaking apart in his actions: in his drunken rage against his wife Lynette and his cousin Albertine, he accidentally breaks apart his aunts' pies. Albertine's lament for the loss of the pies could be read as a lament for any of the above characters and their relationships: "once they smash, there is no way to put them right" (39).

This breaking apart seems to be an experience that all the characters in the novel fear but they deal with it in different ways. As the "child" of alcoholics, Marie keeps herself together by controlling her husband Nestor. As a child pulled between Chippewa and white cultures, Nestor keeps himself together and overcomes his urge to drink by the force of Marie's will and by his own recognition that he cannot meet his responsibilities if he keeps drinking. But June and Gordie and King do not or will not or cannot keep themselves together, so they drink and continue to drink—all in an attempt to keep the breaking apart at bay. In the end, the alcohol fails them. June dies; Gordie hits bottom when he thinks he has killed June; and King loses his connection with the Chippewa community and gambles away the car purchased with his mother's insurance money.

This reading not only foregrounds alcohol addiction and fragmentation on personal and cultural levels, but it also invokes certain questions. What different "hurt places" haunt characters in the novel? How does alcohol affect their body/spirit connections? How, if at all, can other characters intervene in the alcoholic characters' lives? What effect does a character's alcoholism have on other characters, on the families, on the community? And perhaps most importantly, how does my reading reflect an Anglo bias and erase Chippewa concerns; for example, how does interpreting Gordie's scene with the deer as a drunken hallucination affect the fact that in Chippewa theology June's spirit might have indeed entered the deer? As with the previous sets of questions, these questions merge narrative and cultural concerns. That is, they acknowledge addiction as a valid means of interrogating the text, and they invite student's knowledge of or experience with addiction, particularly alcohol addiction, into classroom discussions.

What does such a reading offer? In general, it offers a chance to discuss addiction. In particular in my class where such questions came up, it would have offered a validation of student's concern and of student's interpretations. It would have modeled an educational pedagogy that I believe in: start where students are and move them to more complex grounds; at the same time, don't underestimate the complexity of the students' starting points. So what possibilities does such a reading offer for the discussion of addiction? Like the card game, the alcoholism in the novel appears to be a game of chance. But like Lipsha's marking the cards to win the car purchased with his mother's insurance money, the characters are marked with patterns of dysfunctional behaviors that can be understood via a discussion of addiction.

Love Medicine concludes with Lipsha coming to terms with his mother June Kashpaw, his father Gerry Lamartine, his Chippewa heritage, and himself—a model strategy for coming to terms with discussions of addiction in the classroom. Yet Lipsha is purposely ambiguous about his father, not revealing to readers whether or not Gerry is actually guilty of murder: "Let's just say he [Gerry] answered: 'That's the penetrating mystery of it. Nobody knows'" (269). Lipsha's response functions pretty well as a metaphor for reading and writing about literature; coming to terms with an interpretation does not mean erasing ambiguity. His response also functions pretty well as a metaphor for conducting literature and writing classes that foreground addiction; nobody knows what will happen in the course of class discussions or writing assignments.

But one way this uncertainty can be constructively employed is to follow the pedagogical model implied in this paper: (1) provide students with forums in which to ask their own questions about the text; (2) be ready to recognize questions that could drive class discussions about addiction; (3) have students turn their questions into claims and prove or disprove them; (4) together generate other questions triggered by the claims and proofs; (5) explore these new questions without having prefabricated answers prepared or expected; and (6) let students bring their experiences, their research, and their critical reading, writing, and thinking skills to bear in answering these questions. Whether teachers follow this or some other pedagogical model for discussing addiction, two things can be assumed: one, discussing addiction as a literary trope will inevitably lead to confessions of addictions in oneself, one's relatives and/or one's acquaintances; two, layers of meaning will be constructed in discussion, in writing, and in silence.

Teachers need not let this construction of meaning fall to chance. Classes may unfold like the card game at the end of *Love Medicine,* when Lipsha marks the cards so that he can win the car purchased with his mother's life insurance money. Teachers can, and should, come to class with a marked deck of pedagogical strategies, not to cheat students but to put boundaries on the game of chance. An important element of this pedagogical marked deck includes establishing clear boundaries for what can and cannot be discussed in class, in journals, and in papers. An equally important element is recognizing that these boundaries will inevitably blur. When students' oral or written responses do blur these boundaries, use the blurrings as springboards for discussion, and when these blurrings indicate problems in students' lives, be ready to deal with the consequences. As Jane Lilienfeld reminds us, teachers need to have a repertoire of support systems available for students, for example, names, addresses, and numbers of organizations that students may contact. For while I still contend that teachers should not play therapist, I also contend that we cannot let the metaphor of June, the absent alcoholic mother, become the major trope of pedagogy. To do so is to deny the realities of students' lives, the realities that they will write into their reading and writing assignments whether teachers ask them to or not.

BIBLIOGRAPHY

Aronowitz, Stanley and Henry Giroux. *Education under Siege.* South Hadley, MA: Bergin and Garvey, 1985.

Bauer, Dale and Susan Jarratt. "Feminist Sophistics: Teaching with an Attitude." *Changing Classroom Practices: Resources for Literary and Cultural Studies.* Ed. David B. Downing. Urbana, IL: NCTE, 1994. Pp. 149–66.

Beidler, Peter. "Three Student Guides to Louise Erdrich's *Love Medicine.*" *American Indian Culture and Research Journal.* 16 (1992). Pp. 167–73.

Bizzell, Patricia. "The Teacher's Authority: Negotiating Difference in the Classroom." *Changing Classroom Practices: Resources for Literary and Cultural Studies.* Ed. David B. Downing. Urbana, IL: NCTE, 1994. Pp. 194–201.

Chappell, Virginia. "'But Isn't This the Land of the Free?': Resistance and Discovery in Student Responses to Manzanar." *Writing in Multicultural Settings.* Eds. Carol Severino, Juan C. Guerra, and Johnella Butler. New York: Modern Language Association, 1997. Pp. 172–88.

Downing, David B., ed. *Changing Classroom Practices: Resources for Literary and Cultural Studies.* Urbana, IL: NCTE, 1994.

Flavin, Louise. "Louise Erdrich's *Love Medicine:* Loving over Time and Distance." *Critique.* 31 (Fall 1989). Pp. 55–64.

Freire, Paulo. *Education for Critical Consciousness.* New York: Seabury Press, 1978.

Giroux, Henry. *Theory and Resistance in Education: A Pedagogy for the Opposition.* South Hadley, MA: Bergin and Garvey, 1993.

———. *Teachers as Intellectuals: Toward a Critical Pedagogy of Learning.* Granby, MA: Bergin and Garvey, 1988.

Gore, Jennifer. "What We Can Do for You! What *Can* 'We' Do for 'You'?: Struggling over Empowerment in Critical and Feminist Pedagogy." *Feminisms and Critical Pedagogy.* Eds. Carmen Luke and Jennifer Gore. New York: Routledge, 1992. Pp. 54–73.

Graff, Gerald. "A Pedagogy of Counterauthority, or the Bully/Wimp Syndrome." *Changing Classroom Practices: Resources for Literary and Cultural Studies.* Ed. David B. Downing. Urbana, IL: NCTE, 1994. Pp. 179–93.

Grigg, Russell. "Signifier, Object, and the Transference." *Lacan and the Subject of* Language. Eds. Ellie Ragland-Sullivan and Mark Bracher. New York: Routledge, 1991. Pp. 100–15.

hooks, bell. "Pedagogy and Political Commitment: A Comment." *Talking Back: Thinking Feminist, Thinking Black*. Boston: South End Press, 1989. Pp. 98–104.

Lather, Patti. "Post-Critical Pedagogies: A Feminist Reading." *Feminisms and Critical Pedagogy*. Eds. Carmen Luke and Jennifer Gore. New York: Routledge, 1992. Pp. 120–37.

Lewis, Magda. "Interrupting Patriarchy: Politics, Resistance, and Transformation in the Feminist Classroom." *Feminisms and Critical Pedagogy*. Eds. Carmen Luke and Jennifer Gore. New York: Routledge, 1992. Pp. 167–92.

Lilienfeld, Jane. "But I'm an English Teacher, Not a Therapist." Midwest Modern Language Association Convention, Minneapolis. November 1993.

Louise Erdrich and Love Medicine. Writers Talk: Ideas of Our Time. The Roland Video Collection. Northbrook, IL. 1989.

Luke, Carmen. "Feminist Politics in Radical Pedagogy." *Feminisms and Critical Pedagogy*. Eds. Carmen Luke and Jennifer Gore. New York: Routledge, 1992. Pp. 25–53.

Luke, Carmen and Jennifer Gore, eds. *Feminisms and Critical Pedagogy*. New York: Routledge, 1992.

McLaren, Peter. *Life in Schools: An Introduction to Critical Pedagogy in the Foundations of Education*. New York: Longman, 1989.

———. "On Ideology and Education: Critical Pedagogy and the Cultural Politics of Resistance." *Critical Pedagogy, the State, and Cultural Struggle*. Eds. Henry Giroux and Peter McLaren. Albany, NY: SUNY, 1989. Pp. 174–202.

Rainwater, Catherine. "Reading between Worlds: Narrativity in the Fiction of Louise Erdrich." *American Literature*. 62 (September 1990). Pp. 405–23.

Walsh, Catherine. *Pedagogy and the Struggle for Voice: Issues of Language, Power and Schooling for Puerto Ricans*. New York: Bergin and Garvey, 1991.

Chapter 8

ALCOHOLISM IN THIRD-WORLD LITERATURE

Buchi Emecheta, Athol Fugard, and Anita Desai

Nancy Topping Bazin

Alcoholism is a major problem in most countries; yet in only a few countries has it become a social issue and a topic to be discussed seriously and openly. Within universities, substantive knowledge about alcoholism appears to be confined mainly to medical and sociology departments. Certainly, alcoholism is a neglected topic in literary studies. Almost all critics and teachers of literature are blind to its impact on a surprising number of characters and their relationships—even when alcoholism is the primary cause of suffering. Unless a teacher is a recovering alcoholic or knows well someone who is, ignorance or self-censorship evidently prevents much discussion of alcoholism in the classroom. Because of the shame and secrecy so long associated with alcoholism, revealing any interest in it seems almost taboo (Gilmore 6). Silence about alcoholism allows the kind of abuse and violence that frequently accompanies alcohol addictions to continue.

Until a few years ago, I knew very little about alcoholism. I certainly did not clearly understand the damage it does to physical health and family life. But then, quite unexpectedly, I witnessed a seizure caused by withdrawal from alcohol. The shock of this event raised my consciousness and opened my eyes to the nature and consequences of addictions. Gradually I became aware of the extent to which alcoholism permeates both our social environment and the literature I teach. Not to have directed students' attention to the impact of alcoholism on the lives of many characters in literature was, in fact, to have misread that literature.

Despite a preoccupation with the many sources of the protagonists' pain, critics of third- world literature, for example, fail to point to alcoholism as a significant factor in many literary works. In this chapter, therefore, I shall examine the impact of alcoholism on the characters in Buchi Emecheta's *The Joys of Motherhood,* Athol Fugard's *"Master Harold" . . . and the Boys,* and Anita Desai's *Clear Light of Day.* Although the settings for these works are Nigeria and India, the characters touched by alcoholism suffer in similar ways.

Feminist discussions of Buchi Emecheta's *The Joys of Motherhood* reveal the extent to which the female protagonist, Nnu Ego, is the victim of an arranged marriage, polygamy, son preference, emphasis on fertility, and a belief in male superiority. Yet critics ignore the ways in which the alcoholism of Nnu Ego's husband, Nnaife, made her situation significantly worse. Nnaife's drinking impoverishes his family, makes him abusive, causes him to be violent, and sends him to jail.

Nnaife celebrates the births of his sons by serving and "drinking palm wine" (53). For instance, after the birth of his second son, he is "fully saturated with drink" (80). At the celebration of the naming of another son, "palm wine flowed like the spring water from Ibusa streams" (111). Likewise the arrival of his second wife as well as his son's success in obtaining his first job call for celebrations with palm wine and ogogoro, the local gin (111). He also turns to palm wine for consolation when his brother dies and when girls rather than boys are born. When his wife announces the birth of twin girls, he blames his wife for not giving him something better and leaves the house "to drink with his friends" (127).

Nnaife's drinking is not confined to special occasions; he drinks every evening. When unemployed and suffering from hunger, he still has a fat abdomen from drinking palm wine—"too much of it" (94). He is frequently out drinking until "the early hours of the morning" (113). Thus, his drinking causes his wife and children to suffer from hunger. Whereas his senior wife, Nnu Egos, accepts such behavior as normal for males—"Men, they will always have their fun" (130)—his second wife, Adaku, begins to protest—"Look at us, trying to make ends meet, and he squanders his money on drink" (130). Even Nnu Ego recognizes that they "are not given enough housekeeping money" and says, "I am sure he spends more than we get on his drink" (133–34). Finally Nnu Ego confronts Nnaife directly: "What you spend on a keg of palm wine would buy us all a meal" (134). His response however, is hostile: "'I am not adding a penny to that money,' he said adamantly. 'You can starve, for all I care.' With that he strode out, making his way to the stalls of the palm-wine sellers near Suru Lere" (136).

Nnaife continues to impregnate his wives although he cannot support the children already born, and he continues to waste on alcohol the money needed for food. Nnaife had wrongly assumed he "would no longer have to work and would lead a life of indolence and ease, drinking palm wine with his friends" once his eldest son, Oshia, graduated (198). However, instead of displaying any willingness to support Nnaife's ever-expanding family, Oshia announces that he is saving his money to go to a university in the United States. His enraged father tells him "I do not wish to see you ever again. . . . Out of my house!" (201). This angry response permanently destroys their relationship. Because of Nnaife's quarrelsome, drunken behavior, the other children also flee the turmoil in their home.

Kehinde rebels against her father's wish that she marry a man from the Ibo tribe instead of the Yoruba man she loves. Her refusal to comply with her father's demand angers him so much that he turns again to the consolation of palm wine, drinking before as well as after his dinner. When Nnaife is awakened to help the rest of the family search for Kehinde, he goes off in a drunken rage to kill the Yoruba man's family. Although Nnaife's son is able to warn the family and help restrain his father, Nnaife does slash the shoulder of one of the Yoruba sons. Therefore, he is arrested and tried for attempted murder.

Nnaife's drinking habits condemn him; Nnu Ego unwittingly reveals at the trial his failures as an alcoholic husband and father, and his own testimony shows him to be greedy and naive. Because Nnu Ego believes he "owns" her (217), she states that he pays the children's school fees; in fact, the money he pays with is money *she* earns. Indeed Nnu Ego is the family's primary provider. Furthermore, Nnaife admits in court that he desires the bride price and the "twelve big kegs of bubbling palm wine" he would receive if his daughter marries according to Ibo customs (215–16). Should she marry someone from the Yoruba tribe, neither would be forthcoming. Moreover, times have changed; Nnaife never doubts he had the right to take justice into his own hands. Personal revenge was condoned in the traditional, rural world Nnaife grew up in and he is unaware that such behavior is no longer socially acceptable. Nor does society still condone alcoholism to the extent his wife, Nnu Ego, accepts his.

Nnu Ego seldom complained about his drinking because the traditional culture she grew up in saw alcohol consumption as signifying manliness. The prosecuting attorney asks her if Nnaife has a "nasty temper," and the following dialogue ensues:

> He only gets angry when he is drunk.
>
> And he drinks often, every day?
>
> Well, he is a man, isn't he? Men are expected to be like that. My father—
>
> Ahem. We are talking about your husband, not your father.
>
> My husband is like any other man. I would not have married any man who did not behave like a man.
>
> Even to the extent of carrying a cutlass?
>
> He was drunk and his daughter's honour was at stake. (217–18)

The relationship of alcoholism to gender is indeed interesting. Although Nnu Ego does not like the fact that her husband drinks, she tolerates it. As an expert on alcoholism, Robert J. Ackerman, says: "For the male, there exists a complementary norm of excessive drinking and masculinity" (9). He points out that "a male can become inebriated and engage in drunken behavior and still be permitted to feel masculine. It is difficult for a woman to become inebriated and engage in drunken behavior and feel feminine" (9). This clarifies why a 1983 study showed that, in families with young children, nine out of ten women stayed with an alcoholic husband. Yet, when "the situation is reversed, and she is the alcoholic, only one out of ten males will stay" (9). The alcoholic's wife, like Nnu Ego, is the victim of a variety of patriarchal beliefs that intertwine with the expectation that women should tolerate a man's drinking, no matter what the consequences for her and her children. However, as Nnaife's second wife, Adaku, proves in *The Joys of Motherhood,* Nnu Ego would have been better off without him. A feminist analysis of the ways in which Nnu Ego is victimized by patriarchal attitudes and behavior must include recognition of the destructive role of her husband's alcoholism and of its association with manliness.

Just as alcoholism is intertwined with male dominance in *The Joys of Motherhood,* alcoholism and racism intermingle in Athol Fugard's play *"Master Harold" . . . and the Boys.* Fugard's play is usually analyzed only in terms of South African racial tensions. The play, which is autobiographical, is primarily about a child of an alcoholic. The pain created by the family situation causes the racial conflict that ensues. Hally, the white adolescent protagonist, lashes out at Sam, the black servant he loves, not because he is a racist but because his alcoholic father is about to return from the hospital. He is, therefore, anticipating "the end of the peace and quiet we've been having." Halley's father treats him like a servant, asking him to empty his "stinking chamberpots full of phlegm and piss" (48). Furthermore, his father steals both his money and his mother's in order to have "money for booze." In addition, when alcohol allows his parents' tempers to flare up, Hally is caught in between the two of them, which "makes life hell" for him (48–49). He tells his mother: "I'm not going to be the peacemaker anymore. I'm warning you now: when the two of you start fighting again, I'm leaving home" (49).

As a child, Hally sought refuge in the room of the two black servants Sam and Willie. As Hally tells them: "No joking, if it wasn't for your room, I would have been the first certified ten-year-old in medical history" (25). Hally's visits to the servants' room were not socially acceptable. Repeatedly, he got a "rowing for hanging around the 'servants' quarters'" (25). Yet, he was much happier there than with his alcoholic father and his mother who functioned as an enabler. Sam, the black servant in "*Master Harold,*" was a substitute father. When Sam made a kite out of "tomato-box wood, brown paper and two of [Hally's] mother's old stockings" and they were actually able to fly it, Hally felt proud of himself and Sam: "I was so proud of us! it was the most splendid thing I had ever seen" (30).

Hally wants his mother to protect his peace of mind by insisting that his father stay in the hospital a bit longer. Hally's mother fails her child by letting the father come home early and by forcing Hally to get some brandy for his father (49). When Sam tries to comfort Hally, out of his pain and anger Hally turns on him. Hally forgets how much he loves Sam and decides to put him back into his place as a black servant. By lording it over Sam and forcing Sam to begin addressing him henceforth as "Master Harold," Hally tries to compensate for the powerless and impossible situation in which he finds himself.

Hally feels torn apart emotionally. He loves his father and defends him at the same time that he wants his father to stay away. He tells Sam: "You see, you mustn't get the wrong idea about me and my Dad, Sam. We also have our good times together. Some bloody good laughs. He's got a marvelous sense of humor" (55). Unfortunately, Hally asserts his white dominance over Sam by repeating a racist joke of his father's and proclaiming to Sam that he, too, found it "a bloody good joke" (55). Hally's behavior is self-destructive, for he risks the loss of Sam's love. Sam tells him: "You've just hurt yourself bad. And you're a coward, Master Harold. The face you should be spitting in is your father's . . . but you used mine, because you think you're safe inside your fair skin . . . and this time I don't mean just or decent" (56).

Because of the alcoholism, Hally's father fails to behave as a responsible adult and father. Sam reminds Hally of the time they went to fetch Hally's father—the night he "was dead drunk on the floor of the Central Hotel Bar" (57). As if that were not humiliating enough, Hally and Sam had to wash his father because "he'd messed in his trousers" (58). Sam describes the dilemma faced not just by Hally but by many children of alcoholics: he loves his father and yet he is intensely ashamed of him. Seeing how ashamed Hally has been, Sam comments, "That's not the way a boy grows up to be a man! . . . But the one person who should have been teaching you what that means was the cause of your shame" (58). Worse yet, Hally also felt ashamed of himself. Sam tells Hally how he behaved after they had to fetch his father that night: "You hadn't done anything wrong, but you went around as if you owed the world an apology for being alive" (58).

Additionally, the alcoholism of his father makes Hally despair. Like another victim of alcohol abuse, Martha in Edward Albee's *Who's Afraid of Virginia Woolf,* Hally is an atheist. He claims that the "fundamental law of the Universe" is the "principle of perpetual disappointment." Hally believes that "if there is a God who created this world, he should scrap it and try again" (35).

In *Clear Light of Day* Anita Desai, a novelist from India, depicts the pain of children in the home of dysfunctional parents. However, unlike Fugard, she is silent about the reasons for this situation. Ostensibly the novel is about a family reunion and a sense of time and space as "perceived by the five senses" (Srivastava, 224). Critics celebrate Desai's imagery and narrative structure, but none mention that the power of the novel radiates from what is, out of pain, left unsaid.

In Desai's autobiographical novel published in 1980, the four children—Raja, Bim, Tara, and Baba—are like orphans. Their parents are never home. As adults, they recall that they were "always waiting" for their parents to come home, and even after they came home, "they were still unfulfilled, still waiting" (122). Raja describes his father as dealing with "both family and business by following a policy of neglect" (52). The night their mother dies, she had not felt well, and, "for the first time in twenty years" she had "missed an evening at the club" (53). When the father dies, the children do not miss him because he had never been there anyway: "It was but a small transition from the temporary to the permanent" (64). His absence seems normal; only the presence of his car in the garage seems abnormal (64). When their family doctor says about himself, "It is a great responsibility being an only child of a loving mother," Bim's response is: "I wouldn't know . . . didn't have one" (84). In addition to the parents' "total disinterest in their children," there was "the secret, hopeless suffering of their mother" who had diabetes (130). The neglect and the mother's suffering created a "silent desperation that pervaded the house" (130). Anita Desai does not mention alcoholism as the reason for this neglect or as one of the causes of her mother's agony; nor does she indicate whether the father and perhaps even the diabetic mother drank alcohol every evening at the club. But in her next novel, *The Village by the Sea* (1982), the mother is again ill and the father is unemployed. This time the nonworking father is described as a dipsomaniac.

Despite Desai's silence about the parents addiction in *Clear Light of Day*, there is certainly alcohol and alcoholism in the home. Even before Tara gets married, Aunt Mira, a poor, widowed cousin who has been brought in to take care of the children, is already sneaking drinks "from a familiar looking bottle on her cupboard shelf" (64). The prospect of young Tara's oncoming marriage makes Mira drink "agitatedly, as if to hide from the intolerable prospect" (64). Later in the book Aunt Mira's body is "bony and angular, wrinkled and desiccated" (111), and she is subject to terrifying hallucinations. On one occasion she runs outside naked, crying "'Oh God—the rats, the rats! Rats, lizards, snakes—they are eating me—oh, they are eating me—' and her frantic hands tore the creatures from her throat, dragged them out of her hair. Then she doubled up and rolled and howled" (96). On another occasion, she imagines that she is being engulfed by flames (78; Cf. Gilmore, 20). At this point, Aunt Mira has a "bird-boned wrist" (97) and delirium tremens to such an extent that she cannot drink from her glass, "only spilt it all" (98). Obviously, Aunt Mira has been drinking for years. Because of alcohol, as a parent substitute she too fails to meet the children's needs.

Children of alcoholics adjust to their pain by developing certain types of personalities. The four children in Desai's novel match several of the patterns usually found in alcoholic homes. As the eldest daughter, very early on Bim becomes a hypermature child who manages the house and family (Cf. Ackerman 50). At one point the adult Bim boasts bitterly: "I could have been a nurse—or a matron—in a plague hospital. I can handle it all" (85). Yet when her doctor asserts that she is sacrificing her life for others, she angrily denies it. In contrast, her younger sister, Tara, is the kind of child who is not noticed. She cowers in a corner or under her Aunt Mira's skirts. She does not misbehave, but she performs poorly in school. School is for her a terrifying experience. In contrast, Raja and Bim excel in school in order to gain approval through their own achievements. Also, as a way to survive, both Raja and Tara choose substitute families and spend as much time as possible in these neighbors' homes. The fourth child, Baba, is mentally handicapped. His congenital problems may or may not have been caused by either his mother's diabetes or fetal alcohol syndrome. No explanation is given.

The oldest son, Raja, feels there is "no house as dismal as his own, as dusty and grimy and uncharming. Surely no other family could have as much illness contained in it as his, or so much oddity, so many things that could not be mentioned and had to be camouflaged or ignored" (49). As Raja says, "The restraints placed on him by such demands made him chafe" (49). Eventually, Raja escapes the atmosphere at home by running away. Consciously, Tara escapes by getting married.

Meanwhile, filled with bitterness and anger, Bim stays on in the old house to care for her alcoholic aunt and her mentally handicapped brother. The plight of these four adult children is most poignantly represented by what Bim sees one day on the veranda:

> She nearly stepped on a smashed pigeon's egg and the unsightly corpse of a baby bird that had plunged to its death at birth from its disastrously inadequate nest. The scattered bits of shell, the shapeless smudge of yellow-tipped feathers and bluish-red flesh and outsize beak made Bim draw back for a moment, then plunge on with a gasp of anger, as if the pigeon had made its nest so crudely, so insecurely, simply to lose its egg and anger her and give her the trouble of clearing it. It was a piece of filth—Bim nearly sobbed—not sad, not pathetic, just filthy. (163)

Raja, Bim, Tara, and, perhaps most of all, Baba were the victims of an insecure nest.

Anita Desai's silence about what made the family nest so insecure weighs over the book. Although she is frank about her alcoholic aunt, she has censored the reasons for her parents' behavior. What is absolutely clear, however, is that she is familiar with alcoholism. Desai's *Clear Light of Day* includes moving descriptions of her Aunt Mira's hallucinations and vivid glimpses of the behavior of the drunken brothers who live next door. Yet the inexplicable behavior of the parents suggests that she may still be guarding family secrets. Critics admire her work without commenting on her lack of explanation for the parents' behavior and without noting that the children would have been affected by the central role alcohol played in the life of Aunt Mira.

To fail to notice and analyze the impact of alcoholism on the characters in literature by third world writers is to fail to understand fully the exact nature of the pain they are describing. If we ignore the alcoholism, or speak of it casually, we fail to understand what the writers wish to communicate. Third-world writers describe many problems. However, their condemnation of economic, political, and social injustices should not blind us to how clearly many of them also reveal through their characters the destructive impact of alcoholism on human lives.

BIBLIOGRAPHY

Ackerman, Robert J. *Children of Alcoholics: A Guide for Parents, Educators, and Therapists.* Holmes Beach, FL: Learning Publications, 1983.

Desai, Anita. *Clear Light of Day.* New York: Penguin, 1980.

Emecheta, Buchi. *The Joys of Motherhood.* London: Heinemann, 1980.

Fugard, Athol. *"Master Harold" . . . and the Boys.* 1982. New York: Penguin, 1988.

Gilmore, Thomas B. *Equivocal Spirits: Alcoholism and Drinking in Twentieth-Century Literature.* Chapel Hill: University of North Carolina Press, 1987.

Srivastava, Ramesh K. "Anita Desai at Work: An Interview." *Perspectives on Anita Desai.* Ed. Ramesh K. Srivastava. Ghaziabad: Vimal Prakashan, 1984. Pp. 208–26.

Part IV

Addiction and Literature

CHAPTER 9

NGAIO MARSH AND THE "DRUG SCENE" OF DETECTIVE FICTION

Kathryne S. McDorman

ALL FORMS OF FICTION ARE AN APPROPRIATE source for cultural historians who wish to examine problems, attitudes, and social changes in a particular era. British detective fiction began with Arthur Conan Doyle's Sherlock Holmes stories in the 1890s and reached its apogee in the middle years of the twentieth century during the so-called Golden Age. It continues to be one of the most vital and popular forms of fiction, with its modern practitioners following in the traditions set by Arthur Conan Doyle and his successors, the "Grand Dames," women authors of the Golden Age. Because British detective fiction is a democratic literature that appeals to readers in many strata of British society from the modest working people to the dons of Oxford and Cambridge, it provides rich information about varied concerns. Detective fiction in the late twentieth-century becomes a version of the eighteenth-century novel of manners, revealing in its portrayals the foibles and passions of an age.

By surveying almost a century of detective stories, a historian may discern how attitudes were formed, developed, and shaped by the passage of time and events. From the 1890s to the 1990s, Britain and British society have been subject to tremendous pressures arising from two devastating world wars, her demise as a great imperial power, economic depression, and the rise and fall of Bolshevism. She has been forced to watch her class distinctions dissolve, her former military hegemony crumble, and her Victorian moral certainties succumb to the scrutiny of modern "situation ethics." Nowhere is the strain affecting modern society more clearly delineated than in its attitudes toward drug culture and drug trade, and the legislative and police efforts to control or stop them.

Throughout most of the nineteenth century the development of opiate drugs was considered an improvement in the pharmacology available to treat serious illness and pain. In 1803, a German apothecary assistant first isolated crystalline morphine, and, in 1898, the Bayer Company, also of Germany, developed heroin (Judson, 4). By the middle of the nineteenth century the opium trade had become so profitable in Britain that from 1839 to 1842 she fought a war against the Chinese when they tried to limit the amount of opium brought from British India into China. In all the centuries of drug use up until the twentieth there is only one account of medical concern about the addictive principles of opium, recorded in 1701 by a Dr. Jones of London; the vast majority of doctors regarded it as a staple in their treatments (Judson, 74). Indeed, opium was known in the ancient world as early as the time of the Sumerians and was used by the Greeks and Romans. Its assistance in healing and pain relief was praised in the writing of Paracelsus (1493–1541) who also developed tincture of opium known as laudanum. Furthermore, opium was so commonly used in nineteenth century Britain that it was a major ingredient in many forms of patent medicines (Bean, 18; Parissinen, ix), and in the American Civil War (1861–1865) opium was used so widely to treat pain from wounds that it is estimated that four hundred thousand addicts were inadvertently created. With the invention of the hypodermic needle in mid-century, a medical mythology emerged that if drugs were injected rather than ingested it was possible to avoid addiction because the drug did not reach the stomach (Parissinen, 208).

In addition to the opiates, barbiturate drugs like cocaine were known in Europe at the beginning of the twentieth century. Usually it was "snuffed," but injection of cocaine became increasingly common. As late as 1890, cocaine was deemed acceptable for general use, and was advertised as a drug that cured the "blues" or a "wine for sportsmen." Sigmund Freud was the first doctor to study the pharmacological effects and was a regular user, as were Emile Zola, Henrick Ibsen, and Robert Louis Stevenson (Kobayashi, 125; Parissinen 117). Queen Victoria, that model of rectitude in the age that bore her name, undoubtedly took opiates and barbiturates in her medicines.

Victoria's most famous fictional detective, Sherlock Holmes injected himself with cocaine with the full knowledge, if not the full approval, of Dr. Watson. Indeed one of the first stories, "The Sign of Four," opens with Holmes taking a bottle from the mantle, a hypodermic syringe and

> With his long, white, nervous fingers he adjusted the delicate needle and rolled back his left shirtcuff. For some little time his eyes rested thoughtfully upon the sinewy forearm and wrist, all dotted and scarred with innumerable puncture marks. Finally he thrust the sharp point home, pressed down the tiny piston, and sank back into the velvet-lined armchair with a long sigh of satisfaction. (Doyle, 89)

His friend, Dr. Watson, comments that he had witnessed this ritual three times a day for "many months," but "custom had not reconciled my mind to it." Intimidated by Holmes' superb intelligence and superciliousness, Watson hesitated to speak, but finally overcame his reluctance and asked Holmes which drug it was today, "'morphine or cocaine?' He raised his eyes languidly from the old black-letter volume which he had opened. 'It is cocaine,' he said, 'a seven-per-cent solution. Would you care to try it?'" (Doyle, 89)

When Watson demurs and speculates on the physical strain that it puts upon the body. Holmes responds "Perhaps you are right, Watson . . . I suppose that its influence is physically a bad one. I find it, however, so transcendently stimulating and clarifying to the mind that its secondary action is a matter of small moment" (Doyle, 89). Declaring that his mind "rebels at stagnation," Holmes merely smiles at his friend's further protest:

> Count the cost! Your brain may be as you say, be roused and excited, but it is a pathological and morbid process which involves increased tissue change and may at last leave a permanent weakness. You know, too, what a black reaction comes upon you. Surely the game is hardly worth the candle. Why should you, for a mere passing pleasure, risk the loss of those great powers with which you have been endowed? (Doyle, 89)

Watson also reminds him that as a medical man his opinion has authority. It should be remembered that Sir Arthur Conan Doyle, Holmes' creator, was a qualified physician who also wrote histories, and who went to South Africa at the turn of the century to serve in the Boer War, a war in which more British soldiers died of disease that of wounds. Surely he would have used opiates and barbiturates there to treat the sick and wounded. At the end of "The Sign of Four" Watson laments that the police took the credit for the solution of the case, and everyone but Holmes appears to have been rewarded. Holmes, already bored by his success in solving the knotty mystery replies, "'For me . . . there still remains the cocaine-bottle.' And he stretched his long white hand up for it" (Doyle, 158).

Critics have noted that Holmes' drug use abates during the course of the stories; nevertheless, Doyle's initial portrayal of the drug-stimulated detective seems to offer a rationale for drug use that simply would not have been acceptable after the turn of the century. Attitudes toward drugs and addiction changed radically in the course of the twentieth century (Parissinen, 103). No twentieth-century author would have been likely to make drug use so attractive, nor make their detective an addict. In fact, by the turn of the century most respectable English people believed that most drug abuse was relegated to the slums. In the United States, however, the public and Congress took greater alarm and passed laws like the 1914 Harrison Narcotics Act that sought criminal penalties for those trading or using drugs. Great Britain did not act in a formal way until the 1920 Dangerous Drugs Act that sought to control the manufacturing and sale of opiates and barbiturates. These two responses indicate a growing split in the way the two countries viewed drug abuse. In the United States drug manufacturing, trade, and use were considered criminal acts; in Britain the trade was condemned, but the user was viewed as a victim suffering from a medical problem (Bean, 6; Judson, 21). Indeed, in 1967 methadone maintenance became covered under the National Health Service. British detective fiction quite clearly supports this distinction, not only by the attitudes it displays, but by its rather sanguine response to "the drug problem" in contrast to the hysteria in the United States.

Of the four Grand Dames who wrote classical British detective fiction in the twentieth century, New Zealand born Ngaio Marsh is in a unique position as the colonial "outsider" among the "insider" authors such as Agatha Christie, Margery Allingham, and Dorothy Sayers. The peripatetic Marsh visited England for the first time as an adult in 1928, and would continue to spend a portion of each year until 1974 dividing her time between London and her New Zealand home in Christchurch. According to Marsh, her homeland remained in such a frozen state of Victorian sensibilities that she experienced an acute sense of contrast each time she disembarked at Southhampton. Traveling back and forth between England and New Zealand heightened her sensitivities and developed her special perspective to analyze social change as she observed it. In her work one senses the breakdown of English class distinction, and one perceives in the character of her protagonist, Roderick Alleyn, an aristocrat and a professional policeman, a symbol of that fundamental transformation. It is through a policeman's eyes that Marsh views the problems of modern England's permissive society.

During the years that Marsh wrote (1935–1982), England underwent a revolution in mores that witnessed the emergence of a drug "scene" that eclipsed anything that Sherlock Holmes could have imagined. Of her thirty-two novels about murder mysteries, seven portray drugs and the drug trade not exactly as a cause of crime and social decay, but certainly as a motive for murder and therefore as a threat to the health of the body politic. From her second mystery, *Enter a Murderer,* published in 1935, to her next-to-last novel, *Last Ditch,* published in 1977, Marsh creates addicts, international drug lords, bogus religious sects that feature mind-altering drugs as "worship" experiences, drug smugglers, and, in the midst of it all, the ubiquitous Alleyn who must solve a murder in the presence of all these distractions.

In *Enter a Murderer,* Marsh employs for the first time a locale that will become her trademark—a theatrical setting. Alleyn is attending a drama called "The Rat and the Beaver," with his friend and first "Watson," Nigel Bathgate, when a stage murder turns into the real thing. The play features a group of villains engaged in the opium trade who have discovered that they have been betrayed by one of their own. The murdered actor actually played the part of the suspected "rat." In the course of his investigations, Alleyn finds that the play's producer, the inappropriately named Jacob Saint, had actually been accused of building his fortune on the drug trade. A number of years previously an anonymous article in the tabloids had proclaimed "Ladies and Gentlemen with unattractive portmanteaux under their yellow eyeballs were . . . constantly being obliged with opium and cocaine by some agency controlled by a 'well known theater magnate'" (*Enter,* 86). Saint had survived the charges but had never escaped the scandal entirely. Upon examining the murder victim's apartment, Alleyn, Bathgate, and Inspector Fox discover drug paraphernalia. Marsh allows life to imitate art when the murderer turns out to be another of the actors who had been to heroin parties with the murdered man while at Cambridge, and who had actually been the author of the articles accusing his present producer. A group of villains involved in drugs, indeed! Although illicit drugs are not the focus of the story, they are a back lighting illuminating the web of sordid relationships.

Death in Ecstasy offers a very different and unusual look at drugs as a part of a pseudoreligious experience. Marsh reprised this theme 20 years later in *Spinsters in Jeopardy* with a few new flourishes. In this novel the murder takes place at London's House of the Sacred Flame, which is led by a self-proclaimed priest with the improbable name of Father Jasper Garnette, and is as sanctimonious a bit of goods as Marsh ever created. When one of the more sensible characters, Janey Jenkins, tries to explain to Inspector Alleyn the effect that "Father" Garnette had upon his flock when he preached, that "everything seems to be beautifully dovetailed and balanced," Alleyn remarks that "I believe opium smokers experience it" (86).

This novel has Marsh's first developed portrayal of an addict, Maurice Pringle, who is engaged to Janey. Alleyn immediately recognizes that he is an addict by his erratic behavior and the enlarged pupils. Janey confronts her fiancé, only to get the time-honored promises from Maurice that he will stop soon, tomorrow, someday. Janey laments to Nigel Bathgate "It's frightful. Not only the cigarettes, but—worse than that. He's taking it now, I know he is. You'll see. When he comes back he'll be excited and—dreadfully friendly. He's turning into a horrible stranger. You don't know what the real Maurice is like" (245). Indeed, when Maurice returns from bathing and changing, Nigel is treated to a sample of his new, drug induced personality: "His eyes were very bright. He had an air of spurious gaiety. He was like a mechanical figure that had been over wound and might break. He talked loudly and incessantly, and laughed at everything he said" (247). Of course this euphoria was followed within a short time by flagging energy, a hangover, and extreme irritability. In despair Janey recognizes her helplessness to stop the nightmare of his addiction.

Later when Janey admits to herself that she knows who seduced him into this dependency, she rails "It's Father Garnette. He's responsible. I think that he must be the wickedest, foulest beast that ever lived" (245). Alleyn had already concluded that the bogus priest was in truth simply a tarted-up drug pusher using the ploy of spiritual enlightenment. In one of his flights of verbal fancy he gloats over the discovery of heroin-treated cigarettes in the priest's apartment.

> Oh excellent priest! Perdition catch my soul, but I do love thee. All the top cigarettes as innocent as the wild woodbine, but underneath in a vicious little mob, ten doped smokes. A fairly high percentage of heroin was found, from one-tenth to as much as one-seventh of a grain per cigarette. It is possible that the cigarette tobacco has been treated with a solution of diamorphine? Oh, Jasper, my dear, my better half, have I caught my heavenly jewel? (233)

By the novel's end, the murderer has been caught and "Father" Garnette exposed for the charlatan that he is, largely through Pringle's accusations. For Alleyn the case is officially closed, but he gives a stern lecture to Maurice that "I think that you should go into a nursing home where such cases are treated . . . It won't be pleasant, but is, I believe, your only chance. Don't answer now. Think it over and let me know. In the meantime, I have asked Dr. Curtis to have a look at you and he will help you, I am sure" (311).

Today that bit of advice would be looked upon as naive, ignoring as it does the medical model of addiction, but it is consistent with the then-British view that the addict is not the criminal that United States law insists is the case. Alleyn knows that Pringle's complete cure is uncertain, but leaves the decision in his, and Janey's, hands. As for Jasper Garnette, though he is not the murderer and not criminally culpable by British law in his followers' degradation, he is arrested for fraud connected to the House of the Eternal Flame's business. Alleyn practically spits out his judgment of Garnette, as compared to the murderer: "'Him and his heroin! Devil take me, but I swear he's the nastier sample of the two'" (319).

Marsh's next image of drugs and the drug trade is tied to the Jazz Age. Though jazz and night clubs made their most popular appearance in the twenties just after World War I, Marsh does not write about them until after World War II. The righteous condemned jazz and nightclubs as sleazy entertainment that flaunted decent conventions. Many observers feared that the frank sexuality in jazz sounds and songs, and the nightclub's dimmed lights, sensuous decor, and the smoky, boozy atmosphere were mere rest stops on the path to damnation. Marsh's view is more sophisticated than those who condemned on moral grounds, but her story does confirm the suspicion in the mind of such puritans that jazz and nightclubs are fronts for crime and that many jazz musicians are hooked on drugs.

In *A Wreath for Rivera* (1949), Marsh creates one of the most delightful, aristocratic eccentrics in her canon. Lord Pastern and Baggot is known for his wild and fleeting enthusiasm. His wife describes him as having cycled through fascinations as varying as Central European religious sects, the study of voodoo, nudism, and, most recently, jazz. He has hired a popular band leader, Breezy Bellairs, and his band to rehearse at his London town house in preparation for a nightclub date at which Lord Pastern, himself, will play the drums with the band. Meanwhile his daughter's unsuitable attraction to Carlos Rivera, Bellairs' saxophonist, has alarmed Lady Pastern who has called upon her niece, Carlisle Wayne, to dissuade her daughter. While visiting the house, Carlisle read an exposé on the drug trade in a new popular magazine *Harmony,* a magazine secretly published by Lord Pastern, in which "[t]wo Latin-American business firms with extensive connections in Great Britain were boldly named. An editorial note truculently courted information backed by the promise of full protection" (26). Lord Pastern rather disingenuously praises the boldness of the article: "They're not afraid to speak their minds, b'God. See that thing on drug runnin'? Names and everything and if they don't like it they can damn well lump it. The police . . . are no good; pompous incompetent lot" (29).

Lord Pastern is about to encounter those "pompous" police in an unexpected way. During the band's performance at the Metronome nightclub, Carlos is murdered. Alleyn's ensuing investigation uncovers the world of drugs, nefarious dealings, and murder. While being held for questioning Breezy betrays himself as an addict dependent on his "fix." When he begins withdrawal and experiences the delusional behavior that accompanies it, Alleyn does for him what he did for Maurice Pringle, he arranges for the police surgeon, Dr. Curtis, to give him some of the drug so that he can be questioned. This is consistent with British public policy that views the addict as a victim, not someone to be punished. It is unlikely that American detective fiction would have portrayed an uncorrupted policeman assisting an addict. Alleyn confronts Lord Pastern and accuses him of knowing Bellairs' drug connection and ignoring it. Lord Pastern's sarcastic answer is, "Not bein' a detective inspector . . . I don't have to wait until a dopefiend fits and passes out before I know what's wrong with him" (83). Breezy's band, on the other hand, denies that they knew of the dope; they insisted that it was medicine for nerves.

Alleyn finally succeeds in persuading the timpanist Skelton to talk about the addiction. Skelton's confession adds another twist to the distinctly British view of the drug trade.

> The drug racket . . . is like any other racket in a capitalistic government. The real criminals are the bosses, the barons, the high ups. They don't get pulled in. It's the little blokes that get caught. You have to think it out. Silly sentiment and big talk won't work. I've got no tickets on the police department in this country. A fairly efficient machine working for the wrong ideas. But drug-taking's no good from any point of view. (103)

Following this outburst, Skelton revealed that Breezy got his dope from the victim, Carlos Rivera, and that the nightclub had become a convenient distribution point from suppliers to users.

Skelton's suspicions that dope was really a capitalist plot offers an interesting side light on British policies. Three years before *A Wreath for Rivera* was published, England elected her first real socialist government. The Labour government under Clement Atlee enacted enormous change with the National Health Service and the subsequent nationalization of many private industries. "Damn the capitalists!" would have been fairly common currency at the time. If this sort of sentiment had cropped up in an American novel, it would have been coupled with Skelton's guilt of some sort of heinous crime such as espionage. The one thing that Americans were afraid of even more than dope itself were the "Reds." The Labour Party in Britain was working to improve relations with Stalinist Russia, the greatest socialist state of them all. The post-war disillusion with the Soviets had not set in completely, and the Cold War had not really begun.

Carlos Rivera, as his ledgers revealed, was a fairly successful dealer, undoubtedly connected with one of the larger drug networks that Alleyn and his sidekick, Fox, would love to uncover. As they search his apartment, Alleyn explains to a young constable how drug smuggling works. "This will have come in by the usual damned labyrinth . . . This is probably cocaine or heroin, and has no doubt traveled long distances in bogus false teeth, fat men's navels, dummy hearing aids, phony bayonet fitments for electric light bulbs, and God knows what else" (150). As eager as they are to crack the drug trade, Alleyn and Fox have to remind themselves that it's a murderer they are after, and they refocus their search.

As the novel ends, Alleyn suspects that Breezy, himself, had killed his supplier because of the threat of blackmail and Carlos' arrogant indifference to Breezy's drug needs. Breezy is in desperate shape, frantically trying to bargain and promising to quit taking drugs sometime soon. Fox, whom Alleyn calls "the drug Baron" because of his investigations, continues to pump Bellairs for information about bigger suppliers than Rivera. Bellairs will trade anything he knows to assure that Dr. Curtis will keep him in his supply. His withdrawal becomes worse, "Suddenly and inanely Breezy yawned, a face splitting yawn that bared his gums and showed his coated tongue. He rubbed his arms and neck. 'I keep feeling as if there's something under my skin. Worms or something'" (199). Once again Alleyn and Fox use the offer of drugs for information and finally break the murder case against Bellairs. Alleyn has the further satisfaction of revealing to the wily Lord Pastern, who had dismissed police as "pompous and incompetent," that he knows that Pastern is the moving force behind *Harmony,* the magazine that exposed the drug traders. Lord Pastern's eyes light up, promising a new obsession to replace jazz, as he queries Alleyn about how he might become a detective.

In 1953, Marsh published the most virulent antidrug novel of her 32 books. It is also a rather peculiar novel, returning to the theme of *Death in Ecstasy,* bogus religious cults and the use of drugs for phony religious purposes. The action of *Spinsters in Jeopardy* takes place in Roqueville in the south of France where Alleyn and his family have gone for a holiday. The holiday is partly genuine because Mrs. Alleyn has a relative, P. E. Garbel, in the little French town whom she wishes to contact. This family connection provides the cover that allows Alleyn to do some undercover snooping. In this novel, Marsh takes a gamble that her readers will tolerate rather lengthy and didactic expositions about the history and evils of drugs and the drug trade. The lectures convey information that Marsh must have deemed necessary to justify Alleyn, a domestic cop, being pulled into international intrigue, but it brings the flow of character development, plot, and place to a dead stop. Ironically, if Marsh was motivated to preach against drugs, she creates this unsuccessful mystery as her pulpit and fails her audience. Indeed, here, the exotic elements, extraordinary circumstances, and preaching are so pronounced that the story risks becoming absurd.

The international difficulties in coordinating police activities to stop the drug trade go back to the years before World War I. In those early years of the century the ideas about prescribing or using opiates and barbiturates changed. Gone were the patent medicines that were confident mixtures of opiate brews. The idea that these homeopathic substances created drug addiction shocked respectable opinion. Some of the legitimate drug industry went underground and became the illicit opium racket intent upon supplying users and creating more consumers. Their activities had reached such alarming proportions that international meetings in Shanghai and the Hague considered how nations might act in concert to stop it. A few tentative decisions were reached, but the war intervened and nothing further could be done (Parissinen, 129–32).

After the war the drug traffic resumed and, in fact, surpassed its previous records. Many countries like Bulgaria became havens for drug manufacturing. Drugs were smuggled around Europe in diplomatic pouches as peacemakers and their staffs scurried continuously from one postwar conference to another. Reputable chemists were lured by high salaries into the manufacture of diacetylmorphine, heroin. While fashionable and powerful people made staggering profits, street peddlers and addicts lived in a shadow world of supply, demand, and death. When the mortality rate from drugs became a public scandal, the League of Nations appointed an Advisory Committee that made the first determined efforts to stop it. By 1939, some progress had been made in seeking out and destroying factories and cutting the trade somewhat (Bean, 43–44).

After World War II, the United Nations and its Interpol agency, an attempt at police cooperation across national lines, began the hunt anew (Bean, 45–46). Alleyn sighs as he tells Troy, "The police still catch the sprats at the customs counters and miss the mackerels in high places" (118). The police believed that the factories moved from Bulgaria to postwar Italy and even into southern France. Hence Alleyn's mission is legitimate in its plot and place, but Marsh strays from the conventions of her genre skirting the perimeters of the dubious realm of propagandist literature.

In preparing for the journey, Alleyn tells his wife, Troy, that M.1.5., the British national security branch and the French Surete are "having a bit of a party" with the Narcotics Bureau (14), and that he has been called to do some fieldwork. His mission underlines some of the difficulties of international cooperation when a British citizen living abroad is involved with breaking the laws of both his native and his adopted country. The citizen in question is one Albert George Clarkson, also known as Oberon, spiritual leader of the Children of the Sun in France. If he is a felon, to which country is he accountable? Alleyn's task is complicated by the fact that as the train pulled into Roqueville in the very early hours of the morning, he happened to witness what appeared to be a murder in a lighted room opposite his darkened sleeping car. He learns that this window was in an ancient Saracen citadel occupied by the Children of the Sun cult. As Alleyn and his family prepared to disembark they are distracted by the sudden appendicitis attack of another passenger, a spinster, Miss Truebody. They lift her gently from the train and seek medical assistance. By another happenstance, the only physician in Roqueville at that moment is an Egyptian doctor who is a member of the cult. All these startling coincidences give Alleyn access to the citadel, and he becomes as concerned with catching the murderer whom he believes that he saw as with uncovering the drug connections.

Brought into the citadel through the good offices of Miss Truebody's appendix, Alleyn meets a number of celebrities, actresses, and socialites. All are rather obviously disoriented and ill with hangovers. He is concerned that one of the members of the cult, Annabelle Wells, the actress, knows that he is a policeman. Although Alleyn fears exposure, when he sees her wasted eyes, he cannot overcome the impulse to preach. After she admits that she is a heroin addict he responds:

> Are you asking me if I could help you to cure yourself of drugging? I couldn't. Only an expert and sense of purpose to keep faith, as you put it, perhaps you should have enough guts to go through a cure. I don't know. . . . Go to a doctor in Paris and offer yourself for a cure. Recognize your responsibility and, before further harm

> can come out of this place, tell me or the local commissary or anyone else in a position of authority, everything you know about the people here. . . . The place and all of you speak for yourselves. Yawning your heads off because you want your heroin. Pin-point pupils and leathery faces." (82–83)

Marsh insists that these heroin "junkies" began with the "devil weed," cannabis. Rabid antidrug campaigners believed that the recreational use of soft drugs leads inexorably to experimentation with more potent ones. Although modern research is ambiguous on this assertion, Marsh and her contemporaries believed it. Movies like *Reefer Madness* and the harsh penalties placed upon possession of marijuana in the fifties were certainly predicated upon this belief. In *Spinsters in Jeopardy* Marsh describes the preparation that the Children of the Sun went through to receive their profane sacraments. Part of it involved smoking marijuana, with snacks thoughtfully provided should initiates get hungry. P. E. Garbel later confesses to Alleyn,

> He started me on marijuana—reefers, you know—and I've never been able to break off. They see to it that I get just enough to keep me going. They get me up here and make me nervous and then give me cigarettes . . . When I smoke I get very silly. I hear myself saying things to fill me with bitter shame. But when I've got the craving to smoke and He's given me cigarettes, I well, you've seen. (201)

A contemporary observer might find this unrealistic and even amusing. Current wisdom and research finds certain, unhealthy long term effects in heavy marijuana users, but this kind of craving and dependency is almost nonexistent. It is a poor motive for Garbel's complicity in covering up a murder.

Alleyn learns the ritual babble of the cult, and, in disguise, wends his way into the sacred circle. While there he sees enough to mark the murderer and to arrest the whole sordid crew. Marsh returns to a plot element found in *Death in Ecstasy;* again, Alleyn solves the murder and breaks the drug connection through the assistance of the confessed addict. First Maurice Pringle and now

Troy's cousin, P. E. Garbel, provide evidence that nails a murderer, but by doing so sever their supply of drugs, heroin in Pringle's case and marijuana in Garbel's. The coincidence seems remote that a policeman would be assisted, twice, by the very addicts that were enslaved by their suppliers. Marsh loses her touch for verisimilitude when she ventures into this murky world of seriously addictive drugs and the people who fall prey to its attractions. Inspector Dupont of the French Surete expresses a more cynical and pragmatic approach to those who are not accessories to the murder: "I imagine that we take statements from the painter, the actress Wells and the two young ones and let it go at that. They may be more useful running free. Particularly if they return to the habit" (223).

In the 1960s, England faced some difficult times in the war against drugs. In those years, Joseph Simpson, the police commissioner, established a drug squad within the Criminal Investigation Department, Alleyn's division of Scotland Yard. By April 1970, it was clear that the drug squad had become a secret little empire of its own using such questionable methods as entrapment and becoming agent provocateurs in order to catch the drug lords. As David Ascoli describes it, they operated in an area "ill-defined by law and moral precept"(307). Indeed, one of those ill-defined areas was exactly where the jurisdiction of the drug squad overlapped with the Customs Bureau since most illicit drugs were smuggled into the country. By 1970, twenty officers were involved in scandalous accusations. At this point the Home Office responsible for police management asked for a complete dossier on the drug squad. Some of their worst fears were confirmed in June 1971 when the trial of Basil Sands, a major contact within the drug trade, exposed several questionable drug squad practices. By June 11, the drug squad was officially dissolved, and the detectives assigned to it were sent to other postings.

In July, Scotland Yard announced that an investigation of drug squad activities would be carried out by the assistant chief of constables, Harold Prescott. That the proud London based C.I.D. could be forced to allow an investigation by an officer from the provincial police is an indication of how serious the trouble was presumed to be. Prescott reported in 1972 that there appeared to be no cause for criminal indictments, but the new police commissioner, Robert Marks, ordered two more internal investigations that resulted in six officers being brought up on charges (Ascoli, 319). In 1973, the six drug squad members stood trial for charges of conspiracy to pervert the course of justice, and five were also charged with perjury. All were acquitted of the first charge but three were found guilty of perjury and sent to prison. Despite the acquittals, the message was clear that the C.I.D. must be brought under closer control and scrutiny (Ascoli, 321).

In the midst of this scandal, Ngaio Marsh published *When in Rome,* a mystery that in a similar vein to *Spinsters in Jeopardy* has Alleyn sent to a foreign country to investigate the drug trade only to become inadvertently involved in a murder. This novel is more successful than *Spinsters,* though it flirts with some of the same exotic themes. Modern audiences might find some language in the book quaint, such as when Sebastian Mailer the book's villain and victim, a drug addict and pusher, and a British citizen, first confronts Barnaby Grant, the famous author, he confesses, "I have acquired an addiction for cocaine. Rather 'square' of me isn't it? I really must change one of these days to something groovier. You see I am conversant with the jargon" (12). Marsh also reprises her theme of marijuana as leading to other drugs, but this time she dismisses the arguments of the opposition. As Kenneth Dorne and his elderly aunt discuss drugs, she asks,

> "In Perugia. Did you—did you—smoke?"
>
> "There's no need for the hushed tones, darling. You've been handed the usual nonsense, I see."
>
> "Then you *did?*"
>
> "Of course," he said impatiently.
>
> "Kenneth, what's it like?"
>
> "Pot? Do you really want to know?"
>
> "I'm asking, aren't I?"
>
> "Dire the first time and quite fun if you persevere. Kid stuff really. All the fuss about nothing."
>
> "It's done at parties, isn't it?"
>
> "That's right lovey, want to try?"
>
> "It's not habit-forming. Is it?"

> "Of course it's not. It's nothing. It's O.K. as far as it goes. You don't get hooked. Not on pot. Try a little trip . . . In point of fact I *could* arrange a *fabulous* trip. Madly groovy. You'd adore it. All sorts of gorgeous gents. Super exotic pad. The lot." (27)

These two characters are members of a tour of Rome that is organized by the disreputable Mailer as a way of recruiting new addicts and blackmailing other victims. Roderick Alleyn, billed as R. Allen, is also on the tour since he has been sent to Rome to ferret out new drug trade routes and suppliers. As he explains to his counterpart at Rome's police force, "[t]he whole problem of the drug traffic, as we both know, is predominately an Interpol affair, but as in this instance we are rather closely tied up with them" (29). As Alleyn gets to know his fellow travelers he is startled to meet the respectable Barnaby Grant who is held prisoner in one of Mailer's twisted blackmail schemes. When Sebastian Mailer disappears and is later discovered dead in the catacombs beneath an ancient Roman church, it turns out that everyone on the tour had a motive to wish him dead.

Before Mailer is discovered, Alleyn has an opportunity to observe the Rome drug scene first hand. Kenneth Dorne indiscreetly confides to "R. Allen" that he is thinking of trying new drugs, "The big leap. Pot head to mainliner. Well, as a matter of fact, I've had a taste. You know. Mind you, I'm not hooked. Just the odd pop. Only a fun thing" (101). Yet as much as he protested, Kenneth Dorne is clearly headed for disaster when the late night attractions of Mailer's tour involve a visit to "Toni's Pad." Toni turns out to be a fat, effeminate man who announces the evening's entertainment as "Keenky Keeks." Marsh primly leaves the unnamed sordid entertainment to send Alleyn to make a drug buy. This is just the sort of agent provocateur activity that the drug squad would be excoriated for shortly after the book was published (Collison, 153). Alleyn feigns the symptoms of an addict in need in order to persuade the concierge at Toni's to sell him cocaine, heroin, and the necessary paraphernalia.

Later, when the emphasis shifts to the murder investigation, Alleyn reminds Dorne of the conversation about his conversion from soft to hard drugs. Alleyn reassures him that he is not going to arrest him, he just wants information that will help him trap the killer. Alleyn also uncovers the reason why Barnaby Grant cooperated in such a peculiar enterprise. When Grant reveals the blackmail to Alleyn, the detective's response is that "everything is grist that comes to our grubby little mill. . . . My masters sent me here on the drug-running lay and I find myself landed with . . . murder" (144).

When Alleyn uncovers the murderer, he also links the alleged drunk on the tour, Major Sweet, as a key figure in the drug trade. He confronts Sweet with the knowledge that he has gained about a new entry route for hard drugs being employed by one of the major smugglers, Otto Zeigfeldt. Alleyn discovers that Sweet is really a courier for the Zeigfeldt connection sent to check on Sebastian Mailer. With the death of the disreputable Mailer, Sweet's mission is compromised, with the unpleasant consequence for the drug barons that a policeman now knows too much about their operation. Alleyn also knows that Sweet may be in danger because the unwanted exposure and the possibility that he is involved in a double cross to cut himself in on Mailer's profits may make him expendable to his masters. He offers Sweet a deal: protection for "a complete list of Zeigfeldt's agents and a full account of his modus operandi between Izmir and the U.S.A. Step by step. With particular respect to Mailer" (153). Sweet, cursing and sweating for a drink, agrees to Alleyn's terms. As the mystery concludes, once again a British policeman has released known addicts, made a deal with the drug merchant's agent, solved two murders, and, with scarcely a bow to the limitations of his power as a C.I.D. agent abroad, ridden home in triumph (Collison, 154).

In her next-to-last mystery, *Last Ditch* (1977), Marsh once again weaves the international drug trade into her web of deceit. Ricky Alleyn, Roderick and Troy's grown son, has retired to a small fishing village on an unidentified British island off the coast of France to write a novel. While there he is charmed by the eccentric Pharamond family, puzzled by the late night fishing expeditions of his landlord, and caught up in a murder investigation. The only young man of his age with whom he has contact is a painter, Sydney Jones, who cultivates Ricky's friendship with the hope of an introduction to his famous painter mother, Troy Alleyn. Syd is also a minor villain in the piece, and one who introduces the drug theme. One evening after a convivial drink in the town pub, Syd invites Ricky to his "pad." When Syd offers him a smoke and asks if he's ever taken a "trip," Ricky leaves quickly. Later, upon reflection he realizes that Syd's odd behavior and suspicious trips to France for an imported artist's paint may mark him as both an addict and a smuggler.

This connection is validated when Roderick arrives in the village, supposedly on holiday, to visit Ricky. Alleyn explains his presence to his son: "I'm here on a sort of double job which is my Assistant Commissioner's Machiavellian idea of economy. I'm here because the local police are worried about the death of Dulcie Harkness and have asked us to nod in and I'm also supposed in an offhand, carefree manner to look into the possibility of this island being a penultimate station in one of the heroin routes into Great Britain" (105). The French town opposite Ricky's little village haven has been identified by Scotland Yard as a probable new port of smuggling that the drug runners resorted to after Major Sweet's revelations in *When in Rome*. Alleyn has once again been assigned to chop off another of the hydra heads of the Zeigfeldt drug empire.

The murder investigation yields surprising results when more and more strange events come to light. The police find that the victim's uncle, a fire and brimstone preacher, has amphetamines tucked into his pamphlets on eternal damnation, and Ricky's landlord, Gil Ferrant, emerges as a man with extensive connections with chemical factories near Marseilles that M. Dupont of the French Surete tracked down for Scotland Yard. M. Dupont, whose first appearance was in *Spinsters in Jeopardy*, cooperates with his old friend Alleyn as both lie in wait hoping to catch the biggest dealers, not merely the middle-sized ones. Syd Jones certainly qualifies as a small time operator, barely trusted by the drug pushers because he, himself, has become a junkie. Alleyn explains, "They don't use drug consumers inside the organization . . . they're completely unpredictable and much too dangerous" (159).

He is almost tragically right, for his own son will be taken hostage by Syd and his pal who beat Ricky severely in order to ascertain how much the police know. It is a rash act that only succeeds in hastening Alleyn's intervention and capture of both the dealers and the murderer. When he finds his badly beaten son, Alleyn receives at least some small and legitimate amount of revenge as he withholds Syd's "fix" in order to elicit his frantic revelations about drugs, murder, and smuggling: The murder victim, Dulcie Harkness, discovered that Syd was smuggling pellets of drugs to the island in his paint tubes. She was murdered to protect the route by which illicit drugs were moving into England and the fortunes that even small-time dealers had begun to amass. Although Alleyn does not succeed in landing one of the big fish, he does succeed in identifying the director of the island operation, Louis Pharamond, one of Ricky's delightful hosts.

As in *Spinsters in Jeopardy* and *When in Rome,* Alleyn does not overstep his authority completely in *Last Ditch.* He is, after all, on British soil. *Spinsters in Jeopardy* and *When in Rome* underscored the problem of international cooperation necessary among national police forces; *Last Ditch* comments upon another area of tension, that is, between the domestic police and customs officials as blame shifts back and forth about whose responsibility it is to protect England from the intrusion of drugs. Justice certainly has her day at the end of *Last Ditch,* but Marsh and Alleyn both acknowledge that ending a portion of the trade is but one battle in a long and frustrating war.

All of Marsh's books that weave the drug trade into their fabric of murder and mystery reveal a policeman's revulsion at the wasting of human quality and potential in addictive drugs, but the more common cause of such waste, alcoholism, is never mentioned. A good deal of social drinking is going on in these books, but the drunk is in no way compared with the doper. Drunkenness is an ugly part of the victim's personality in *Enter a Murderer* and a kind of menacing violence accompanies it, but it represents little more than a social inconvenience, or as the smart young set averred, a "bore." A drunk was not quite a gentleman, but he was tolerated in society. Even the hapless Maurice Pringle of *Death in Ecstasy* is considered quite acceptable while he, Janey, and Nigel drink highball after highball. It is only when he retires to his closet to drug himself that he appears so dangerously changed. In *A Wreath for Rivera* the smart young people of the jazz clubs also drink a good bit, but evidently with no unfortunate results. In another of Marsh's novels, *Scales of Justice,* Commander Syce, a retired military officer, is an alcoholic, but when he succumbs to a fit of lumbago, he also succumbs to the maternal charms of Nurse Kettle who sets about to straighten him out, spine and habits, and does so. Is Marsh suggesting that all the drunk needs is the love of a good woman?

Two other retired military men who are drunks, villains, and in one case a murderer appear in *When in Rome* and *Black As He's Painted.* In *When in Rome* Major Sweet craves his bottle and stays half drunk throughout the infamous tour of Rome that results in Sebastian Mailer's death. Though Alleyn knows that some of the Major's befuddlement was an act to provide cover for his drug activities, some of it was real. As he sees the Major cleaned up after a night of hard drinking, Alleyn notes, "[p]erhaps the Major was all he seemed to be and all of it gone to the bad" (150). Major Sweet was in fact a "bad 'un" who falsified his military identity, aided in covering up one murder, and betrayed his drug boss. No benign old drunk was he, but a manipulative thorough scoundrel.

Another ex-military man and a drunk appears in the 1973 novel, *Black As He's Painted.* Colonel Cockburn-Montfort is credited with the excellent organization and training of the army of Ng'ombwana, a fictional African nation emerging from colonial status to independence. Like many of his breed, Cockburn-Montfort knew no other life but the military and, after spending many years there, thought of Ng'ombwana as his home. When the new rulers of the nation relieved him of responsibility and turned over the army to an African officer, he withdrew into drink and became embittered and vengeful. His alcoholic ways hide the anger and bitterness, and Alleyn at first tends to dismiss him as an impotent drunk incapable of a terrible double murder of two repulsive ex-colonials who were suspected of ties to the drug trade. As Alleyn views the Colonel shortly after the murder, his tendency, as with Major Sweet, is to see him as ludicrous rather than evil.

> Colonel Cockburn-Montfort lay in an armchair, with his mouth open, snoring profoundly and hideously. He would have presented

> a less distasteful picture, Alleyn thought, if he had discarded the outward showing of an officer—and ambiguous addition—gentleman: the conservative suit, the signet ring on the correct finger, the handmade brogues, the regimental tie, the quietly elegant socks and, lying on the floor by his chair, the hat from Jermyn street—all so very much in order. And Colonel Cockburn-Montfort so very far astray. (207)

As with Major Sweet, Alleyn discovers that Cockburn-Montfort was the murderer of the two victims. He murdered them, returned to his home, had a drink, and passed out as Alleyn finds him. Surely in these two, drink is an unpleasant habit, but not roundly condemned. Alleyn cannot rouse himself to the same sense of moral outrage at their drunkenness, even when it has destroyed character as certainly as marijuana and heroin.

Critics have argued that those who write detective fiction are, by nature, social meliorists, intent on righting wrongs and serving the cause of justice. Other critics point to this as the genre's greatest flaw—the tendency to tie up all stray ends, tidy up the moral issue of murder with definitive notions of "Right" always prevailing in the end. The murder victim is frequently an unpleasant or unpopular person, often ungrieved for by survivors. The murderer is always discovered, whether by police methods or private investigator ingenuity, and the conclusion promises a world purged of doubt and murder. Leaving aside for the moment that modern practitioners of the craft like P. D. James and Ruth Rendell are transforming the genre, critics complain that the world simply is not as the classic writers make it appear. The "Grande Dames" of the Golden Age are looked upon by these critics as little better than romance novelists who provide an artificial resolution to all conflicts by the end of the story.

Murder, the act upon which so many mysteries focus, is always portrayed as arising from individual responsibility. There is perhaps no more existential, defining moment in life aside from the moment of birth than the moment in which a person commits murder. It has been regarded as a crime by most known societies regardless of social context or provocation. Methods of proof, trial and punishment may differ from one society to another, but the crime itself remains constant. When it occurs, the general efforts are bent towards purifying the world by resolving the loss, solving the puzzle and apprehending the perpetrator.

To some readers, the blending of murder mysteries and drug addiction is an odd combination, an uneasy alliance. Drug abuse is most often seen as a social crime, not a moral one, and it is an act requiring a vast network of resources from supplier to user. Drug use may, in fact, be a social act performed with others as companionable associates. Murder is most often a lonely crime requiring only two parties: the murderer and the victim. Addiction to drugs remains a denizen of the gray areas of an individualistic, capitalistic society's conscience. Unlike murder, where the crime is defined as doing unto others, addiction is, to many, a matter of doing unto oneself. What is the moral issue, and how can it be consistent with individual freedom? Certainly only the addict's first experience can be defined as existential, most subsequent use is because of a physical or psychological imperative.

Certainly reasonable men and women can disagree on whether the individual user is a victim of or a coconspirator in the illegal drug trade. The United States and Britain developed totally different policies in the early and middle years of the twentieth century. Surely both nations have been frustrated in their attempts to shut down the trade and the bastard children that it spawns—prostitution, gambling, and money laundering. Yet, typically, the big drug barons do not relish murder—their trade is most lucrative in the shadows, and a murder investigation can turn up the lights to the great discomfiture of pusher and user alike.

The link between the use of drugs and bogus religious sects in Marsh's novels offers the most plausible climate for the inclusion of the drug trade in a murder mystery. Both drug use and religious sects demand an individual shaman, the surrender of individual will, and, Holmes notwithstanding, a strong community identity. Alleyn makes this connection in *Death in Ecstasy* when he notes that both Father Garnette's hypnotic preaching and opium both deliver a sense of transcendence and euphoria. Yet bogus religious sects seem out of place in the refinement of classic detective fiction, "A bullet creasing a well tailored dinner jacket, tea gently laced with arsenic in the Spode teapot, were the stuff of the English school of crime writing, served up with relish and wry" (Budd, xi).

All this exotica seems remote from the cozy little murders that the Grande Dames were most famous for producing. Murder is most often motivated by greed, fear, or jealousy, not a search for transcendence. Traditional detective fiction is an odd dwelling place for addicts. Addicts take the emphasis off the plot and place it on reading character—typically the weakest part of Golden Age stories. Marsh is more skilled than many other writers in character development, but she is always concerned more with their actions than with their psyches. Yet addicts demand attention to their psyche; they cry out to be understood. Her novels that employ addiction as a theme are among her weaker novels. As brilliantly concocted as some of Marsh's plots are, the addition of addiction to the brew produces an odd hybrid—not a typical mystery and not a psychological character study. The fact that she chose to make the attempt tells us more about the social concerns of her day than whether or not these individual mysteries are successful. We see in her treatment of addiction and the drug trade her troubled reading of a troubled world. Surely the two world wars, the threat of total nuclear annihilation, and concurrently the threat of losing a generation not to war but to addiction shaped the world in which Marsh wrote her stories.

BIBLIOGRAPHY

Ascoli, David. *The Queen's Peace: The Origin and Development of the Metropolitan Police, 1829–1979*. London: Hamish Hamilton, 1979.

Bean, Phillip. *The Social Control of Drugs*. New York: John Wiley and Sons, 1974.

Bejerot, Nils. *Addiction and Society*. Springfield: Charles C. Thomas, 1970.

Budd, Elaine. *Thirteen Mistresses of Murder*. New York: Ungar, 1986.

Collison, Mike. *Police, Drugs and Community*. London: Free Association Books, 1995.

Dorn, Nicholas, Karim Murji, and Nigel South. *Traffickers: Drug Markets and Law Enforcement*. London: Routledge, 1992.

Doyle, Arthur Conan. "The Sign of Four." *The Collected Stories of Sherlock Holmes.* Garden City, New York: Doubleday, 1930.

Edwards, Griffith and Carol Busch, eds. *Drug Problems in Britain: A Review of Ten Years.* London: Academic Press, 1981.

Judson, Horace Freeland. *Heroin Addiction in Britain: What Americans Can Learn from the English Experience.* New York: Harcourt Brace Jovanovich, 1973.

Kobayashi, Tsukasa, Akane Higashiyama, and Masaharu Uemura. *Sherlock Holmes's London: Following the Footsteps of London's Master Detective.* San Francisco: Chronicle Books, 1986.

Marsh, Ngaio. *Black As He's Painted.* New York: Jove Books, 1978.

———. *Death in Ecstasy.* New York: Berkeley, 1977.

———. *Enter a Murderer.* London: Fontana Collins, 1964.

———. *Last Ditch.* Boston: Little Brown, 1977.

———. *Scales of Justice.* New York: Jove Books, 1980.

———. *Spinsters in Jeopardy.* Boston: Little Brown, 1953.

———. *When in Rome.* New York: Jove Books, 1980.

———. *A Wreath for Rivera.* Boston: Little Brown, 1949.

Parissinen, Terry M. *Secret Passions, Secret Remedies: Narcotic Drugs in British Society, 1820–1930.* Philadelphia: Institute for the Study of Human Issues, 1983.

Schur, Edwin M. *Narcotic Addiction in Britain and America: The Impact of Public Policy.* Bloomington: Indiana University Press, 1968.

CHAPTER 10

ALCOHOLIC IMPLICATIONS

A Catalyst of Valencian Culture

Jeffrey Oxford

VICENTE BLASCO IBÁÑEZ IS UNDOUBTEDLY one of the most widely recognized hispanic writers in the nonhispanic world and one of the, if not the, first millionaire Spanish novelists. Although Cervantes has been translated into many languages, his renown lies primarily in the universal character of don Quijote de la Mancha. Vicente Blasco Ibáñez's acclaim, however, is derived not only from a single work, but from various translations, dramatizations, and cinematographic adaptations of multiple narratives. Perhaps the most widely applauded of these by the American audience are the 1922 version of *Blood and Sand,* starring Rudolph Valentino, and the 1962 film *The Four Horsemen of the Apocalypse,* starring Glen Ford.

The primary critical analysis of Vicente Blasco Ibáñez revolves around a turn-of-the-century collection of novels commonly referred to as the Valencian cycle. Composed of six different novels written between 1894 and 1902, this group includes *Arroz y tartana* (*The Three Roses*), 1894; *Flor de Mayo* (*The Mayflower*), 1895; *La barraca* (*The Cabin*), 1898; *Entre naranjos* (*The Torrent*), 1900; *Sónnica la cortesana* (*Sónnica*), 1901; and *Cañas y barro (Reeds and*

Mud), 1902. The central theme of these is Valencia, Spain, both the region itself and the people inhabiting it. Vicente Blasco Ibáñez is considered Valencia's favorite son and enjoys great popularity there to this day in spite of the fact that his treatment of the area reveals its "ignorancia, vicios y brutalidades" (ignorance, vices, and brutalities) (Smith, 19; all translations are mine). The seeming emphasis placed upon these different elements has been one of the causes for the critical world's association of naturalism with these novels.

Naturalism, a late nineteenth-century literary movement, evolved out of the earlier literary movement of realism as a result of the studies by Darwin, the philosophy of Comte, and the sociological impacts of the Industrial Revolution. "Those in favour of a naturalistic approach to and interpretation of life concentrated on depicting the social environment and dwelt particularly on its deficiencies and on the shortcomings of human beings" (Cuddon, 416). These novelists' works purportedly "objectively" examined life without the interference of authorial directives guiding the plot to its ultimate denouement in a literary experiment influenced by the scientific method. Emile Zola, the critically acclaimed French master of naturalism, used the points of heredity and environment to expand upon these views and develop what he called the experimental novel. This art form allows for character development but only up to the limits imposed by the two aforementioned constraints. Consequently, a predisposed affinity/proclivity toward animalistic behaviorism is quite common in these narratives. However, naturalist authors should not be regarded as fatalists. Zola distinguishes between determinism and fatalism by referring to the issue of extracorporal forces: According to determinism, humans always have a choice, but their selection is predestined to be the negative outcome. Fatalism is the belief that humans have no choice; the negative is always forced upon the person.

Typical Spanish naturalist writers, meanwhile, differ from the French master by not adhering completely to these tenets of predestination in spite of the fact that, like Zola's, their novels exhibit a marked emphasis on the baser instincts, genetic influences, addiction, and environmental causality. However, to accept completely the philosophical statements of the naturalist movement would mean a denial of the *libre albedrío* (free will), a basic principle of Catholicism, the dominant religion of Spain, since the French naturalistic predestination relegates humans to simple bestiality, with no ability to improve themselves or their society; genetics and environment overrule any latent human abilities. Contrastingly, "un trait qui distingue ces romanciers [espagnols] du naturalisme français et donné à leur réalisme un caractère original et national, c'est bien la présence de l'humour, de l'ironie, de l'expression parodique dans leurs oeuvres" (one trait which distinguishes these [Spanish] novelists from French naturalism and gives their realism an original and national character is the presence of humour, of irony, of expression of parody in their works) (Clemessy, 51).

Consequently, Spanish naturalists found themselves walking a fine line between their religious teachings and traditional aesthetics, which accept that a person has an inherent ability to choose either good or evil, and the naturalistic literary tendencies emphasizing a predilection toward evil. Pardo Bazán, the most important female Spanish writer to laud Zola, later tempered her support even further upon his publication of the provocative, and unpopular in Spain, *La Terre*. Blasco Ibáñez, on the other hand, was the most renowned Spanish novelist to maintain continual support for the movement and its French master even in the face of subsequent ostracism by his contemporaries. His resultant Valencian cycle, although certainly not the only, is one of the most widely recognized examples of naturalism in Spanish literature.

In spite of this recognition, in the critical corpus over Blasco Ibáñez there has appeared only one study entirely devoted to using alcohol as a point of departure for analysis, even though various critics have mentioned the element in passing. That article, "The Reliable Determinant: Alcohol in Blasco Ibáñez's Valencian Works," is primarily a comparative exposition of alcohol usage in various novels by French and Spanish writers.

A review of Smith's analysis is in order, however, due to its scope and the foundation it provides for this investigation. In his article, Smith surveys the presence of alcohol in Zola's *L'Assommoir* and in other Spanish writings of the nineteenth century such as those by Wenceslao Ayguals de Izco, Emilia Pardo Bazán, and

Benito Pérez Galdós. His discussion focuses on the Spanish writers' "certain evasiveness or nonseriousness with regard to [alcohol's] constituting a problem of any consequence" (188). The critic's thesis is that Blasco Ibáñez's contrasting portrayal of alcoholism depicts the illness as an integral part in the society of the impoverished, causing the author to be uncharacteristically associated with the French novelist Zola.

The three novels Smith focuses his attention on are *Flor de Mayo, La barraca,* and *Cañas y barro.* All of these, as mentioned earlier, come from the Valencian cycle. The examination of *Flor de Mayo* primarily limits itself to a plot summary delineation of alcohol's constant presence. "*La barraca* . . . turns at critical moments on [alcohol's] use and abuse by certain protagonists" (193), and with *Cañas y barro* Smith notes that the novelist works with the determinist ideas of heredity and environment. In his examination of all three novels, the critic primarily limits himself to a basic examination of the plot and statements as to where alcohol abuse occurs. This present study, although acknowledging Smith's valuable contribution to the topic, will be an even more intensive examination of alcohol addiction and misuse showing that, in fact, alcohol becomes the catalyst of destruction in *La barraca,* and without it the story ceases to exist.

An examination of the basic plot will show, in part, why alcoholism plays such an integral part of *La barraca.* Barret, a farmer who has fallen on hard times, is evicted from his rented parcel of land when he cannot pay the ever-increasing rent to the unsympathetic Salvador. After becoming intoxicated, Barret spends the afternoon asleep outdoors, awakening upon Salvador's approach. During Salvador's futile attempt to protect himself, Barret decapitates his former landlord with his sickle. Ten years later, Batiste, an outsider, is recruited by the rich landowners to break the rural farmers' control over Salvador's uncultivated land. Tòni, the local bully, who has been the peasants' champion in their disputes with the landowners, attempts to affect the newcomer's departure. When Obispo, Batiste's youngest son, dies, animosities temporarily cool. Soon thereafter a gargantuan drinking competition occurs; Batiste goes to observe, and the drunken Tòni attacks him. In spite of his prior ability to drive off other would-be settlers, this time Tòni is rebuffed by the newcomer's self-defense. Tòni, upon recovering from the head wound, vengefully ambushes Batiste at night but receives a fatal gunshot in return. After the local hero's death, Batiste's home, barn, crops, and possessions are mysteriously burned leaving the farmer and his family homeless and pennyless.

The structure of Barret's history reveals the importance of alcohol in the narrative; his story microcosmically foreshadows the novel's denouement. Barret is not a drinker, but the function of the bar as the community social center leads him there every Sunday for entertainment. When the foreclosers come—a forewarned, but unbelieved, occurrence—he is forced to leave his house. Early the next morning, "sin saber adónde iba" (without knowing where he was going) (493), he passes by the bar, enters and drinks. He leaves the bar in search of Salvador because "el aguardiente se había apoderado de él" (the brandy had overpowered him) (494). With murder etched in his mind, he falls asleep in one of his former landlord's orchards, but upon awakening "su honradez primitiva le hizo avergonzarse de este envilecimiento, e intentó en pie para huir" (his primitive honor made him ashamed of this debasement, and he rose up to flee) (494). Upon standing up, however, he sees Salvador, and, immediately, "Barret sintió que . . . reaparecía su borrachera" (Barrett felt his drunkenness reappear) (494).

It is the disinhibiting *and* personality altering force of alcohol that converts this peace-loving farmer who "había sido siempre de los dóciles, votando lo que ordenaba el cacique y obedeciendo pasivamente al que mandaba" (had always been among the docile, voting as the boss ordered and passively obeying he who was in command) (495) into a homicidal beast. Barret's entire personality changes under the influence of alcohol, which he consumes only out of desperation and/or dejection upon losing the farm. As Jacques Dérrida states: "Those 'products' otherwise considered as dangerous and unnatural are often considered fit for the liberation of this same 'ideal' or 'perfect body' from social oppression, suppression and repression" (14). This belief, as evidenced by Barret, and the subsequent action nevertheless only causes the drinker additional problems.

After Salvador falls dead into a canal, a terrified Barret leaves, fleeing justice; alcohol has forever changed his life. The *Guardia Civil* captures him, and he is carted off to prison "hecho una momia" (now a mummy) (495) after which he soon dies. His family, too, must suffer the consequences of his moment of drunkenness: "Disolvióse su familia; desapareció como un puñado de paja en el viento" (His family dissolved; it disappeared like a fist-full of straw in the wind) (495).

Batiste, the farmer finally recruited by the landlords to toil the idled acreage, is "a man without malice or evil in his heart upon his arrival" (Anderson, 34). He, like Barret, does not imbibe; rather, he is a "hombre sobrio, incapaz de beber alcohol sin sentir náuseas y dolores de cabeza" (sober man, unable to drink alcohol without feeling nausea and headaches) (545). The simile, however, is that his desire to work the land and earn a living becomes the family's addiction: "En punto a laboriosos, eran como un tropel de ardillas" (As to hard-working, they were like a bunch of squirrels) (499), "sudando y jadeando la familia desde el alba a la noche" (sweating and panting from dawn to dark) (499). "Aquel hombre era una hormiga infatigable para la rebusca" (That man was an untiring ant for gleaning) (500), and "embriagándose en su labor" (intoxicating himself with his labor) (501). The control that this addiction, work, has over Batiste causes him to ignore the warnings of impending danger. Like the story's drunkard, Tòni, he believes himself capable of controlling his circumstances. This naiveté, combined with his curiosity about the drinking competition, tempts him to view the quasi dipsomniacs: "¿Por qué no había de ir él a donde iban los otros?" (Why shouldn't he go where others went?) (545)

Once in the bar, however, Batiste's interest in the competition is soon overpowered by the environment in which he finds himself. "En el ambiente flotaban vapores de alcohol" (In the air floated vapors of alcohol) (547) and "era . . . intolerable . . . el olor del alcohol" (the smell of alcohol was intolerable) (547). His reasoning is impaired to the point that "tuvo que beber. . . . No le gustaba; pero un hombre debe probar todas las cosas" (he had to drink. . . . He didn't like it, but a man should try everything) (547). Unlike Zola, who would have detailed the alcohol-dependent heritage of the protagonist, Blasco Ibáñez does not offer the reader information about Batiste's ancestry. In spite of this, he does seem to imply that alcoholism, or at least Batiste's susceptibility to alcohol, is inherited; the author suggests this in his description of Batiste as a "hombre sobrio, incapaz de beber alcohol sin sentir náuseas y dolores de cabeza" (sober man, incapable of drinking alcohol without feeling nauseous and headaches) (545). Environmental factors alone could not cause such malaversion.

This one drink, consequentially, changes him irrevocably: "Sintió gran dolor en el estómago y en la cabeza una deliciosa turbación. Comenzaba a acostumbrarse a la atmósfera de la taberna . . . Hasta [Tòni] le resultó un hombre notable" (He felt great pain in his stomach and in his head a delightful confusion. He was beginning to become accustomed to the atmosphere of the tavern. . . . Even [Tòni] seemed a noble man) (548). Alcohol exerts such control over him that he finds it impossible to leave the situation even when he knows he should: "Batiste . . . sentía un vago deseo de irse. . . . Pero, sin saber por qué, permanecía allí como si este espectáculo tan nuevo para él pudiese más que su voluntad" (Batiste . . . felt a vague desire to leave. . . . But, without knowing why, he remained there as if this show so new for him were stronger than his will) (548).

Tòni, on the other hand, becomes antagonistic and orders Batiste to leave. Batiste refuses, realizing that the order implies not just the bar but the farm as well. A fight breaks out, and Batiste, having seriously wounded Tòni, "permanecía inmóvil, con los brazos caídos . . . asustado de lo que acaba de hacer" (remained inmobile, with his arms fallen . . . frightened by what he had just done) (551). Unlike Barret, however, Batiste can not flee immediately; he must first escape the threatening crowd before he can begin to run. The reader can see that the strength of alcohol imposes itself on all those present, with a terrifying result, until circumstances are beyond their control.

Batiste is able to escape the offensive repercussions of alcohol consumption one time: When Batiste's horse dies and he buys another (531), propriety demands that he share a drink with the seller. This they do, and no ill effects or negative social implications arise from the action. With this the author demonstrates that alcohol, instead of being simply a cause of savagery, is rather an impetus toward a stronger than usual reaction in the same emotional direction, which may result in a temporary change of character. Zinberg and Shaffer recognize this varying influence that alcohol has, even on the same person, stating that such "depend[s] on the preexisting conditions" (58). Textually, this is exemplified by both Tòni and Batiste: Tòni is inherently a bully; drink makes him more so. Batiste, although possessing no malice, is a stubborn person; he refuses to heed the warnings and leave the farm. Alcohol exacerbates his desire to defend what he considers his. After buying the horse, and sharing drinks, he proudly mounts the horse and rides it home, passing by the bar so that all would be "convencidos de que era difícil hincarle el diente, de que sabía defenderse solo" (convinced that it was hard to force his hand, that he knew how to defend himself) (531).

Early statements in the novel concerning the bar give an idea of its cultural influence and social significance. The establishment is initially introduced as "la taberna de Copa . . . [donde Tòni] jugaba al truco" (Copa's tavern . . . [where Tòni] played pool) (485). Inextricably associated with idleness, the bar is for those under its power a place of refuge and leisure activities. For those unaccustomed to entering, however, alcoholic powers and gothic metonymies transpose this edifice into a dungeon where drink and evilness are intertwined:

> Allí estaba la cueva de la fiera . . . Rumor de voces, estallidos de risas, guitarreos y coplas a grito pelado salían por aquella puerta roja como una boca de horno que arrojaba sobre el camino negro un cuadro de luz cortado por la agitación de grotescas sombras. Y, sin embargo, [Roseta, hija de Batiste], al llegar cerca de allí, deteníase indecisa, temblorosa, como las heroínas de los cuentos ante la cueva del ogro. . . . [Era] la rojiza boca que despedía el estrépito de la borrachera y la brutalidad (512).
>
> There was the cave of the wild beast . . . Rumor of voices, outbursts of laughter, guitar strummings, and ballads shouted out came out through that red door like the mouth of an oven that cast over the black road a picture of light cut by the movement of grotesque shadows. And, however, [Roseta, Batiste's daughter],

> upon arriving close to there, stopped indecisive, trembling, like the heroines of the stories in front of the cave of the ogre. . . . [It was] the red mouth that was discharging the racket of drunkenness and brutality.

However, the most overt statement by the author of the cultural importance of the neighborhood bar occurs when Batiste enters:

> Batiste se fijó por primera vez detenidamente en la famosa taberna. . . . Tenía las paredes zócalos de ladrillos rojos y barnizados, a la altura de un hombre, con una orla terminal de floreados azulejos. Desde allí hasta el techo, todas las paredes estaban dedicadas al sublime arte de la pintura, pues Copa . . . (h)abía traído un pintor de la ciudad, manteniéndolo allí más de una semana, y este capricho de magnate protector de las artes le había costado, según declaraba él, unos cinco duros, peseta más que menos.
>
> Bien era verdad que no podía volverse la vista a ningún lado sin tropezar con alguna obra maestra, cuyos rabiosos colores parecían alegrar a los parroquianos, animándolos a beber. Arboles azules sobre campos morados, horizontes amarillos, casas más grandes que los árboles y personas más grandes que las casas . . . Un portento de originalidad que entusiasmaba a los bebedores (546).
>
> Batiste for the first time looked closely at the famous tavern. . . . It had walls of red and varnished bricks to the height of a man, with an edge of flowered tiles. From there to the roof, all the walls were dedicated to the sublime art of painting, because Copa . . . had brought a painter from the city, keeping him there more than a week, and this caprice as high protector of the arts had cost him, according to what he said, some five *duros,* not a *peseta* less.
>
> It was very true that one could not look anywhere without encountering some masterpiece whose rabid colors seemed to gladden the parishioners, enlivening them to drink. Blue trees over purple fields, yellow horizons, houses larger than the trees and people larger than the houses. . . . A prodigy of originality that enthused the drinkers.

As a symbol of the cultural axis around which the community revolves, Copa's establishment serves as the local museum of art.

Just as the churches contain murals concerning Christendom, many of which were painted by professionals who were reimbursed for their services, so Copa's kingdom is embellished. In fact, it is not surprising that this establishment would be described in ecclesiastical terms; the bar, in effect, becomes the community's church. The murals, thematically related to the edifice's raison d'être, serve as an inspiration to a higher calling. The counter behind which Copa stands reflects the ministering duties of the priesthood when "vigilaba la borrachera de sus parroquianos" (he watched over the drunkenness of his parishioners) (546).

In a more overt statement, the author semiotically transposes the religious onto the real neighborhood force: "[Copa] era el sumo sacerdote de este templo de alcohol" ([Copa] was the high priest of this temple of alcohol) (545). Additionally, in Blasco's thesis novel *La bodega,* which condemns the wine industry's control over its workers' lives, the owner of the winery is so religiously fanatic that the workers "vivían sujetos a la voluntad del jefe, cuidándose, más que de los trabajos de la oficina, de asistir a todas las ceremonias religiosas que organizaba don Pablo en la iglesia de los padres jesuitas" (lived subjected to the boss's will, being careful, more than to the office jobs, to attend all the religious ceremonies that don Pablo organized in the Jesuit fathers' church) (1219).

Blasco Ibáñez recognizes the cultural importance of alcohol to the Valencian society. He writes: "La Naturaleza generosa le ha dado [al hombre] cuanto tiene de más hermoso y seductor; le ha dado la mujer, el vino y la primavera, las tres grandes inspiraciones del arte" (Generous Nature has given [man] everything he has that is beautiful and seductive; it has given him woman, wine and spring, the three great inspirations of art) (VI 1124). However, he also notes that "(e)l español que menos bebe es el valenciano; la embriaguez no tiene disculpa para él" (The Spaniard that drinks the least is the Valencian; drunkenness has no excuse for him) (VI 1157). Jellinek notes that although "alcohol addiction [in Spain] is low . . . marked damage may arise through violence and impairment of the family budget occasioned by 'fiesta drinking' and weekend bouts which are not individual in nature but involve drinking in large groups" (16). Certainly, Batiste suffers violence; he is shot; he mortally wounds

Tòni; and he suffers economic collapse due, indirectly, to the binge drinking. In short, although genetics and environment both may play a role in a person's inebriety and the amount of alcohol a person may safely consume, *La barraca* reflects more the strength of alcohol and its potential impact when consumed in excess.

Quantitatively, alcohol plays an important role in the novel. An examination of chapter 9, which contains the drinking contest between Tòni and his two competitors, reveals how strongly alcohol impacts the narrative. There are, in this one chapter, 13 references to the contest, variously called the "apuesta," "porfía" or "lucha." Another 51 designations of drink or drinking are contained in such statements as "embriaguez, bebiendo, ebrio, aguardiente, vino, alcohol, porrón," and "líquido" (drunkenness, drinking, inebriety, brandy, wine, alcohol, wine bottle, and liquid). The author refers 37 times to the bar where the bout takes place, with an additional 2 mentions of other local bars; 14 instances of either the bar owner or other drunken folk add to the portrait.

All five senses are employed in this presentation of alcohol's strength: Of the preceding references, 31 are Batiste's first observation of the bar's decor. Moreover, "brillaban en [Tòni's] pupilas una chispa azulada e indecisa, semejante a la llama del alcohol" (a blue and indecisive spark similar to the flame of alcohol shone in Tòni's eyes) (547), and "Pimentó lo miraba con demasiada frecuencia, con sus ojos molestos y extraños de borracho firme" (Pimentó was looking at him too frequently, with his eyes upset and strange with a strong drunkenness) (548). The smell of alcohol is pervasive: the bar "exhalaba un vaho de alcohol" (exhaled a fume of alcohol) (545), as do the patrons: "[Tòni] olía a vino" ([Tòni] smelled like wine) (549). Other sensory allusions are inherent in the "habitación, oscura y húmeda, [que] exhalaba un vaho de alcohol, un perfume de mosto, que embriagaba el olfato y turbaba la vista" (room, dark and humid, that exhaled a fume of alcohol, a perfume of must, that intoxicated the nose and upset the vision) (545). The sound of drinking is also present: "Circulaba el porrón, soltando su rojo chorrillo, que levantaba un tenue *glu-glu* al caer en las abiertas bocas" (The wine bottle was circulating, releasing its red stream that was raising a tenuous "glug-glug" upon falling in the open mouths)

(547). "Se pasaban de mano en mano los jarros pagados a escote, y era aquella una verdadera inundación de aguardiente, que, desbordándose fuera de la taberna, bajaba como oleada de fuego a todos los estómagos" (The jars paid by all passed from hand to hand, and that was a true flood of brandy that, overflowing outside of the tavern, was coming down like a wave of fire to all the stomachs) (547).

> Pimentó . . . sintió caer de un golpe sobre su cerebro todo el aguardiente bebido en dos días. Había perdido su serenidad de ebrio inquebrantable, y al levantarse, tambaleando, tuvo que hacer un esfuerzo para sostenerse sobre sus piernas. Sus ojos estaban inflamados, como si fuesen a manar sangre; su voz era trabajosa, cual si tirasen de ella, no dejándola salir el alcohol y la cólera.
>
> Pimentó . . . felt all the brandy drunk in two days fall all at once on his head. He had lost his serenity of unbreakable inebriety, and upon standing up, tottering, he had to make an effort to stay on his feet. His eyes were inflamed, as if they were going to pour out blood; his voice was laborious, as if alcohol and anger would not let it come out. (551)

The fact that this chapter should be so overwhelmed with references to alcohol is not surprising considering that it describes a drinking contest. Alcohol and the drinking bout give rise to the ambushing of Batiste, the death of Tòni, and the burning of Batiste's possessions. Perhaps the author could have created another history without alcohol that would have resulted in the misfortune of Batiste's family, but this particular novel would necessarily end with chapter 8 when all is going well, crops are producing bountifully, and the neighbors are passively permitting the idled lands to be farmed again.

Certainly, then, alcohol is central to the story. Barret, a simple farmer whose ancestors toiled the same patch of ground, can only obtain his revenge on Salvador when the strength and influence of alcohol prevails over him. Although angered, sobriety causes him to shudder at the murderous act. This prehistory of the novel's narrative serves as a simple microcosmic foreshadowing of the later conflict between Batiste and the community at large.

When Batiste goes to watch the much-publicized drinking bout, Tòni is able to repel Batiste through his drinking. Sympathy for

Batiste's dead child is forgotten and the threat to the idled land must be confronted. It is evident that alcohol is more than a mere disinhibiting agent; it changes a simple bully into a violent madman, rendering the narrative a depiction of how alcohol can be truly a catalyst of destruction.

BIBLIOGRAPHY

Anderson, Christopher L. "Vicente Blasco Ibáñez: The Evolution of a Novelist in His Imagery." Diss. Indiana University, 1982.

Blasco Ibáñez, Vicente. *Obras completas,* vol 1. Madrid: Aguilar, 1978.

Chamberlin, Vernon. "Las imágenes animalistas y el color rojo en *La barraca.*" *Duquesne Hispanic Review* 6 (1967). Pp. 23–36.

Clemessy, Nelly. "Sur la question du naturalisme en Espagne." *Cahiers d'études romanes* 8 (1983). Pp. 41–56.

Cuddon, J. A. *A Dictionary of Literary Terms.* Middlesex: Penguin Books, 1986.

Dérrida, Jacques. "The Rhetoric of Drugs. An Interview." *Differences.* 5 (Spring 1993). Pp. 1–25.

Jellinek, E. M. *The Disease Concept of Alcoholism.* New Haven, CT: Hillhouse Press, 1960.

Smith, Paul. "The Reliable Determinant: Alcohol in Blasco Ibáñez's Valencian Works." *Ideologies and Literature.* 2 (1987). Pp. 185–99.

———. *Vicente Blasco Ibáñez: Una nueva introducción a su vida y obra.* Santiago de Chile: Andrés Bello, 1972.

Zinberg, Norman E. and Howard J. Shaffer. "The Social Psychology of Intoxicant Use: The Interaction of Personality and Social Setting." *The Addictions: Multidisciplinary Perspectives and Treatments.* Ed. Harvey B. Milkman and Howard J. Shaffer. Lexington, KY: Lexington Books, 1985. Pp. 57–74.

Zola, Emile. *The Experimental Novel, and Other Essays.* Tr. Belle M. Sherman. New York: Cassell, 1893.

CHAPTER 11

"TO KEEP FROM SHAKING TO PIECES"

Addiction and Bearing Reality in "Sonny's Blues"

Sandy Morey Norton

HEROIN ADDICTION IS A BAD THING. Almost anyone would agree with this statement, even the average junkie. In his story "Sonny's Blues," James Baldwin uses this consensus about heroin addiction and the intense social stigma attached to it to challenge the mainstream cultural values of America in the 1950s. He suggests that only the creation of dialogue can break down the structure of "us versus them" that contributes to the denial of the reality of human suffering.

As the story opens, Baldwin's implied reader confidently determines where value is to be placed. The narrator, a high school algebra teacher, is stunned to read in the paper that his brother, Sonny, has been arrested for "peddling and using heroin" (103). Although the first-person narrative is full of stress and distress, it is probable that Baldwin intended that the teacher, who is trying to redeem his life growing up in Harlem through education, embody the socially valuable, while the drug addict, Sonny, be either a lost cause (once a junkie, always a junkie) or, at best, be rehabilitated into another version of his brother, the narrator.

Different readers begin to understand and listen to Baldwin's shifting and moderating of these values at different points in the story. Baldwin very effectively draws many readers into sympathy with his narrator. Yes, this older brother is afraid, but who wouldn't be? Sure, the "icy dread" (113) he feels when Sonny returns from treatment isn't terribly endearing, but wouldn't most of us react in the same way? Indeed, for some readers, the addict by definition must always remain, if not the bad guy, at least an irreparably flawed character. But by the time we hear the narrator respond to his younger brother's devotion to jazz by asking if he can make a living at it and then abjuring him to "[start] thinking about [his] future" (122), most readers begin to sense that something is amiss.

The story of "Sonny's Blues" is finally the story of the narrator's struggle out of denial. He is, in fact, a man full of fear, trying to use his relatively privileged social position to protect himself from emotional reality. Only when his young daughter dies of polio, for instance, does he begin to feel sympathy for his brother: "My trouble," he says, "made his real" (127). Baldwin traces this process of recovery through an associative, memorial narrative chronology; a masterful use of repetition; an unusual and complex weaving of images of darkness and light as well as of music; and an invocation of highly spiritualized religious allusions.

The narrator is associated from the outset with the values of the dominant American culture. Though he lives in Harlem, because he is a teacher, he has, in some sense, "escaped." But he is full of fear and denial. As the story opens, the narrator has just read about his brother's arrest, and he repeatedly insists, "I couldn't believe it" and "It was not to be believed" (103). "I couldn't believe it," he says again, and "what I mean by that is that I couldn't find any room for it anywhere inside me. I had kept it outside me for a long time. I hadn't wanted to know. I had had suspicions, but I didn't name them, I kept putting them away" (103). As the narrator repeatedly articulates his denial and fear—"I was scared, scared for Sonny" (103)—many of Baldwin's readers recognize that this is precisely how the average, middle-class white person in similar circumstances is expected to react.

The narrator's language early in the story reflects what Mikhail Bakhtin calls "monologic" discourse, language that

> denies the existence outside itself of another consciousness with equal rights and equal responsibilities, another I with equal rights (*thou*). With a monologic approach . . . *another person* remains wholly and merely an object of consciousness, and not another consciousness. No response is expected from it that could change everything in the world of my consciousness. Monologue is finalized and deaf to the other's response, does not expect it and does not acknowledge in it any *decisive* force. Monologue manages without the other, and therefore to some degree materializes all reality. (292–93)

The narrator's interaction with a junkie friend of Sonny's just after he hears the news of the arrest represents a nervous attempt to maintain just such perceptual righteousness. But it's a righteousness that depends on a failure to hear: responding to the junkie, the narrator thinks, "All this was taking me some place I didn't want to go. I certainly didn't want to know how [heroin] felt. It filled everything, the people, the houses, the music, the dark, quicksilver barmaid, with menace; and this menace was their reality" (107). This menace is, of course, part of the narrator's reality also, but he will not face it.

His early conversations with Sonny repeat his rigidity and denial, for in playing jazz piano, Sonny attempts to confront and articulate instead of denying the suffering and pain that includes and, at least to some extent, accounts for addiction. Baldwin never wants his reader to forget that, in the historical time and place out of which he writes, addiction represents a dis-ease of the community, a response of an individual to a collective economic, social, and political oppression that is not general but particular, that is not abstract but achingly and agonizingly specific. Once asked by an interviewer what it meant to be "tight," Baldwin living and growing up in such a community: "when you walk out of your door in the morning you are not sure whether you will get back in it at night. You have got to face whatever you have to face all day long. And hope you get home. Every day, twenty-four hours of everyday" (Weatherby, 235).

This is the world of "Sonny's Blues," post–World War II Harlem, and for Sonny and his brother, these are "the vivid, killing streets of our childhood" (112).

But the narrator and Sonny respond very differently to the reality of that agony. The narrator's fearful reaction to his brother's addiction moves him to try to control Sonny: "I sensed myself in the presence of something I didn't really know how to handle," he says, "so I made my frown a little deeper as I asked: 'What kind of musician do you want to be?'" (119). Baldwin emphasizes the narrator's fear when Sonny, moved to laughter, says, "I'm sorry. But you sound so—*scared!*" (120). Though the reader may still be confident that the addict, Sonny, should be devalued, Baldwin certainly begins to suggest that the narrator's attitude, which probably reflects his reader's, is very limited and deeply flawed.

This kind of denial is a strategy for dealing with pain that many adults teach their children. Baldwin describes it as being, in the culture he depicts, an absolutely necessary survival mechanism. The mother of these two men, for instance, tells the narrator that she asked their father never to repeat to them the story of his own brother's murder by drunken white men. The father's anguish at watching his younger brother be run over on a moonlit Saturday night is a secret he shared only with her: "Your father always acted like he was the roughest, strongest man on earth. And everybody took him to be like that. But if he hadn't had me there—to see his tears!" (118). The story she finally tells her son is indeed one of horrific racism; the narrative of the murder is extremely painful to read, a tale not only of murder but of a deeply wounded brotherly love. Yet because the father and mother feel they can only protect their children from that wound by denying it, this also becomes a story of shutting down dialogue and therefore emotional connection between a father and his sons, a theme Baldwin dealt with repeatedly in his work.

The associative chronology of the story, which is fueled by the desperation of the narrator to account for and psychologically contain his own fear of his brother's addiction, opens up the possibility of hearing a rejoinder, the necessary first step in entering a true dialogue. The unconscious nature of association loosens control over meaning and, therefore, what someone who listens might hear or understand. Seemingly unbeknownst to the narrator himself, for instance, a reader is constantly reminded of the narrator's need to listen; Baldwin repeats some form of the verb "to listen" over and over again, in a variety of contexts. When the junkie wants to talk about his responsibility in Sonny's addiction, for instance, the narrator "beg[ins] to listen more carefully" (107), but when he and Sonny talk about jazz, Sonny insists, "I hear you. But you never hear anything I say" (124). Finally, when Sonny returns from treatment, the narrator realizes that he has "begun, finally, to wonder about Sonny, about the life that Sonny lived inside" (110). The narrative thus becomes what Bakhtin would call double-voiced, often "serv[ing] two speakers at the same time and express[ing] simultaneously two different intentions: the direct intention of the character who is speaking, and the refracted intention of the author. In such discourse there are two voices, two meanings and two expressions" (Bakhtin, "Discourse," 324). Both the narrator's cruelty to the junkie friend—"Look," he says, "Don't tell me your sad story" (106)—and his completely ineffectual responses to his brother create such a double-voicedness: the narrator speaks out of his monologic worldview but, through his words, Baldwin at the same time demonstrates the inadequacy of this character's position.

That double-voicedness, however, eventually does influence the narrator's attitude toward his brother, as if he hears his own problematizing of the story he tells in the way he tells it. By using the form of the story to bring the narrator to confront reality, Baldwin suggests that the narrator's denial parallels both Sonny's art and his drug use as a way of attempting to manage pain and suffering. If anything, Sonny's art, if not his heroin addiction, is offered as the most meaningful and fulfilling response to feeling, precisely because it depends on dialogic interaction; it takes "responsibility" in the Bakhtinian sense of recognizing a duty to offer a rejoinder to the other.[1] Baldwin thus turns the accepted notion of the addict as the one in denial on its head: in this case the addict is presented as the more sensitive, more perceptive person who refuses to deny the reality of human pain, even when that suffering, because it has become culturally institutionalized, seems utterly unchangeable.

When the narrator goes into the army, leaving his brother with his in-laws and his new wife, for instance, Sonny emerges as such a figure in his constant piano playing: "It wasn't like living with a person at all," says Isabel, the narrator's wife,

> it was like living with sound. And the sound didn't make any sense to her, didn't make any sense to any of them—naturally. They began, in a way, to be afflicted by this presence that was living in their home. It was as though Sonny were some sort of god, or monster. He moved in an atmosphere which wasn't like theirs at all. . . . it was as though he were all wrapped up in some cloud, some fire, some vision all his own; and there wasn't any way to reach him. (125)

But, the narrator realizes, when Sonny plays, he is "at that piano playing for his life" (125). What the addict represents, Baldwin suggests here, particularly in his lack of control, is so threatening to non-addicts—in this case, the narrator's in-laws—that they run from the notion that they might have anything to learn from such a sufferer and they are unable to listen to him. Yet it is Sonny who can show them the transformative power that might reshape their pain.

When no one hears him, he uses heroin to dull his hurt, but the drug has hard consequences, not the least of which is that it reinforces isolation, pushing the dialogue that he desires even further out of reach. An artist, as does everyone else, needs an audience—someone to listen and respond. For art to be an adequate answer to suffering, it cannot be static; it must initiate a dynamic sharing of experience between at least two people. Denial makes many people unable to enter into dialogue, for they might hear what they are totally invested in rejecting. Thus, it is only when the narrator himself suffers that he can begin to hear Sonny's story; only when his daughter dies does he experience a pain that cannot be outfaced by his denial; he cannot refuse to hear it and know it. Then he is finally moved to communicate with Sonny and open himself up to the reality of his brother's addiction.

"Sonny's Blues" describes the process of recovery for both the narrator and his brother as realized through listening and the dialogue that results. That dialogue is the very foundation of art for Baldwin: the title, "Sonny's Blues," describes both the music Sonny plays and the refusal of so many to listen to and hear it. The price of that failure to listen is enormous. When art succeeds in articulating feelings that are shared by another, that is a spiritual act, spiritual in the sense that while an artistic act is always fully embodied in the material self—the fingers on a piano, the words of a text, the body of a speaker—that materiality creates a space that exists outside the self. The dialogue is never solely one's own, nor does it belong to the other. Indeed, it is more than both. The journey of Sonny and the narrator in this sense reflects quite clearly the process of 12-step recovery, though of course not consciously for Baldwin, as this would have been fairly unlikely in 1957.[2] But the emphasis in the story on trusting what is not the self enough to enter into dialogue with it and on the importance of listening as part of that psychological and spiritual movement is unmistakable. Dialogue makes possible the creation of a narrative, a story through which people can express, understand, and through that understanding—with luck—to some extent contain human experience. In 12-step meetings, participants constantly give this kind of dialogic narrative form to their lives.

For Baldwin, telling the story is nothing less than standing as a witness that "deep water and drowning [are] not the same thing" (138). Heroin addiction is drowning, but it represents a desperate attempt to contain feeling in much the same way as art. At the end of this story, Sonny describes his addiction to his brother just before the narrator describes Sonny's playing to us, and Baldwin thus emphasizes the functional similarity between addiction and art. Using heroin is not an escape for Sonny—the narrator is the one who would escape—but a way of bearing the suffering of seeing and hearing reality. Heroin, says Sonny, makes one feel "distant. And—and sure" (131), words often used to describe the perspective of the artist. Heroin "makes something real for [the user]" (132). Baldwin explores this power of both drugs and art to make an experience real in his portrayal of the street revival meeting that the narrator and Sonny watch. After describing the sense of the reality heroin brings, Sonny says, "listening to that woman sing, it struck me all of a sudden how much suffering she must have had to go through—

to sing like that. It's *repulsive* to think you have to suffer that much" (132). Drug use, finally, is a way "to *stand* it, to be able to make it at all. On any level. . . . In order to keep from shaking to pieces" (131). Heroin keeps things from fragmenting in the face of unbearable pain, as does art.

The psychodynamic literature on addiction does offer an understanding of addiction as self-medicating in this way; yet the discourse of that literature serves to reinforce the distinction between a "normal," presumably middle-class and educated "us" that is opposed to a deviant, often lower-class, addicted "them" that parallels precisely the gap Baldwin portrays between the two brothers in "Sonny's Blues." Discourse theory suggests that in order to be published in a social science or medical journal even the most caring clinician is required to adopt a language that necessarily reinscribes the social hierarchy. Thus the language of even a very compassionate analysis of addiction, such as Edward Khantzian and Robert Schneider's "Treatment Implications of a Psychodynamic Understanding of Opioid Addicts," still performs this kind of cultural work. These authors theorize that "narcotics are used by addicts to compensate for defects in affect defense, particularly against feelings of rage, shame, hurt, and loneliness" and note that "narcotics can actually reverse regressive states through the direct antiaggressive action of opiates; this action counteracts disorganizing influences of rage and aggression on the ego" (325). Khantzian and Schneider proceed to give a compelling analysis of the opiate addict's deficient ego defenses, and they suggest appropriate treatment modalities to help put such mechanisms in place. The dysfunction of addiction results, they say, from "early developmental difficulties in managing . . . emotions and coping with external reality," which in turn, "trigger psychological fragmentation and disorganization" (326). An effective treatment program thus introduces and consistently maintains psychological structures, even in the face of aggression and rage.

According to this theory, then, Sonny would be understood to have deficient ego defenses that are unable to shield him from the suffering around him. The theory entirely fails, however, to consider that the narrator's very well-developed defense of denial—in other words, a very well-developed ego defense mechanism—*might be a problem,* which is at the heart of Baldwin's story and exists in contrapuntal relationship to Sonny's addiction. Indeed, I would argue that Khantzian and Schneider's theory represents a discourse that works to obfuscate the central problem of massive cultural denial as a part of the dynamics of addiction. While these writers clearly care deeply for the human beings they work with, they employ the distanced, disinfected, medicalized language of the professional social sciences, which plays deeply against the very subject the authors are discussing.

Only in the brief reference to "early developmental difficulties in managing . . . emotion and coping with external reality" do Khantzian and Schneider acknowledge the profound weight of suffering in the lives of many addicts. Moreover, in African American communities, much of this suffering is institutionalized by the racism of the dominant culture. But even the language of "developmental difficulties" continues to place the responsibility for the deficient ego on the addict, or in this case the child, him/herself. Valerie Polakow, in her powerful book *Lives on the Edge: Single Mothers and Their Children in the Other America,* poignantly and angrily critiques this kind of discursive cultural domination. She insists that culture as a whole—and not just the privileged, because many of those who are victims of social and economic domination nevertheless adopt the very structural categories that oppress them—must change; we must all

> act and see differently[, which] means to develop an understanding that enables us, in Sartre's words, "to change, to go beyond oneself." And to go beyond oneself is to build another way of seeing, beyond the deficit pathology frames that have made poverty an individual problem and a private affair—not a public responsibility, not a consequence of the political economy of distribution, of public policies that have constructed the poor. (172)

Thus the "low self-esteem" that Khantzian and Schneider suggest 12-step programs can help to alleviate is exacerbated by the discourse of deficiency that is consistently used to theorize addiction and treatment modalities. If, in fact, the struggle against addiction is a struggle against the denial of suffering, whether socially generated or not, to adopt the ego defense of cultural denial is not an option for the addict. He or she is left to fight not only against the drug but against the defensive protection of the society at large. In this theorization—and in Baldwin's story—the tables are thus turned on the dominant culture; all people, not just the addict, are called to recover and face their own pain and the pain of their communities courageously and in solidarity.[3] This is the opportunity that 12-step recovery offers.

The monologic voice of social policy that Polakow takes to task in her book parallels the monologic voice of Baldwin's narrator. But the narrator finally begins to realize toward the end of the story how he has crippled his brother by failing to listen to him. He has never opened himself to Sonny as someone who could "change everything in the world of [his] consciousness" (Bakhtin, 293). Sonny speaks, really calling to his brother out of his isolation: "It's terrible sometimes, inside," says Sonny,

> that's what's the trouble. You walk these streets, black and funky and cold, and there's not really a living ass to talk to, and there's nothing shaking, and there's no way of getting it out—that storm inside. You can't talk it and you can't make love with it, and when you finally try to get with it and play it, you realize nobody's listening. So you've got to listen. You got to find a way to listen. (133)

And in this scene, the narrator acknowledges that he has not listened and responded: "there stood between us, forever, beyond the power of time or forgiveness, the fact that I had held silence—so long!—when he had needed human speech to help him" (132). Because in his denial he could not listen, the narrator failed to be a person who can hear and respond to Sonny's voice, allowing him to create a containing narrative or, in this case, a blues.

Help comes in 12-step recovery precisely through listening and response that allows the alcoholic/addict to give form to his or her situation. And the willingness to enter into such a dialogue constitutes a statement of faith that this act might actually get participants somewhere. Not surprisingly Baldwin understands and writes this account of addiction and recovery very much as a spiritual journey, but a journey based on one's own personal understanding of the spirit. In all his work, he borrows metaphors and images from the black American evangelical tradition in which he was raised, a tradition he finally had to abandon in his teens because the complexity of his life was no longer congruent with its teaching.[4] The process of separation was extraordinarily painful for Baldwin, however, at least in part because so much of his religious practice continued to realize for him a passionate sense of connectedness to other human beings and to God. The street revival observed by the narrator and Sonny, for instance, provides a locus for such connection between them. The reader hears both of their perspectives. First, the narrator gives a fairly straightforward—and monologic—description of the scene, but then he turns inward, articulating what that group of witnesses represents for him and for the Harlem community around them. And he gives voice to a change in himself:

> It was strange, suddenly, to watch, though I had been seeing these meetings all my life. So, of course, had everybody else down there. Yet, they paused and watched and listened and I stood still at the window. "'Tis the old ship of Zion," they sang, and the sister with the tambourine kept a steady, jangling beat, "it has rescued many a thousand!" Not a soul under the sound of their voices was hearing this song for the first time, not one of them had been rescued. Nor had they seen much in the way of rescue work being done around them. Neither did they especially believe in the holiness of the three sisters and the brother, they knew too much about them, knew where they lived, and how. The woman with the tambourine, whose voice dominated the air, whose face was bright with joy, was divided by very little from the woman who stood watching her, a cigarette between her heavy chapped lips, her hair a cuckoo's nest, her face glittering like coal. . . . As the singing filled the air the watching, listening faces underwent a change, the eyes focusing on something within; the music seemed to soothe a poison out of them; and time seemed, nearly, to fall away from the sullen, belligerent, battered faces, as though they were fleeing back to their first condition, while dreaming of their last. (128–29)

The narrator then observes his brother in the circle of listeners. When Sonny enters the room, he offers another version of the revival, a version focused on the suffering of the singer. Through this juxtaposition of the brothers' two narratives, Baldwin embodies the process of dialogue as a shaping of consciousness, a shaping that honors differences between people while at the same time giving voice to what they share. Thus religious practice in "Sonny's Blues" becomes a vehicle for articulating an individual character's situation in the context of his community. Similarly, at a 12-step meeting, one listens to narratives that are not one's own but are significantly similar to one's own, spoken out of the subjectivity of a person who is, in an absolute sense, other than the self. Indeed, a participant normally does not even respond directly to what is shared by others at a meeting, but instead simply listens and then speaks out of his or her own "experience, strength, and hope." This format creates an almost palpable sense of dialogue that is both bound inextricably to the lives of individual speakers and at the same time has a reality independent of any one of them. Dialogue in this way creates a locus for creatively engaging pain.

In "Sonny's Blues," Baldwin creates not only the central dialogue between Sonny and the narrator, but various metadialogues: between the narrator and the ideal reader, using double-voiced language; between himself as author and both the narrator and Sonny; and certainly between Sonny and the ideal reader, as we empathize with him in the context of his brother's judgments. Like a 12-step meeting, these dialogic spaces offer the possibility of coming to new understandings of feeling. Baldwin is particularly gifted on this level of metadialogue at portraying both the specificity of the experience he describes and suggesting its broader human quality. But in Baldwin's writing, as in a 12-step meeting, the notion of shared human experience is never privileged over the particular. The setting in Harlem of "Sonny's Blues," for instance, is critical to understanding the two main characters. The ghetto that the narrator sees himself and his brother as trying to escape from is central to everything that happens in the story. Even the narrator's students, described early on, can be understood only in the context of the Harlem Baldwin creates as context:

> These boys, now, were living as we'd been living then, they were growing up with a rush and their heads bumped abruptly against

> the low ceiling of their actual possibilities. They were filled with rage. All they really knew were two darknesses, the darkness of their lives, which was now closing in on them, and the darkness of the movies, which had blinded them to that other darkness, and in which they now, vindictively, dreamed, at once more together than they were at any other time, and more alone. (104)

These generalized boys are like the narrator and Sonny; they are like the junkie the reader meets soon after reading this passage, but on some level—if only in the power found to empathize because of the poetry of this language—Baldwin challenges the reader to believe they themselves are like these boys.

In one of the story's most powerful passages, Baldwin paradoxically evokes a universality that seems to arise precisely out of the same qualities that make his scene culturally specific. In recollecting his parents, the narrator thinks of Sunday afternoons "when the old folks were talking after a big Sunday dinner . . . and night is creeping up outside, but nobody knows it yet" (114):

> You can see the darkness growing against the windowpanes and you hear the street noises every now and again, or maybe the jangling beat of a tambourine from one of the churches close by, but it's real quiet in the room. For a moment nobody's talking, but every face looks darkening, like the sky outside. . . . Maybe a kid is lying on the rug, half asleep. Maybe somebody's got a kid in his lap and is absent-mindedly stroking the kid's head. Maybe there's a kid, quiet and big-eyed, curled up in a big chair in the corner. The silence, the darkness coming, and the darkness in the faces frighten the child obscurely. He hopes that the hand which strokes his forehead will never stop—will never die. He hopes that there will never come a time when the old folks won't be sitting around the living room, talking about where they've come from, and what they've seen, and what's happened to them and their kinfolk. (114–15)

Abruptly, someone will turn on a light, and

> when the light fills the room, the child is filled with darkness. He knows every time this happens he's moved just a little closer to that

> darkness outside. The darkness outside is what the old folks have been talking about. It's what they've come from. It's what they endure. The child knows that they won't talk any more because if he knows too much about what's happened to *them,* he'll know too much too soon, about what's going to happen to *him.* (115)

The reader must make no mistake that the "darkness outside" is the violence and the danger of Harlem's streets. It is the menace of drugs that the narrator strives to deny and avoid. It is the cold-blooded murder of a young brother on a moonlit Saturday night by drunken, racist white men. But while these realities bring the emotional power to the narrator's recollection, Baldwin constructs his language so that every reader, regardless of race, will enter the psychic space he creates. White readers—and particularly white academics—may protest that they don't belong in this scene; as good postmodern readers, they don't want to practice cultural appropriation or textual imperialism. But Baldwin insists that "*You* can see the darkness growing . . . and *you* hear the street noises." He demands his reader's presence in this scene. And the general quality of "a kid" and "the child," of the plural "old folks," as well as his use of the present tense further draw the reader in. Finally, of course, it is the fear, the "darkness in the faces [that] frighten[s] the child obscurely" that readers truly share. It is a fear that, in this story, reverses the traditional symbolism of light and dark; while darkness remains dangerous and fearful, the light in this passage would deny it, thus rendering it more dangerous still. It is what people don't know, don't say, won't tell that would kill them.

It is, of course, particularly difficult to try to explore the nature of spiritual experience using words, especially in the empirically formed, expository prose of critical discourse. It's like trying to communicate in a language when the discursive participants don't agree about even the most basic conventions of meaning. Baldwin certainly levels such obstacles, but then he's writing fiction, and even so, he recognizes the inadequacy of language to speak for the spirit.[5] Thus, while thematically Baldwin's writing and the narrator's telling of the story parallel Sonny's playing, it is music rather than language that realizes spiritual experience and connection in the story: "the man who creates the music is . . . dealing with the roar rising from the void and imposing order on it as it hits the air. What is evoked in him, then, is of another order, more terrible because it has no words, and triumphant, too, for that same reason. And his triumph, when he triumphs, is ours" (137).

The spirituality Baldwin calls for demands that the narrator—and the reader along with him—stay in the real, a place that Sonny can create in his piano playing. Baldwin never romanticizes heroin addiction in "Sonny's Blues"; Sonny makes it very clear that being strung out is no picnic. But Baldwin refuses to allow the culture to continue to use the addict as a figure that separates "us" from "them," the "haves" and the "have nots," the "good" from the "bad." Everyone has a story to tell, but to tell it, and to listen to the stories of others, takes immense courage, because every story is absolutely personal and particular and at the same time absolutely shared. As the narrator listens to Sonny play in the story's final scene, he sees that his brother "had made it his: that long line, of which we knew only Mama and Daddy. And he was giving it back, as everything must be given back, so that, passing through death, it can live forever" (140). Then he sees the faces of his own pain: his mother, his father's brother, his little girl, and his wife. Seeing such pain must call out a response: it calls out denial, calls out addiction, and calls out art—the telling of a story. In this last scene, the narrator finally understands that recovery is about facing the blues, which are "not about anything very new." But Sonny and the musicians he plays with "were keeping it new, at the risk of ruin, destruction, madness, and death, in order to find new ways to make us listen. For while the tale of how we suffer, and how we are delighted, and how we may triumph is never new, it always must be heard. There isn't any other tale to tell, it's the only light we've got in all this darkness" (141).

NOTES

1. See especially Bakhtin's essay, "Author and Hero in Aesthetic Activity."
2. I want to make clear that I do not claim to speak in any way for 12-step programs in general. Experience of the 12 steps is, by definition,

the experience of an individual as they struggle with the steps in the company of those they meet at a particular meeting. Any abstracting and generalizing I do here about 12-step meetings, then, is no more than abstracting and generalizing of my own personal, individual experience.

3. The complex dynamic of denial as both personal and social is illuminated by the history of Baldwin's very heavy drinking. He lived and worked with a group of people who virtually all drank heavily, so his behavior was to some extent socially sanctioned. Yet he seems to have been unusually prone to find himself in situations where argument took on the kind of virulent edge that only alcohol can give it. After narrating numerous instances of this kind, Baldwin's biographer, W. J. Weatherby, feels compelled to address the question of Baldwin's alcoholism in what reads as a peculiarly defensive tone of denial. He quotes Baldwin as saying, "'I don't know any writers who don't drink. Everybody I've been close to drinks. But you don't drink while you're working.'" Weatherby continues: "American literary history seems to bear him out. Of seven American Nobel laureates in literature, at least four were more or less alcoholics for much of their lives" (164). Yet such an assertion is very curious, especially in a biographer, as it serves to deny—by shutting down as insignificant—the question of Baldwin's addictive behaviors and their role in his life and work. At the very least these behaviors seem to be profoundly bound up with Baldwin's experiences of racism, his writing, and his struggle with hostility toward his homosexuality.

   Baldwin's story is, moreover, historically placed in its failure to acknowledge the interrelationship of addictive behaviors. In the 1990s, many readers are taken aback by the fact that both Sonny and his brother drink alcohol throughout the story and find it shocking that the climactic moment comes at the end when the narrator buys a round of drinks for the band, including a "Scotch and milk" for his brother. In fact the final words focus on the drink, describing it in the language of the prophet Isaiah: "For me, then" says the narrator, "as they began to play again, it glowed and shook above my brother's head like the very cup of trembling" (141). This powerful symbol is variously interpreted by critics, but Byerman's reading is perhaps the most compelling. The drink, he points out, is itself "an emblem of simultaneous destruction and nurture to the system; it cannot be reduced to one or the other. Sonny's acceptance of it indicates that he will continue on the edge between the poison of his addiction and the nourishment of his music" (371). It is interesting and poignant to note that Baldwin, who often claimed that only his heavy drinking helped him to get through some of the more traumatic moments of living in a racist culture, was an inveterate drinker of scotch, and so in this final redemptive gesture, as the artist really chooses to continue to walk the dangerous line between addiction and creation, Sonny most fully comes to represent Jimmy Baldwin himself.

4. Baldwin's final decision to leave the church was significantly but certainly not solely precipitated by the intransigent insistence of American fundamentalist Christianity—an insistence in many African American churches even today—to deny the spiritual humanity of homosexuals. Fortunately for Baldwin, he was brought through this difficult period in a supportive relationship. As Weatherby says, "soon after he turned sixteen, he met a Harlem racketeer, a man in his late thirties, who 'fell in love with [him].' Baldwin wrote over forty years later, 'I will be grateful to that man until the day I die'" (29).
5. I strongly disagree, therefore, with Keith E. Byerman, who understands the narrator as consistently trying to control experience through language from the beginning to the end of the story. He insists that the narrator, in the "terrible wordlessness of what he is hearing" in the jazz club of the story's final scene, "undertakes to explain the music through the metaphor of conversation. . . . If the terror of the music is its lack of words, then to explain it as language is to neutralize its power" (370). But this is to entirely overlook the dialogic and transformative power of the "conversation," as Byerman calls it. This is not "mere speech" in a vacuum, but language in the indeterminate and uncontrollable context of dialogue.

BIBLIOGRAPHY

Bakhtin, Mikhail. "Author and Hero in Aesthetic Activity." *Art and Answerability.* Ed. Michael Holquis and Vadim Liapunov. Tr. Vadim Liapunov. Austin: University of Texas Press, 1990.

———. "Discourse in the Novel." *The Dialogic Imagination.* Ed. Michael Holquist. Tr. Caryl Emerson and Michael Holquist. Austin: University of Texas Press, 1981.

———. *Problems of Dostoevsky's Poetics.* Ed. and tr. Caryl Emerson. Minneapolis: University of Minnesota Press, 1984.

Baldwin, James. "Sonny's Blues." *Partisan Review.* 24 (1957). Pp. 327–58. Reprinted in *Going to Meet the Man.* New York: Vintage, 1995. Pp. 103–41.

Byerman, Keith E. "Words and Music: Narrative Ambiguity in 'Sonny's Blues.'" *Studies in Short Fiction.* 19 (1982). Pp. 367–72.

Khantzian, Edward J., and Robert J. Schneider. "Treatment Implications of a Psychodynamic Understanding of Opiod Addicts." *Psychopathology and Addictive Disorders.* Ed. Roger E. Myer. New York: Guilford Press, 1986. Pp. 322–33.

Polakow, Valerie. *Lives on the Edge: Single Mothers and Their Children in the Other America.* Chicago: University of Chicago Press, 1993.

Weatherby, W. J. *James Baldwin: Artist on Fire.* New York: Donald Fine, 1989.

CHAPTER 12

JOHN BERRYMAN'S TESTIMONY OF ALCOHOLISM

Through the Looking Glass of Poetry and the Henry Persona

Matts Djos

JOHN BERRYMAN'S LIFELONG BATTLE with alcohol had a major impact in determining the character and focus of his writing. In evaluating the consequences of his addictive perception, critics like Sarah Provost and Luke Spencer have provided considerable insight on Berryman's confessional mode and his preoccupation with sublimation and idealization; Manly Johnson has written a first rate analysis of the protective function of the poet's creative impulse; and Carol Frost and Kathe Davis have explored the problem of substituting the personality of the poet for his work, especially as it relates to the "Henry" poems.

Certainly, it must be acknowledged that Berryman felt himself to be like a great many alcoholics in protecting his delusions of power and in nurturing the fallacious image that he was somehow emotionally stable. Even so, it is not easy to discern whether he uses the Henry persona as an objective disguise for his own addictive problems or whether he is developing an alcohol-dependent caricature that has no direct, personal relationship.

Fear was the mainspring of Berryman's addictive perception, which was frequently manifested in quasi-psychotic illusions of power and in a rather puzzling complex of shame, denial, and depression. Thus, in "Henry by Night," an escapist Henry is self-imprisoned by a vicious cycle of intemperate scribbling, drinking, coughing, and wandering:

> . . . Henry, lost
> at 3 a.m., off for more drugs or a cigarette,
> reading old mail, writing new letters, scribbling
> excessive Songs;
> back then to bed, to the old tune or get set
> for a stercoraceous cough, without quibbling
> death-like. (*Collected,* 255)

Poor Henry's "nocturnal habits" drive his women insane. He is lost and hyperactive. He drinks; he smokes; he thrashes and snores in a nonsensical, stercoraceous resignation to circumstance:

> . . . you'll admit it was no way to live
> or even keep alive.
> I won't mention the dreams I won't repeat
> sweating & shaking: something's gotta give:
> up for good at five" (*Collected,* 255).

Henry's "sweating," "shaking," and craving are obsessive and convulsive. He is defused and histrionic, but he can't get anywhere. He is badly broken, but he is a master of self justification. In "Dream Song 311," Berryman amplifies this preoccupation with self-engorgement; but this time he reverses his position and insists that Henry's insatiability is messianically self-destructive and "constitutional": "Hunger was constitutional with him, / women, cigarettes, liquor, need need need / until he went to pieces" (*Dream,* 333). In truth, the narrator may complain that Henry "needs" cigarettes and women and liquor, but there is nothing "constitutional" in his paleourgency because it is thoroughly reductive.

A different kind of urgency is found in "Drunks" where Berryman describes the ludicrous shenanigans of a New Year's party in which,

> poor H got stuck in an upstairs bedroom
> with the blonde young wife of a famous critic
> a wheel at one of the book clubs
> who turned out to have nothing on under her gown
> sprawled out half-drunk across her hostess's bed
> moaning "Put it in! Put it in!"
> He was terrified.
> I passed out & was put in that same bed. (*Collected,* 176)

The image of the poet-narrator "half drunk" (half?) on the hostess's bed, having been dismantled and dismasted by a prodigious intake of liquor, has a certain gallows humor. Adult misbehaviors under the influence, and a tenuous cache of indignations, affronts, and immoral behaviors provide readers with a portrait of the insults and the dishevelment which invariably accrue from excessive drinking.

A great deal of Berryman's poetry describes the generic alcoholic cycle of drunkenness, insolence, guilt, recrimination, anger, and the resumption of drunkenness. In "Dream Song 351," this self-destructive pattern of behavior and response is made clearly evident in the declared intentions of the Henry persona. Although he is trying to recover from one hangover, Henry is already planning his next drunk. Indeed, it is masochistically presupposed that more liquor, another hangover, and an unrestrained appetite will propel "animal Henry" to a new query, to intimacy with new demons, and, of course, to another thrashing and another hangover:

> Animal Henry sat reading the *Times literary supplement*
> with a large Jameson & a worse hangover.
> Who will his demon lover
> today become, he queried (*Dream,* 373).

Henry's most intimate relationships are contaminated by "demon" images, hard liquor, and a preoccupation with self-justification, misanthropy, and provocation. In a moment of sobriety, he admits,

> Nothin very bad happen to me lately.
> How you explain that?—I explain that, Mr Bones,
> terms o' your bafflin odd sobriety.
> Sober as man can get, no girls, no telephones,
> what could happen bad to Mr Bones? (*Dream,* 83)

Here, in "Henry's Confession," sobriety is "bafflin" and "odd"—an alien normality that is neither crisis-driven nor catastrophic. For Henry, who is inclined to be catastrophic in the extreme, it is an odd mental state in which circumstances are generally boring and insipid. Without liquor, there are no girls, no marathon phone calls, no problems to evade. Life without liquor amounts to little more than death in life—a pointless test of human endurance that is invariably dull, boring, and glum.

Henry is not unlike many alcoholics who are reluctant to acknowledge their personal responsibility in contaminating their own life and the lives of others. The AA publication *Twelve Steps and Twelve Traditions* describes the twisted relationships, the irresponsibility, and the pitfalls that accrue from alcohol abuse and dependence. Because of his own monumental history of recovery and relapse and his involvement with Alcoholics Anonymous, Berryman would have been familiar with this perspective:

> But it is from our twisted relations with family, friends, and society at large that many of us have suffered the most. We have been especially stupid and stubborn about them. The primary fact that we fail to recognize is our total inability to form a true partnership with another human being. Our egomania digs two disastrous pitfalls. Either we insist upon dominating the people we know, or we depend upon them far too much. If we lean too heavily on people, they will sooner or later fail us, for they are human, too, and cannot possibly meet our incessant demands. In this way our insecurity grows and festers. (*Twelve Steps,* 53)

According to AA, a manipulative, self-centered impulse is a primary aspect of the alcoholic perception. Perhaps this is why fiction and poetry may have had such a profound appeal for Berryman. They evoked judgements that were invested with an extraordinary perspective on the connection between creativity, alcoholic spirituality, power-centeredness, and unrestrained self-indulgence. The crisis of loving thus triggered illusions of selective dependence in which intimacy was predicated on betrayal and a loss of identity. In "His Helplessness," Berryman writes,

> I know a young lady's high-piled ashen hair
> and she is miserable, threatened a thoroughfare
> for pants in their desire
> fondless: she drinks too dear, & feels put down,
> "no one is friendly to me" she scribbles here,
> of all them griefs the crown
> having been her lay by her father age'd ten
> from which she grew up slowly in the world of men
> who headed ha [*sic*] for her. (*Dream,* 397)

Here, Berryman describes the common alcoholic strategy of substituting sex for companionship and erotic liberality for love. Such behavior leads inevitably to misery, self-pity, and promiscuity. The lady with the "high-piled ashen hair" is burned out, both emotionally and physically. She has been incested, and, like so many of her sisters, she has tried to resolve her anger and her loneliness by drinking "too much." At the same time, she believes—as do most victims—that alcohol and intercourse might provide her with some degree of love and affection because she has not learned to distinguish sexual abuse from real intimacy. Berryman goes on to tell us that she has tried suicide to evade the darkness that shrouds "her disordered soul / whose last letter flew like a prayer" (*Dream,* 397).

Berryman's victim is especially tragic because—like so many of her gender—she must bear the burden of moral condemnation that far exceeds society's ethical judgments against alcoholic men. And, like so many alcoholics, she persists in her anguished search for control and affection with strategies that are inherently self-destructive by their power to isolate and condemn and by their inability to transcend the limitations of self.

For the Henry persona, the hunger for relief from the alcoholic bludgeon of self-sufficiency is a powerful force. In "Love & Fame, # 3," he prays to be reconciled, to accept, to be at peace and unforsaken:

> Forsake me not when my wild hours come;
> grant me sleep nightly, grace soften my dreams;
> achieve in me patience till the thing be done,
> a careful view of my achievement come.
> Make me from time to time the gift of the shoulder.
> When all hurt nerves whine shut away the whiskey.
> Empty my heart toward Thee. (*Love & Fame,* 88)

Henry yearns for some means of acceptance. He prays to resolve his compulsions, and he prays that he learn compassion, patience, and tenderness; that the hunger for whiskey be lifted; that his d.t.'s subside; and that he find some means of surrendering unreservedly to God. The prayer is terrifying because it admits helplessness without the redeeming features of grace. It also embodies a fundamental inability to discover any degree of congruence between the spirit, the body, and the mind. His hunger persists despite his "grand endeavors," and it persists because of his lust for fulfillment and his refusal to be reconciled to circumstances over which he has no control.

Henry cherishes the illusion that his self-inflicted martyrdom may serve to dampen his feeling of guilt and his fear of personal worthlessness. In "Opus Dei," he is confronted with the agonies that accrue from an emotional and spiritual imbalance, a lack of focus, an absence of humility, and the catastrophic consequences of his aberrant behavior. He tells us that he, "falleth into the fire, and oft into the water. / And he did evil, because he prepared not / his heart to seek the Lord" (*Collected,* 225). The dementia inherent in this bleak mood of social hatred and self-pity is oddly gratifying. It justifies Henry's posturing as a prophet and martyr, thereby elevating him above the common lot of humanity.

The futility of trying to overwhelm some uncertain prospects through self-mastery and through the creative process may lead to despair. In "Of Suicide," Berryman writes,

> I drink too much. My wife threatens separation.
> She won't 'nurse' me. She feels "inadequate."
> We don't mix together.
> . . . .
> Rembrandt was sober. There we differ. Sober.

> Terrors came on him. To us they come.
> Of suicide I continually think. (*Collected,* 206)

The poet-narrator is fed up with the insults, irritations, and ambiguities of circumstance. He is fed up with adulation, reproach, and marital alienation. His instincts point to suicide, the ultimate rebellion, but he recognizes the futility of this option. The poem ends in a fatuous resignation to fate and circumstance. "I'll teach Luke," he says, but his resignation is transparent, self-serving, and hypocritical.

According to Dardis and Gilmore, most alcoholic writers feel that there is some kind of connection between creativity and spirituality. They claim to apprehend more than the immediate and apparent, and they hope for some means of creativity and re-creation that will provide them with an extraordinary measure of spiritual control. Alcoholic's Anonymous is only too familiar with this defiant, control centered perspective; *Twelve Steps and Twelve Traditions* states,

> As psychiatrists have often observed, defiance is the outstanding characteristic of many an alcoholic. So it's not strange that lots of us had our day at defying God Himself. Sometimes it's because God had not delivered us the good things of life which we specified, as a greedy child makes an impossible list for Santa Claus. More often, though, we had met up with a major calamity, and to our way of thinking lost out because God deserted us. (31).

AA would suggest that, as an alcoholic, a writer may be tempted to invest his/her art with a spiritual perspective that insists on meanings, actions, and expectations that border on the extreme.

In spiritual matters, then, alcoholics like the Henry persona—and perhaps Berryman himself—are a dichotomy. Many imagine themselves to be both irresistibly attractive and unreasonably repulsive, eloquent and stupefied, sexually powerful and hopelessly inadequate. Henry regards himself as a compendium of all experiences good and bad. In "Love & Fame, #6," Berryman describes the spiritual bankruptcy, the double nature, and the adamant passion for self-sufficiency that typify the chronic drinker. The narrator yearns to identify with everyone on a quasi-universal scale. Perhaps such a grand identification will be his means of spiritual reconciliation; perhaps it will endow his soul with some kind of cosmic connectedness; perhaps it will even defuse his carnal appetites. He prays:

> Under new management, Your Majesty:
> Thine. I have solo' mine since childhood, since
> my father' blow-it-all when I was twelve
> blew out my most bright candle faith, and look at me (*Love & Fame,* 91).

The poet-narrator inventories his childhood faith, his obsession with self, and his intolerable confusion. In contrast with his own limited spiritual perspective, he describes God's benevolent discipline, the agonies of the crucifix, the grace of understanding when He,

> . . . pierced the roof
> twice & again. Finally you opened my eyes.
> My double nature fused in that point of time . . . (*Love & Fame,* 91)

The narrator perceives the human condition in terms of catastrophic oppositions and irreconcilable patterns that can only be resolved through some kind of hypermagical grace. It is evident that he yearns for a savior who is intimate, mortal, and perfect; and, indeed, in "Eleven Addresses to the Lord, #1," he writes, "Master of beauty, craftsman of the snowflake, / inimitable contriver, / endower of Earth so gorgeous. . . ." (*Collected,* 215) Here, the narrator praises the radiance and measureless perfection of the Creator who is Lord and Ruler. God is incomparable, extravagant, omnipotent, and whole. The poet claims that he is willing to surrender and to turn his life over to the care of God, "according" to his will; but his hymn of praise is centered on a highly personal, elective perspective of God formed in the Calvinistic tradition:

> You have come to my rescue again & again
> in my impassable, sometimes despairing years.
> You have allowed my brilliant friends to destroy themselves
> and I am still here, severely damaged, but functioning.

Unknowable, as I am unknown to my guinea pigs;
how can I "love" you?
I only as far as gratitude & awe. . . . (*Collected,* 215)

The narrator hungers for a personal connectedness with God, but he is restrained by God's appalling power, the equivocations of divine mercy, and his own peculiar, personal degradation. As such, his equation hardly serves as a loving assurance of any kind of personal relationship with the Infinite; indeed, it is profoundly troubling because of its diminutive connotations and its suggestions of spiritual disorientation.

A similar theme is developed in "The Facts & Issues." Here, the possibility of a personal God appears freakish and illogical. Any kind of unqualified spiritual connectedness is unthinkable because it requires a transcendent perspective that is both constant and perfect:

Let me be clear about this. It is plain to me
Christ underwent man & treachery & socks
lashes, thirst, exhaustion, the bit, for my pathetic and disgusting vices,
to make this filthy fact of particular, long after,
far-away, five-foot-ten & moribund
human being happy. Well, he has!
I am so happy I could scream!
It's *enough! I* can't BEAR ANY MORE.
Let this be it. (*Collected* 263)

The narrator is tortured by the prospect of grace. He masochistically renounces salvation, the suppression of his thirst for alcohol, humiliation, and the bridging of the infinite distance from mortal poet to perfect Savior. He is being killed with kindness. Grace is catastrophic because it threatens to alienate the poet from the common lot of humanity and from his own penchant for self-indulgence. The poem ends on a note of utter despair: God's great glory is incomprehensible; the narrator is estranged, overwhelmed, and confounded; he is satiated and exhausted to the point where he must give up, but his surrender is inflated, cynical, and grotesque.

As an alcoholic, then, John Berryman tried to escape personal commitments and the terrifying burden of frustration and loneliness in drunkenness or in romantic fantasies of power and creativity. Ultimately, he appears to have charged his most intimate relationships with an extraordinary complex of aggressive prejudices that found expression in the "Henry" persona and in related poems. Perhaps this is why so much of the "Henry" canon reflects the limited perspective of a misanthrope; perhaps this is why it is so heavily charged with an element of alcoholic insanity. In any case, the "Henry" persona is probably a vivid, personal testimony to Berryman's own experiences and attitudes, especially as those experiences and attitudes related to his own problems with alcohol and his difficulty in obtaining a perspective that transcended his own addictive limitations.

BIBLIOGRAPHY

Alcoholics Anonymous: The Story of How Many Thousands of Men and Women Have Recovered from Alcoholism. 3rd ed. New York: Alcoholics Anonymous World Services, 1976.

Berryman, John. *Collected Poems, 1937–1971.* Ed. Charles Thornbury. New York: Farrar, Straus and Giroux, 1991.

———. *The Dream Songs.* New York: Farrar, Straus and Giroux, 1970.

———. *Love & Fame.* New York: Farrar, Straus and Giroux. 1969.

Crowley, John W. *The White Logic: Alcoholism and Gender in American Modernist Fiction.* Amherst: University of Massachusetts, 1994.

Dardis, Tom. *The Thirsty Muse: Alcohol and the American Writer.* New York: Ticknor and Fields, 1989.

Davis, Kathe. "The Li(v)es of the Poet." *Twentieth Century Literature* 30 (1984). Pp. 46–68.

Forseth, Roger. "Ambivalent Sensibilities: Alcohol in History and Literature." *American Quarterly* 42.1 (1990). Pp. 127–35.

Frost, Carol. "Berryman at Thirty-Eight: An Aesthetic Biography." *New England Review* 16 (1994). Pp. 36–53.

Gilmore, Thomas B. "John Berryman and Drinking: From Jest to Sober Ernest." *Equivocal Spirits: Alcoholism and Drinking in Twentieth Century Literature.* Chapel Hill: University of North Carolina Press, 1987. Pp. 140–42.

Goodwin, Donald W. *Alcohol and the Writer.* Kansas City, MO: Andrews and McMeel, 1988.

Haffenden, John. "Drink As a Disease, John Berryman." *Partisan Review* 44 (1977). Pp. 565–83.

———. *The Life of John Berryman.* Boston: Routledge and Kegan Paul, 1982.

Hill, Art. "The Alcoholic on Alcoholism." *Canadian Literature* 62 (1994). Pp. 33–48.

Hyde, Lewis. "Alcohol and Poetry: John Berryman and the Booze Talking." *Recovering Berryman: Essays on a Poet.* Eds. J. Kelly and Alan K. Lathrop. Ann Arbor: University of Michigan Press, 1993. Reprinted from *American Poetry Review* 4 (1975). Pp. 7–12.

Johnson, Manly. "John Berryman: A Note on the Reality." *World Literature Today* 64 (1990). Pp. 422–25.

McClatchy, J. D. "John Berryman: The Impediments to Salvation." *Modern Poetry Studies* 6 (1975). Pp. 246–77.

O'Reilly, Edmund B. *Sobering Tales: Narratives of Alcoholism and Recovery.* Amherst: University of Massachusetts Press, 1997.

Provost, Sarah. "Erato's Fool and Bitter Sister: Two Aspects of John Berryman." *Twentieth Century Literature* 30 (1984). Pp. 69–79.

Roth, Marty. "Carnival, Creativity, and the Sublimation of Drunkenness." *Mosaic* 30 (1997). Pp. 1–18.

Spencer, Luke. "'The pieces sat up & wrote': Art and Life in John Berryman's *Dream Songs.*" *The Critical Quarterly* 29 (1987). Pp. 71–80.

Twelve Steps and Twelve Traditions. New York: Alcoholics Anonymous World Services, 1953.

CHAPTER 13

THE BARNES COMPLEX

Ernest Hemingway, Djuna Barnes, *The Sun Also Rises*, and *Nightwood*

Ellen Lansky

IN *DJUNA: THE LIFE AND TIMES OF DJUNA BARNES,* Andrew Field recounts a juicy story that places Ernest Hemingway and Djuna Barnes together in the Select—a busy Parisian café:

> It was [the barman] Jimmy's night off at the Dingo, and he dropped in very late for a drink before bed at the Select. Apart from Djuna Barnes and Thelma Wood [Barnes' partner], who were drinking with another girl whom he does not name, he recalls that the only other customers in the Select were [Robert] McAlmon and a friend. And then, according to Jimmy, an internationally known American newsman [Hemingway] burst into the bar roaring drunk. He lunged over to the three women and sat down without ceremony next to Miss Barnes, whom he began to paw and maul. . . . Jimmy asked him to come out on the terrace to have a mock session of fisticuffs, calculating that by this means he could both mollify Djuna and Thelma and draw the journalist away from the cafe. Unfortunately, Miss Barnes followed them outside and offered a commentary on her assailant's character,

> whereupon he slipped quickly out of Jimmy's hold and flattened her with a well-placed punch on the chin. . . . [Jimmy] had to knock the journalist down three times before he was finally subdued, with a gash that required three stitches. (132–33)

I believe this scene typifies the lives of alcoholics, for whom this kind of catastrophic melodrama is ordinary. Furthermore, this scene could easily have been included in either Hemingway's *The Sun Also Rises* or in Barnes' *Nightwood.* Both novels feature drinking, betrayal, fighting, tantrums, tears, and more drinking: the same kind of catastrophic melodrama in fiction that the alcoholic authors experienced in their lives. Though it would be false to imply conscious collaboration between Hemingway and Barnes, the intertexts between Hemingway's *The Sun Also Rises* and Barnes' *Nightwood* begin with Hemingway's gesture to Djuna Barnes made through his narrator Jake Barnes, and they culminate with casts of drinking expatriate characters who are configured into similar complicated drinking partnerships. An intertextual reading of these novels produces a figure that I propose to call, in honor of Jake and Djuna, the Barnes Complex. The Barnes Complex is an interpretive tool for understanding how alcoholics such as Ernest Hemingway, Brett Ashley, Robin Vote, and Djuna Barnes interact with alcohol and their partners—Jake Barnes, Nora Flood, and other friends, spouses, associates, and readers of their novels.

The Barnes Complex's distinguishing features bear some superficial resemblances to "codependency," but the problem with the term codependency is that its own promulgators have failed to provide it with intellectual currency. It is a concept with nebulous parameters. The social scientist Sharon Wegscheider-Cruse attempts to define codependency as "a specific condition that is characterized by preoccupation and extreme dependency (emotionally, socially and sometimes physically) on another person or object" (Mashberg, 29). The problem with this definition is that its field is too large. One of the most popular "codependency experts," Melody Beattie, claims that "codependency has a fuzzy definition because it is a fuzzy, gray condition" (31). She defines a codependent person as "one who has let another person's behavior affect him or her, and who is obsessed with controlling that person's behavior" (31). This definition includes people who are obsessed with controlling the behavior of an alcoholic, but it does not exclude anyone and so it seems that everyone is or can be codependent. In her book *Women with Alcoholic Husbands,* Ramona Asher tries to move codependency to the ostensibly firmer terrain of theory and cultural studies. She asserts that "we need to recognize codependency as a construct, as a way of talking about modes of thinking, feeling, and acting" (191). Her language is more sophisticated than Beattie's, but her research on the "codependency construct" is only applied to heterosexual women.

Recently, the term "codependency" has been the subject of much debate, with many feminist health professionals and social scientists questioning its validity. In their article "Codependency and Gender-Stereotyped Traits," Gloria Cowan and Lynda Warren summarize the feminist argument against the concept of codependency as follows:

> [T]he charge is that much of the behavior and traits identified as codependent are culturally prescribed for women. Women are then pathologized for following these cultural prescriptions and blamed for their behavior as well as for the behavior of those they love. The solution proposed is both personal and internal, ignoring the social context. (634)

Cowan and Warren find that "the present data do not support the idea that codependency is a label that pathologizes women for being feminine. Rather, codependency is associated primarily with traits that are pathological from the standpoint of being socially undesirable for both genders" (643). They caution "codependency advocates" who "are far too global in labeling people codependent," and they also warn against a similar kind of unilateral dismissal of codependency as some kind of oppressive plot against women (644).

The prevailing arguments for and against codependency theories have gotten bogged down in their own lack of parameters and their heterosexist assumptions: mainly, that in a relationship, the problem person—usually, but not necessarily, a drug addict or an alcoholic—is always a heterosexual man (probably white and middle class) and the codependent is always his wife. Still another big problem with the codependency theory is that neither its proponents nor its opponents are addressing codependency as a condition related to specific alcoholism and drug addiction issues, which are the site of its initial promulgation.

The Barnes Complex applies only to those alcoholics who try, but fail, to drink themselves into a state of permanent intoxication that comes with no negative consequences, and to their partners who try, but fail, to rescue or save the alcoholics from their own self-destructive behavior. The Barnes Complex is inscribed clearly in Hemingway's and Barnes' novels, and an intertextual reading of the two novels demonstrates and illuminates what the Barnes Complex is and how it works.

In *The Sun Also Rises* and *Nightwood,* Jake, Brett, and Mike and Robin, Nora, and O'Connor compose the Barnes Complex. Brett and Robin are alcoholics. Jake and Nora are both respectively devoted to Brett and Robin and preoccupied with controlling their behavior—especially around alcohol. O'Connor and Mike are alcoholics who drink respectively with Robin and Brett, and they foster Jake's and Nora's preoccupation with their alcoholics. Jake's and Nora's role is to ward off negative consequences associated with the alcoholics' drinking, to drink right along with the alcoholics sometimes, and generally to protect the drinkers from any outside influences, forces, thoughts, people, places, or things that may impede the alcoholics' drinking and the behavior they exhibit while drunk. In this way, Jake and Nora give themselves the illusion that they have power and control over Brett and Robin, respectively. Furthermore, both Jake and O'Connor and perhaps Mike encode their sense of their own "potency" as men in their attempts to control Brett and Robin.

Unfortunately, while all these characters enable and perpetuate each other's drinking, they also foment and precipitate each other's misery. This is a predictable effect of the Barnes Complex. At the end of the two novels: Jake is drunk; Mike is drunk and broke; Brett is drunk and silent; O'Connor passes out after a drunken rage; Robin growls and barks with Nora's dog; and Nora curses and then is speechless. The Barnes Complex guarantees frustration and despair for its constituents. In her work on alcoholism in Malcolm Lowry's *Under the Volcano,* Catherine MacGregor makes this important observation: "Lowry knew enough about his own addiction and the reactions of those around him to recognize, paradoxically, that although some sort of help was desirable, nothing anyone does to rescue the alcoholic seems to accomplish anything" (152). MacGregor's observation is eminently applicable to the characters in Barnes' and Hemingway's novels, and to their own experiences in their personal lives. Nothing anyone did to rescue Ernest Hemingway or Djuna Barnes, or any of their alcoholic contemporaries, seemed to have accomplished anything; Hemingway killed himself, and Barnes lived a mostly wretched existence for the second half of her 90 years. Furthermore, nothing anyone does to try and rescue the alcoholics in their novels seems to accomplish anything either.

Futility and paradox are words that characterize the general experience of people such as Jake and Nora who try to help, save, or rescue alcoholics. Nora follows Robin all over Paris, all the way to Tangier, but she must admit to O'Connor: "[s]ometimes Robin seemed to return to me . . . for sleep and safety . . . [but] she always went out again" (139). She can't control Robin, she can't rescue Robin, and she can't accept the fact that she can't. Jake's rescue attempts are equally impotent. In Pamplona, when the fiesta is over, Jake provides services for Mike. He and Bill drop the flat-broke Mike at a hotel that will extend him credit, and Jake pays Mike's share of the limousine bill. Having situated Mike, Jake tries to take some time to himself in San Sebastian, but then Brett sends a terse telegraph message: "COULD YOU COME HOTEL MONTANA MADRID AM RATHER IN TROUBLE BRETT" (238). Instead of wiring her some money, Jake cuts short his vacation and takes an express train to Madrid so he can personally facilitate Brett's salvation or rescue. But Brett and Mike are not saved or rescued at the novel's end by Jake or anyone else, and neither is Robin. This is another predictable effect of the Barnes Complex.

Jake and Nora both locate their personal power or "potency" in their capacity to enable and control the alcoholics' drinking. Because of a war wound, Jake is unable to function as Brett's sex partner. Therefore, drinking provides a way for Jake to give Brett "what she wants"—or, more precisely, what he thinks she wants, or what he wants her to want. Brett's first significant utterance to Jake is "I say, give a chap a brandy and soda" (22), and he does. Later, when Brett pays Jake a visit at half past four in the morning, Jake gets "brandy and soda and glasses" (32) without being asked. When he knows she's out on a drinking and sex bender, he simply waits for her to return. She always does. Jake can't serve Brett's sexual needs, but he can serve her drinks, and he must glean some pleasure or satisfaction from this kind of service.

Nora also devotes herself to serving others. Before she meets Robin, Nora is depicted as a calm, sober figure who presides over a strange salon composed of drunks: "[of] all that ranting, roaring crew, she stood out. The equilibrium of her nature, savage and refined, gave her bridled skull a look of compassion" (50). Unfortunately, her seeming equilibrium and compassion come at a price, and in the course of maintaining her "ranting and roaring" salon, she "robbed herself for everyone; incapable of giving herself warning, she was continually turning about to find herself diminished" (51). So diminished, Nora seems oddly distanced from people—disconnected and spectatorial. Rather than participating in the world, "the world and its history were to Nora like a ship in a bottle; she herself was outside and unidentified, endlessly embroiled in a preoccupation without a problem. Then she met Robin" (53).

Robin, who has "the shakes" when Nora first meets her at the Denckman circus, provides the perfect problem for Nora's preoccupations. Robin drags Nora into the "bottle"—the Parisian cafe culture of drinking and sex. Before long, they are utterly enmeshed, "so 'haunted' of each other that separation was impossible" (55). In her relationship with Robin, Nora goes beyond robbing herself and instead "Robins herself." Robin takes over Nora's body and mind: "in Nora's heart lay the fossil of Robin . . . and about it for its maintenance ran Nora's blood. . . . [Nora's] mind became so transfixed that, by the agency of her fear, Robin seemed enormous and polarized, all catastrophes ran toward her, the magnetized predicament" (56). Nora becomes clearly and completely identified with Robin.

Like Jake and his involvement with Brett and her exploits, Nora is a silent partner in Robin's café catastrophes.

Like Jake Barnes, her counterpart in the Barnes Complex, Nora also finds that she cannot accommodate Robin's compulsions for sex and alcohol. She soon realizes that trying to keep up with Robin's desire to get drunk and have sex with strangers is an exercise in futility. At last, Nora is "unable to endure the knowledge that she was in the way or forgotten, seeing Robin go from table to table, from drink to drink, from person to person" (59). Like Jake, Nora realizes that she can't give Robin what she wants, so she stays home and waits, and eventually Robin returns. Jake and Nora may seem like martyrs, waiting for Robin and Brett to return from their escapades. However, the fact that Robin and Brett always do return must provide Jake and Nora with satisfactory proof that they have power over Brett and Robin—which is what they want.

In addition to providing their partners with an opportunity to enact their desire for control and power, the alcoholics also provide their partners with the opportunity to get drunk. Jake responds to Brett's successful sexual encounter with Pedro Romero—which he helped precipitate—by getting thoroughly drunk. After the bullfight, and with the intuitive knowledge of Brett's imminent departure with Romero, Jake drinks too much absinthe and tells Bill Gorton he feels "low as hell." He wants to give Brett her bullfighter, but he also wants her not to want the bullfighter enough to run off with him, and because she doesn't do what he wants, he gets drunk. Mike also uses Brett's sexual infidelities as a reason to get roaring drunk. He announces, "I think I'll stay rather drunk. This is all awfully amusing, but it's not too pleasant" (203).

Similarly, Nora finds herself mimicking the same behaviors she finds most abhorrent in Robin: drinking and promiscuity. She tells O'Connor, "I haunted the cafes where Robin had lived her night-life; I drank with the men, I danced with the women; but all I knew was that others had slept with my lover and my child" (156). O'Connor's participation in Nora's and Robin's relationship facilitates his own drinking project. Nora's misery over her inability to control Robin provides O'Connor with an opportunity to get drunk. He drops in on Nora one afternoon, and his first move is to help himself "to a generous port" (124). Their conversation begins as a genuine exchange, and Nora does have a dim epiphany about her relationship with Robin. Meanwhile, Dr. O'Connor can't enlighten Nora because he's too busy drinking her port. Their discourse disintegrates. The doctor drinks port and prattles on about Robin's beauty and Robin's perpetual child-like state. Nora gives a speech to the doctor that ends: "In that bed we [Nora and Robin] would have forgotten our lives in the extremity of memory, moulted our parts, as figures in the waxworks are moulted, down to their story, so would we have broken down to our love" (158). Robin's sexual escapades seem to be a "turn-on" for Nora, and in her speech she indicates a certainty that she and Robin could solve their problems in bed—if only she could get Robin in bed. The thrill lies in its promise of control and power; if Nora could get Robin in bed, then she could control not only Robin's drinking but her sexual desires and activities as well.

Nora's corporeal meltdown speech stuns the doctor into an unusual silence. Perhaps he is speechless because he recognizes in her words an intense preoccupation with other people's sexuality. His opening line to her is "'Can't you be quiet now?' . . . and now he staggered as he reached for his hat and coat. He stood in confused and unhappy silence—he moved toward the door. Holding the knob in his hand he turned toward her. Then he went out" (158). From Nora's flat, the doctor stumbles to the *Café de la Mairie VIe*. There, he drinks until he can no longer move, and he babbles himself to angry tears. "Wrath and weeping"—which echoes Mike's "not too pleasant," Jake's "low as hell," and Nora's "all I knew was that others had slept with my lover and my child"—are his last drunken words. Jake and Nora can "blame" their drunkenness on the alcoholics, whose behavior has evidently "driven them to drink." What is clear, though, is that their drunkenness is connected to their frustration over not being able to control the alcoholics' behavior and desires.

Jake's final observations and remarks reveal the way in which his futile rescue missions are inscribed in his sexual incapacity or impotence. As they ride in a carriage along the Gran Via, Brett laments that she and Jake "could have had such a damned good time together" (247). Jake notes "a mounted policeman in khaki directing traffic. He raised his baton" (247). The uniformed man, equipped with a fully functional baton, is able to dictate and control people's actions; "the car slowed suddenly" (247). Jake, on the other hand, does not possess such a potent baton. The slowing car presses Brett against him, which suggests a sexual opportunity, but he has already made it clear that "there's not a damn thing we could do" (26). Furthermore, his three martinis plus five bottles of Rioja Alta wine at lunch would practically guarantee sexual impotence for any man.

The rescue missions Jake Barnes undertakes to try to give himself the feeling of potency turn out to be futile; they merely underscore his impotence. Thus, Jake's final remark, "Yes. . . . Isn't it pretty to think so?" (247) has two functions. First, it emphasizes—through the agency of irony—his despair over the fact that a "potent" sexual encounter, a "good time," for Jake and Brett is impossible. Second, Jake's ironic remark that is ostensibly aimed at his "impotence" must also be understood as a comment on his relationship with Brett. Alcoholics and their partners rarely have "a damned good time together;" the Barnes Complex prohibits it. Finally, the novel's overtones of futility spring not only from Jake's "lack" but also from the frustrating, repetitive, and desperate nature of alcoholism.

The final futility scene in *Nightwood* reinscribes the futility of the final scene in *The Sun Also Rises.* The last paragraphs in *Nightwood* have accrued much attention because they suggest to some readers, the most recent being Edmund White, a sort of bestial sex scene involving Robin and Nora's dog. To summarize briefly, in the novel's final paragraph, Robin is on the floor with Nora's dog in Nora's dilapidated chapel. In response to the dog's barking, Robin "began to bark also, crawling after him—barking in a fit of laughter, obscene and touching" (170). As the dog cries, Robin is "grinning and crying with him, crying in shorter and shorter spaces, moving head to head, until she gave up, lying out, her hands beside her, her face turned and weeping" (170). Though Hank O'Neal recalls that Djuna Barnes consistently denied that Robin and the dog are "getting it on," her denial has not done much to quell this popular interpretation (Broe 353). Nor does Barnes' denial illuminate this opaque moment in her novel.

I would like to suggest that the dog scene has a metonymic connection to Robin, Nora, and O'Connor's relationship. In Nora and O'Connor's last conversation, O'Connor observes that Nora's heart is in her hand. He advises her, "Put it back. The eater of it will get a taste for you; in the end his muzzle will be heard barking among your ribs" (139). The simultaneous appearance of Nora's dog in the novel's last scene and of Robin in Nora's chapel suggests, through metonymy and transubstantiation, that this dog/Robin is the eater of Nora's heart. Thus, O'Connor's predictions come true; in the end the dog's muzzle is heard barking.

This scene also supports O'Connor's conviction at the end of chapter 5, "Watchman, What of the Night," that "Nora will leave that girl some day; but though those two are buried at opposite ends of the earth, one dog will find them both" (106). And so one dog does find them both at the end of the novel. Robin's bloodhound search for Nora seems "romantic" and her posture in the last scene—"she gave up, lying out, her hands beside her, her face turned and weeping" (170)—signals utter prostration and surrender. However, the presence of the two women together with that barking dog suggests that their "hearts" are enmeshed again—or still. Between Robin and Nora, nothing is resolved and nothing is clear, including the role and function of that heart-eating dog. Furthermore, the dog scene distracts the reader's attention from the novel's central unresolved issue: Nora, Robin, and O'Connor's alcoholism and codependency. If one can pry one's prurient gaze from Robin and the dog, in the same way that one has to pry one's gaze from Jake Barnes' crotch in order to examine what is really wrong with his relationship with Brett, what is clear is that Jake and Brett and Nora and Robin and O'Connor and Mike seem doomed to continue their destructive cycle of control, manipulation, futility, and abjection. This destructive repetition is the essence of the Barnes Complex.

Readers are also implicated in the Barnes Complex. A problem of interpretation that alcoholic authors and their texts present to readers is that alcoholism resists distinctions between "fiction" and "life." To some alcoholics, life may resemble fiction. Alcoholics often begin with a factual event and bring imagination and invention to bear on it in order to produce a cohesive, powerful narrative.

In the alcoholic's case, he or she hopes the fictional narrative will provide compelling explanations, excuses, or reasons for insane behavior. The alcoholic's partner, drinking buddy, spouse, lover, friend, or associate corroborates the narrative because he or she needs to believe in the verisimilitude of the alcoholic's fiction in order to preserve his or her own sanity—paradoxical as that may sound.

Alcoholic writers such as Hemingway and Barnes lived lives that were sometimes indistinguishable from the fiction they wrote. Trying to separate their lives from their fictions is frequently futile, especially when the authors themselves may not concern themselves with maintaining a boundary or aesthetic distance between life and fiction. In 1925, for example, it is well documented that Ernest Hemingway went to Pamplona and got drunk day and night for a week, danced with the natives, and ran with the bulls. Right after the fiesta, he began writing *The Sun Also Rises*. There is not much distance between the "real life" events and people and the fictional events and characters. In fact, although Hemingway wrote to his editor Maxwell Perkins that "[i]t is going to be a swell novel with no autobiography and no complaints" (Mellow, 303), many Hemingway biographers and readers have shown that the novel does contain autobiography. James Mellow notes:

> with a few noticeable exceptions, he began with the real names: Nino de la Palma, Hemingway himself, Loeb, Duff, Pat Guthrie, Bill Smith, Don Stewart. Even Hadley made an appearance in the novel to be. . . . Hemingway—"Hem" in the first draft—eventually became the narrator, Jake Barnes; Bill Smith and Don Stewart merged to become . . . Bill Gorton. . . . Pat Guthrie became Mike Campbell. And Duff, after a stint as Duff Anthony, settled into the novel as Lady Brett. (304)

Both the fictional characters and their real-life counterparts enact the same kinds of scenes in the same places.

As in *The Sun Also Rises*, characters in *Nightwood* find their counterparts in the author's life. Again, biographers and critics have taken pains to establish that Barnes began writing *Nightwood* not long after her relationship with Thelma Wood disintegrated. *Nightwood* is a catastrophic melodrama about an alcoholic relationship that disintegrates. The "wood" in *Nightwood* invokes Thelma Wood. Andrew Field notes that "Thelma Wood found the portrayal of Robin Vote all too accurate and was very bitter about it. . . . [S]he evidently went to considerable lengths to dissuade her friends from reading the novel. She knew, after all, that even the name Robin was taken from one of Peggy [Guggenheim]'s dogs" (160). Djuna Barnes's alcoholic friend Dan Mahoney provides another compelling example of the alcoholic's blurred boundaries between "life" and "fiction" and "reader" and "text." Mahoney was the model for Barnes' character Dr. Matthew O'Connor: quack abortionist, cross-dresser, notorious drunk, a lover of roles and melodrama. Mahoney loved O'Connor's debut in Barnes' 1928 novel *Ryder* enough to correspond with Djuna Barnes about O'Connor's role in *Nightwood.* In *Djuna,* Field notes that "When *Nightwood* was being prepared for publication there was substantial editing being done both by Barnes herself and T. S. Eliot, her editor at Faber's, and one of the sections marked for exclusion concerned the childhood of Dr. O'Connor. Mahoney wrote to Djuna Barnes begging her not to excise that portion" (138). For the alcoholic Mahoney, there were no boundaries between author, character, reader, or text; life was fiction.

I am inclined to give credence to Jackson Benson's assertion that "the burden on the professional reader of Hemingway's work to maintain a sense of separateness and otherness is particularly demanding. We succeed or fail as critics of his work not just in pointing to his failures in distance but in maintaining our own" (356). One can easily extend this assertion to apply to Barnes' readers. However, I also think that maintaining this distance is a challenge because Hemingway wants his readers to participate in his drinking enterprise, and so does Barnes. Hemingway enlists his readers as drinking partners through pronoun shifts and other rhetorical strategies, and Barnes enlists her reader/partners through omissions and "scapegoating" characterizations. Both need participant readers in order to validate their own drinking projects, and readers who are alcoholics may find validation for their own drinking inscribed in these novels. This relationship is a key element of the Barnes Complex.

Hemingway constructs the reader as a drinking buddy, someone who will drink right along with him and assure him that his drinking is fine. By using pronoun shifts from Jake's first-person "I" to the second-person "you," Hemingway not only acknowledges the reader's presence, but he also makes room for the reader as a character—the "you" that Jake addresses in the novel. For example, in Chapter 2, Jake comments on Robert Cohn's preoccupation with W. H. Hudson's "The Purple Land," and he makes a significant address to the reader: "You understand me, he made some reservations, but on the whole the book was sound to him" (9). Later, Jake makes the same move toward the reader in his description of Pernod cocktails: "Pernod is greenish imitation absinthe. When you add water it turns milky. It tastes like licorice and it has a good uplift, but it drops you just as far" (15). Although one might argue that Hemingway's use of "you" is an impersonal "you"—the equivalent of the third person singular "one"—certain dynamics still enable a reader to consider himself or herself the "you" that Jake addresses, especially if the reader wants to be part of the novel's public drinking crowd. Jake explains what happens when you drink Pernod, and you can follow his instructions. You can go to Pamplona and run with the bulls; you can go to the Closerie des Lilas and the Select and other cafés in Paris. These spots have become real-life tourist traps due in large part to the success of Ernest Hemingway's fiction. Hemingway doesn't want distance; Hemingway wants you to participate in his novel. He wants you to have a drink. For the "drinking buddy" reader of *The Sun Also Rises,* verisimilitude becomes virtual reality.

While Hemingway constructs a "drinking buddy" reader to validate his intense preoccupation with alcohol, Barnes' reader's purpose is to help the author deny her own alcoholism. Barnes knew that her novel would be received as autobiographical and that readers in the know would connect Nora Flood to Barnes, Robin Vote to Thelma Wood, and Matthew O'Connor to Dan Mahoney. As Shari Benstock, and Constance Perry note, Nora and Robin's relationship is clearly modeled on Barnes' own relationship with Thelma Wood, except that Barnes effectively erases Nora's drinking.

Robin's alcoholism surfaces on the night that she goes into labor and delivers her son. When the pains begin, she "began to curse loudly. . . . [S]he was drunk—her hair was swinging in her eyes" (48). From that point in the novel, Robin hardly draws a sober breath. By contrast, Barnes deploys Nora Flood as the suffering partner: "Nora robbed herself for everyone; incapable of giving herself warning, she was continually turning about to find herself diminished" (51). Nora Flood serves as a decoy to deflect attention from Barnes' own alcoholism.

Many readers have been more than willing to truncate or obliterate these traditional boundaries between reader and text and fiction and life, and this willing participation marks another key component of the Barnes Complex. Both novels have been received as romans à clef—a mode of fiction that invites readers to make connections between people, places, and things in fiction and "real life." The drinking characters model behavior that readers can replicate: they can get drunk in the same way that the characters and their authors do. Readers can go to cafés in Paris and Spain and Berlin and drink in the same places as the authors and characters. Readers who cannot literally go to Europe can imagine themselves going to those cafés while they read and drink. In *A Moveable Feast,* Hemingway explains how the process works: "I was writing about up in Michigan and since it was a wild, cold, blowing day it was that sort of day in the story. . . . In the story the boys were drinking and this made me thirsty and I ordered a rum St. James. This tasted wonderful on the cold day and I kept on writing" (5). This kind of combined literal and imaginary activity blurs the conventional boundary between fiction and life.

Furthermore, these novels publicize drinking and authorize readers to participate in the drinking culture. Beyond offering the reader a vicarious experience, Barnes, Hemingway, and other alcoholic writers may enable their readers to participate in the alcoholism they represent in their fiction. Readers can drink along with the author and the characters and reenact the scenarios that the author describes; they can "live the novels." Hemingway's novel in particular became a culturally iconic narrative that authorized drinking for its readers when it first appeared in Prohibition America. In *Exile's Return,* Malcolm Cowley reports that *The Sun Also Rises* "was a good novel and became a craze—young men tried to get as imperturbably drunk as the hero, young women of good families took a succession of lovers in the same heartbroken fashion as the heroine, they all talked like Hemingway characters and the name was fixed" (3). The key for both Hemingway and Barnes' drinking characters was that this public drinking required control. The "problem" drinkers in both novels—Mike Campbell, Robin Vote, and Matthew O'Connor—are the ones who publicize their drunkenness, who are out of control. The other drinking characters—Brett, Jake, and Nora—get "imperturbably drunk." In public, they appear to be in control of their drinking, and this is the behavior that readers are encouraged to emulate or enable. Consequently, when Jake Barnes observes "we're none of us sober," his use of first person plural easily encompasses all the characters in *The Sun Also Rises* and applies equally well to their counterparts in *Nightwood,* the two authors, and some of their readers as well.

Finally, the two novels are both agents and products of alcoholic melodrama. The novels are informed by the catastrophic melodrama in their authors' lives, and they serve as "conduct books" for their readers. In *After the Lost Generation,* John Aldridge recalls trying to conduct his life according to Hemingway's novels. Acknowledging Hemingway's influence on the next generation of writers, he writes

> I remember hikes we took in the country when we carried along with us the big loaf of hard bread, the wedge of sour cheese, and the dry red wine of those magnificent moments at Caporetto, the Swiss ski lodge, and the fishing stream in Spain. I remember nights of drinking in front of an open fire when everybody sooner or later began talking like Nick Adams and trying to seduce somebody else's girl with the practiced indifference of Harry Morgan. I remember too the nice girls who came to those parties and drank too much and tried to live up to Brett's frantic example, and how some of them were never quite the same afterward. (24–25)

Unfortunately, as those "nice girls" found out, readers who live the novels often find themselves telling the same story of sadness, frustration, and despair. The destructive cycle of the Barnes Complex continues until someone resists; this resistance can begin with a reader who refuses to accept the role these alcoholic authors offer.

BIBLIOGRAPHY

Aldridge, John. *After the Lost Generation.* Freeport, NY: New York Books for Libraries, 1951, 1971.

Asher, Ramona. *Women with Alcoholic Husbands: Ambivalence and the Trap of Codependency.* Chapel Hill: University of North Carolina Press, 1992.

Babcock, Marguerite and Christine McKay. *Challenging Codependency: Feminist Critiques.* Toronto and Buffalo: University of Toronto Press, 1995.

Baker, Carlos. *Hemingway: The Writer As Artist.* 3rd ed. Princeton, NJ: Princeton University Press, 1963.

Barnes, Djuna. *Nightwood.* New York: New Directions, 1937.

———. *Nightwood: The Original Version and Related Drafts.* Ed. Cheryl Plumb. Normal, IL: Dalkey Archive, 1995.

Beach, Joseph Warren. *American Fiction, 1920–1940.* New York: Macmillan, 1941.

Beattie, Melody. *Codependent No More.* San Francisco: Harper San Francisco, 1987.

Benson, Jackson. "Ernest Hemingway: The Life as Fiction and the Fiction as Life." *Hemingway: Essays of Reassessment.* Ed. Frank Scafella. New York: Oxford University Press, 1991. Pp. 155–68.

———. *Hemingway: The Writer's Art of Self-Defense.* Minneapolis: University of Minnesota Press, 1969.

Benstock, Shari. *Women of the Left Bank Paris, 1900–1940.* Austin: University of Texas Press, 1986.

Broe, Mary Lynn. "Djuna Barnes." *Gender of Modernism.* Ed. Bonnie Kime Scott, et al. Bloomington, IN: Indiana University Press, 1990. Pp. 19–27.

———. "My Art Belongs to Daddy: Incest as Exile, the Textual Economics of Hayford Hall." *Women's Writing in Exile.* Ed. Mary Lynn Broe and Angela Ingram. Chapel Hill: University of North Carolina Press, 1989. Pp. 41–86.

———, ed. *Silence and Power: A Re-Evaluation of Djuna Barnes.* Carbondale and Edwardsville: Southern Illinois University Press, 1991.

Bruccoli, Matthew. *Some Sort of Epic Grandeur: The Life of F. Scott Fitzgerald.* New York: Harcourt, Brace, Jovanovich, 1991.

Cowan, Gloria and Lynda Warren. "Codependency and Gender-Stereotyped Traits." *Sex Roles* 30 (May 1994). Pp. 631–45.

Cowley, Malcolm. *"The White Logic:" Alcoholism and Gender in American Modernist Fiction.* Amherst: University of Massachusetts Press, 1994.

Cowley, Malcolm. *Exile's Return.* New York: Viking, 1964.

Dardis, Tom. *The Thirsty Muse: Alcohol and the American Writer.* New York: Ticknor and Fields, 1989.

Diliberto, Gioia. *Hadley.* New York: Ticknor and Fields, 1992.

Djos, Matts. "Alcoholism in Ernest Hemingway's *The Sun Also Rises;* A Wine and Roses Perspective on the Lost Generation." *Hemingway Review* 14.2 (Spring 1995). Pp. 64–78.

Donaldson, Scott. *By Force of Will: The Life and Art of Ernest Hemingway.* New York: Viking, 1977.

Douglas, Ann. *Terrible Honesty: Mongrel Manhattan in the 1920s.* New York: Farrar, Straus, and Giroux, 1985.

Fawcett, Jan. "Comorbidity, Dual Diagnosis, and Addictions—We Can't Ignore Them." *Psychiatric Annals* 24.8 (August 1994). Pp. 397–98.

Felman, Shoshana. *What Does a Woman Want? Reading and Sexual Difference.* Baltimore, MD: John Hopkins University Press, 1993.

Fetterley, Judith. *The Resisting Reader: A Feminist Approach to American Fiction.* Bloomington: Indiana University Press, 1978.

Fiedler, Leslie. "Men Without Women." *Hemingway: A Collection of Critical Essays.* Ed. Robert P. Weeks. Englewood Cliffs, NJ: Prentice Hall, 1962. Pp. 86–92.

———. *Waiting for the End.* New York: Stein and Day, 1964.

Field, Andrew. *Djuna: The Life and Times of Djuna Barnes.* New York: Putnam, 1983.

Forseth, Roger. "Alcohol and the Writer: Some Biographical and Critical Issues (Hemingway)." *Contemporary Drug Problems* 13.2 (Summer 1986). Pp. 361–86.

Gilbert, Sandra, and Susan Gubar. "Infection in the Sentence: The Woman Writer and the Anxiety of Authorship." *Madwoman in the Attic.* New Haven, CT: Yale University Press, 1979. Pp. 45–92.

———. *No Man's Land: The Place of the Woman Writer in The Twentieth Century, vol 1. The War of the Words.* New Haven, CT: Yale University Press, 1988.

Haaken, Janice. "A Critical Analysis of the Codependency Construct." *Challenging Codependency: Feminist Critiques*. Eds. Marguerite Babcock and Christine McKay. Toronto: University of Toronto Press, 1995, Pp. 53–69.

Hanscombe, Gillian and Virginia L. Smyers. *Writing for their Lives: The Modernist Women 1910–1940*. London: Women's Press, 1987.

Hemingway, Ernest. "Hills Like White Elephants." *The Complete Short Stories of Ernest*

Hemingway. Ed. Finca Vigia. New York: Scribners, 1987. Pp. 211–14.

———. *A Moveable Feast*. New York: Scribners, 1964.

———. *The Sun Also Rises*. New York: Scribners, 1926.

Hemingway, Mary Walsh. *How it Was*. New York: Knopf, 1951.

Herring, Phillip. *Djuna: The Life and Works of Djuna Barnes*. New York: Viking, 1995.

Hoffman, Frederick. *The Modern Novel in America*. Chicago: H. Regnery, 1963.

———. *The Twenties: American Writers*. New York: Viking, 1949, 1955.

Iser, Wolfgang. *The Act of Reading: A Theory of Aesthetic Response*. Baltimore: John Hopkins University Press, 1978.

Kannenstine, Louis. *The Art of Djuna Barnes: Duality and Damnation*. New York: New York University Press, 1977.

Kanner, Melinda. "That's Why the Lady is a Drunk: Women, Alcoholism, and Popular Culture." *Sexual Politics and Popular Culture*. Ed. Diane Raymond. Bowling Green, OH: Bowling Green State University Popular Press, 1990. Pp. 183–98.

Kazin, Alfred. "'The Giant-Killer': Drink and the American Writer." *Commentary* March, 1976. Pp. 44–50.

———. *On Native Grounds*. New York: Reynal and Hitcock, 1942.

Keller, Mark and John Doria. "Defining Alcoholism." *Alcohol Health and Research World* 15.4 (1991). Pp. 253–59.

Lanier, Doris. "The Bittersweet Taste of Absinthe in Hemingway's 'Hills Like White Elephants'." *Studies in Short Fiction* 26.3 (Summer 1989). Pp. 279–88.

Lender, Mark and James Kirby Martin. *Drinking in America: A History*. New York: The Free Press, 1982.

Levine, Nancy J. and Marian Urquila. "Introduction." *Review of Contemporary Fiction* Special Issue. 13.3 (Fall 1993). Pp. 7–16.

Lupton, Mary Jane. "Ladies Entrance: Women and Bars." *Feminist Studies* 5.3 (Fall 1979). Pp. 571–88.

Lutz, Tom. *American Nervousness, 1903: An Anecdotal History.* Ithaca, NY: Cornell University Press, 1991.

MacGregor, Catherine. "Conspiring with the Addict: Yvonne's Co-Dependence in *Under the Volcano.*" *Mosaic* 24.3–4 (Spring/Fall 1991). Pp. 145–62.

Marcus, Jane. "Laughing at Leviticus: *Nightwood* as Women's Circus Epic." *Silence and Power.* Ed. Mary Lynn Broe. Carbondale and Edwardsville: Southern Illinois University Press, 1991. Pp. 221–51.

Mashberg. Amy. "Co-Dependency and Obsession in *Madame Bovary.*" *Dionysos* 2.1 (Spring 1990). Pp. 28–40.

Mellow, James. *Hemingway: A Life without Consequences.* Boston: Houghton Mifflin, 1992.

Messent, Peter. "Reconstructing Papa: New Directions in Hemingway Criticism." *Journal of American Studies* 26.2 (1992). Pp. 269–75.

Meyers, Jeffrey. *Hemingway: A Biography.* New York: Harper and Row, 1985.

O'Neal, Hank. *"Life is painful, nasty and short . . . only in my case it has only been painful and nasty:" Djuna Barnes: An Informal Memoir.* New York: Paragon House, 1990.

Perry, Constance. "A Woman Writing under the Influence: Djuna Barnes and *Nightwood.*" *Dionysos* 4.2 (Fall 1992). Pp. 3–14.

Reynolds, Michael. *Ernest Hemingway Annotated Chronology: An Outline of the Author's Life and Career Detailing Significant Events, Friendships, Travels, and Achievements.* Detroit: Omnigraphics, Inc. 1991.

Ronell, Avital. *Crack Wars: Literature, Addiction, Mania.* Lincoln: University of Nebraska Press, 1992.

Rorabaugh, William. *The Alcoholic Republic: An American Tradition.* New York: Oxford University Press, 1979.

Ruben, Douglas. *Family Addiction: An Analytical Guide.* New York: Garland, 1993.

Schweickart, Patricinio. "Reading Ourselves: Toward a Feminist Theory of Reading." *Gender and Reading: Essays on Readers, Texts and Contexts.* Eds. Elizabeth A. Flynn and Patricinio Schweickart. Baltimore, MD: John Hopkins University Press, 1986. Pp. 31–62.

Seabrook, William. *Asylum.* New York: Harcourt Brace, 1935.

Showalter, Elaine. *The Female Malady: Women, Madness, and Culture in England, 1830–1980.* New York: Penguin, 1985, 1987.

Sontag, Susan. *Illness As Metaphor.* New York: Vintage, 1979.

Sournia, Jean-Charles. *A History of Alcoholism.* Cambridge, MA: B. Blackwell, 1990.

Spilka, Mark. "The Death of Love in *The Sun Also Rises*." *Hemingway: A Collection of Critical Essays*. Ed. Robert P. Weeks. Englewood Cliffs, NJ: Prentice-Hall, 1962. Pp. 127–38.

Whitfield, Charles. *Co-Dependency: Healing the Human Condition. The New Paradigm for Helping Professionals and People in Recovery.* Deerfield Beach, FL: Health Communications, 1991.

Young, Philip. *Ernest Hemingway: A Reconsideration*. University Park: Penn State University Press, 1966.

CHAPTER 14

"I COULD DRINK A QUARTER-BARREL TO THE PITCHING"

The Mayor of Casterbridge Viewed as an Alcoholic

Jane Lilienfeld

MICHAEL HENCHARD, THE ONE-TERM MAYOR of Casterbridge, is well aware that he has a problem with alcohol. He tells his new friend Donald Farfrae early in their relationship that ""I am sometimes that dry in the dog days that I could drink a quarter-barrel to the pitching"" (Hardy, 38). But he does not, he continues, because "'I did a deed on account of which I shall be ashamed to my dying day'" (Hardy, 38). He is thus aware that had he not been drinking, he would not have sold his wife. When he once again meets his wife he had sold, 19 years later, the first thing he tells her is that he does not drink (56). He rises to become mayor of a hard-drinking town, and his refraining from drink gives him a clear head that others perhaps did not have. Henchard's abstinence from drink includes all liquor, and indicates that Hardy was most likely familiar with some of the numerous abstinence pledges on which Michael Henchard's ""gospel oath"" (Hardy, 14, 27) is based.[1] However, Henchard has sworn a time-bound oath, and once he drinks again he loses control of his drinking and his destiny, eventually dying in self-imposed exile from the human community like a King Lear of the heath.

There can be little doubt that Hardy intended this "man of character" to be a portrait of an alcoholic man, nor are possible biographical referents for Michael Henchard lacking from Hardy's biography. Hardy was the maternal grandson of a "violent" alcoholic (Millgate, 12); his well-born mentor Horace Moule committed suicide partly because of an alcohol addiction his attempt at temperance could not cure (Millgate, 154–56); Hardy's maternal uncle John Antell died of an illness contracted while lying drunk all night "in a ditch" after a "drunken bout" (Gittings, 15; Millgate, 107–8), and other relatives were kept from rising in life due to drink (Millgate, 15; Gittings, 13–16). Thomas Hardy's recognition of alcoholism and his compassionate understanding of it are clear, too, in his portrait of Tess's friend Marian who becomes drink-dependent later in her life in *Tess of the D'Urbervilles,* in his open-minded recognition of the causes of Joseph Poorgrass's "multiplying eye," in *Far from the Madding Crowd,* and in his understanding of the part that alcohol plays in Jude Fawley's tragic life choices in *Jude the Obscure.* Hardy's comprehension of alcoholism was quite sophisticated, as my essay will suggest.[2]

In spite of the fact that definitions of alcoholism are the site of competing interpretations, several definitions illuminate aspects of Michael Henchard's complicated character.[3] Many current models of alcoholism agree that it is a multicausational illness, has a physiological component, may be genetic,[4] but occurs within an individual embedded in a family system that is located in a particular social class, historical time, and socioeconomic reality. For if there ever were a portrait of a certain kind of alcoholic male, Hardy has delineated it in the figure of Michael Henchard.

How can this assertion be made when many theorists of alcohol have concluded, after years of investigation, that there is no such thing as "the" alcoholic personality (Syme; Ludwig, 77)? In fact, many clinicians now refer to "alcoholisms" (Cox, 147–48), arguing that "alcoholism is anything but a unidimensional disorder" (Vaillant, *Revisited,* 156). The emphasis of the medical debate, unlike literary studies, is not on an avoidance of "essentialism" per se, but is based on the fact that alcoholism is a more complex illness than is suggested by the simplified medical model of the 1930s on which Alcoholics Anonymous is based.

A clinical portrait of one subgroup of male alcoholics can be found in varied sources. Publications by psychologists, psychiatrists, and alcohol counselors form a composite portrait of the North American late twentieth century male alcoholic client, drinking or sober. Facets of this composite picture are substantiated by the results of numerous empirical tests that have been administered to North American male alcoholics for decades.[5] Evidence drawn from longitudinal studies such as those by Vaillant, substantiates the composite picture emerging from psychological and psychiatric clinical studies. The varied diagnostic criteria used to assess alcoholism,[6] the divergence of patients' class, race, gender, age, and potential problems of countertransference (Vaillant, *Revisited,* 368, 372; Wallace, 32–53) need to be considered when synthesizing clinical and research findings. Even so, the resulting overlapping descriptions of a specific kind of North American male drinker are remarkably consistent.

Many North American clinicians have noted consistent patterns of behavior, attitudes and defenses of specific groups of male alcoholics (Levin, *Counseling,* 129–33; Ludwig, 19, 78; Kinney and Leaton, 159–70; Wallace, 26–32; Bean, 343). For example, Ludwig states "the lack of a typical alcoholic personality does not mean that there is not a constellation of inchoate attributes common to alcoholics, or most individuals for that matter, which can become exaggerated . . . in response to a growing dependence upon alcohol" (78). After an extensive review of the medical literature through 1979 about "the alcoholic personality," Gordon Barnes concluded that a clinical alcoholic personality could be postulated (622–23). In his recent book, *Introduction to Alcoholism Counseling,* Jerome Levin agreed that "the few facts that have been determined do hold up across studies and populations . . . [these] describe the clinical alcoholic personality" (*Counseling,* 124; see also Bean, 343).

In the original search for the prototypic alcoholic personality, researchers hoped to establish which predisposing psychological problems might lead to alcoholism. As more became known about the disease, controversy continued about whether certain consistent characteristics of alcoholism may lead to or result from the illness (Miller and Chappel, 202; Miller and Gold, 285; Bell and Khantzian, 273–75). For my purposes, the question is not whether certain physiologies, genetic markers, character traits, and defense structures predispose the alcoholic to the illness, but that once the illness is established, certain traits and defenses—ways of construing life and others—occur as an inextricable part of alcoholism. Clinicians and empirical test results present extensive evidence that certain subsets of male alcoholics have poor self-esteem; grandiose and primitive defenses; sudden and severe rages as part of poor impulse control, which leads them to act out rather than reason through choices about behavior; and little ability to conceptualize the long-range consequences of their actions (Wallace, 26–32; Ludwig, 18–24; Brown, *Recovery,* 97; Khantzian, 30–31).

Several North American clinicians who believe alcoholism leads to characteristic behavioral and perceptual patterns view the loss of control of drinking as central to the definition of alcoholism. As loss of control increases, they note, alcohol becomes the organizing principle of the drinker's life. Distortions in thinking develop, which the alcoholic needs to maintain a central focus on alcohol while denying such a focus. Because alcohol, not themselves or others, becomes their primary concern, alcoholics lessen their physical and emotional self-care; their interpersonal relations suffer. Consequently alcoholism causes decreased work capacity, shame, guilt, self-preoccupation, and increasingly lowered self-esteem (Brown, *Recovery,* 3–26, Bean, 339–45; Wallace, 28–32; Vaillant, *Revisited,* 33–34, 48, 79–80, 82–85, 107, 118–19, 136–37, 142, 270, 274–75, 365, 371–73).

Still other clinicians, such as Jerome Levin and E. J. Khantzian, focus on what some term the "weak ego structures" of certain alcoholics, although Levin postulates such ego-permeability as being the result of alcoholism and Khantzian as a probable precondition. Among the painful characteristics caused by alcoholism, Levin cites low tolerance for frustration, low self-esteem, feelings of shame, and an inability to assess long-range consequences of actions or to control impulsive behavior (*Counseling*, 129–133). The psychiatrist E. J. Khantzian concludes from his clinical work with addicts and alcoholics that specific behaviors of addiction are an attempt to palliate pre-existing severe psychic distress. Such "[d]isturbances in psychic structures" cause problems with "affect life, self-esteem, relationships and self care" (Bell and Khantzian, 275). Khantzian argues that "substance abusers' self-protective, survival deficiencies are the consequences of deficits in a capacity for self-care" ("Self Regulation," 30). Michael Henchard demonstrates many of the characteristics associated with this postulated weak ego-structure in his self-devaluation, lack of impulse control, belligerence, and aggressivity.

The narrative insists on the loneliness and suffering of this man who longs for human connection and can neither make healthy connections nor sustain those he has made. However he came by these characteristics, either as the result of his drinking or as part of the cause, Michael Henchard has those specific difficulties that arise because his core self is poorly developed; he perceives other people as objects, and he experiences his own feelings as intolerable attacks. Repeatedly he seems unable to think through the consequences of behavior, as is evident when one considers the impulsivity of the sale of his wife.

As Langbaum has pointed out in the original manuscript of the novel, Henchard justifies his behavior when citing wife sales he had witnessed (128). Even though Hardy points out in his 1895 introduction to the novel that wife sales were still known in the Wessex of 1820, as Langbaum shows, Hardy excised Henchard's self-justifying memory of such evidence from the final draft of the novel (128). This deletion suggests that Henchard's is an impulsive, aggressive action, the consequences of which Henchard is unable to imagine. Under the influence of the excess of rum he drinks, the short-term gratification of blaming his wife and child for his troubles and expelling them as scapegoats from his life is Henchard's primary focus (Hardy, 3–12). Hardy's manuscript deletions thus suggest that this rash deed is couched more as a personal failure in self-control, an antisocial choice, than as a culturally sanctioned use of a wife as chattel goods. As such, the wife sale, made possible because Henchard is so drunk, is the originating cause of all the events that form the plot of the novel.

When called upon to explain or to defend himself appropriately, Henchard is unable to do so. For instance, he remains silent when confronted by an angry Elizabeth-Jane at her wedding (Hardy, 248–50; Giordano, 93–94), even though he, too, had not known until his wife's death the truth about Elizabeth-Jane's parentage. He is unable to tell his adopted stepdaughter the depth of his love and dependence on her, those feelings that had made him hope and wish that she might like to see him at her wedding (Hardy, 245–46). Elizabeth-Jane's rage is the precipitating cause of his withdrawal from all human contact, an incipiently suicidal choice.

As another indication of Henchard's low self-esteem and lack of impulse control resulting from the impaired self-care of alcoholism, he refuses to lie and discredit the furmity woman when she confronts him. Instead, he agrees with her denunciation of him as a drunken wife-seller (Hardy, 154–55). He might, like the others in court, have discounted her statements as the besotted ravings of a beggar-woman, and used his social position to join in the chorus of disgust and misogyny with which Mrs. Goodenough might have been silenced. But he identifies with her instead of denouncing her, using the occasion to clear his conscience. Michael Henchard's agreement with the furmity woman's denunciation is a classic Aristotelian scene of recognition and reversal. "[I]t formed the edge or turn in the incline of Henchard's fortunes," as the narrator says, and is the moment at which his precipitous "descent" began (Hardy, 167). His self-devaluation renders him incapable of defending himself even when the most important things in his life depend on it.

Discussions of the mayor's weak ego illuminate Henchard's inability to interact with others as an adult human being. He lost his position in Casterbridge for many reasons, but drunk or sober, his rages consistently cost him allies. When he learns that Farfrae's rival grain business is established, for instance, his tantrum could be heard "as far as the town pump" (Hardy, 86). This episode illustrates his lack of self-care skills, as observed in the intolerable and thus uncontrollable nature of his rage, and his inability to recognize and accept long term consequences of ill-advised behavior. His rage indicates his lack of skill in human interaction, as it proves the occasion for the town councilmen, "who had been made to wince individually [by Henchard's temper] on more than one occasion" (Hardy, 86) to align themselves with Farfrae, now Henchard's increasingly popular and prosperous business rival. These unwilled behaviors of Henchard's are characteristics of alcoholism (Wallace, 26–32; Ludwig, 18–20; Brown, *Recovery,* 97; Khantzian, "Self-Regulation," 30–31).

If alcoholism is a biopsychosocial disease, then cultural and sociological variables will affect its development and course. Cross-cultural studies that investigate interpersonal dependency as a factor in alcoholism are pertinent to any discussion of Michael Henchard as an alcoholic (Heath, 393–94). Feminist theory, further, has long argued that the construction of masculinity is the partial result of the rejection of traits culturally marked as "feminine" (Chodorow, 180–90). In his recent book, Terence Real has explored a strong cultural link between expectations of prowess in drinking and the cultural imperatives about what might be termed "American manhood" (34–36). These assertions are pertinent to Howard Blane's speculations about what would now be termed the construction of masculinity within middle-class Caucasian American norms of dependency (Blane, 13–14, 37, 85). Blane suggests that North American alcoholics can be categorized into three types: openly dependent alcoholics who expect others to meet their primary needs, counterdependent alcoholics who cannot admit dependency except under the influence of alcohol, and dependent-independent alcoholics who swing from one extreme to the other. Jerome Levin pointed out that Blane's suppositions have recently been updated and substantiated by newer psychodynamic clinical studies of alcoholic clients that suggest that "the alcoholic is often enraged at those on whom he or she depends" (Levin, *Counseling,* 169), a finding pertinent to Henchard's complicated feelings about Farfrae.

Although it is problematic to advance Blane's ideas about the Caucasian male in North American middle-class culture as scientifically verifiable, his speculations provide an excellent metaphor for Henchard's behaviors in the novel. Michael Henchard sells his wife and child because they do not exist for him as subjects; he experiences them as nuisances who impede his rise. Once having shed his dependence on his wife, he lives superficially with other men and concentrates on work. His one sexual relationship[7] before his wife reappears takes place when he visits the island of Jersey on business. There he becomes physically ill and then falls into a severe depression, which weakens his resolve not to rely on others.

Once Henchard becomes interested in Farfrae, he is overcome by his need for the young man, a need that he goes to extreme lengths to satisfy. When Farfrae refuses to remain in his stranglehold, the mayor veers away from his dependence to a haughty independence that cloaks a fantasy of fused dependence on Farfrae, so that the majority of his actions relate either symbolically or directly to the young man. Michael Henchard thus embodies Blane's theories about dependent-counterdependent male alcoholics. In all these relations, Henchard demonstrates what John Wallace has described as the extreme self-referentiality and consequent flattening of other human beings to objects that is characteristic of certain of his male alcoholic clients who "tend to . . . perceive the happenings around them largely as they impinge upon self," and "screen out" and "distort" other "information" (30). I believe that Michael Henchard's struggle with dependency, both on alcohol and on Donald Farfrae, forms the crux of the plot of *The Mayor of Casterbridge*. Both struggles are inextricable from Henchard's views of his own manhood, and both are connected to his severe, recurrent depressions. As in contemporary American life, Henchard's alcoholism is subtly reflective of cultural ideas about what being a man requires and implies (Real, 34–36).

An alcoholic's dependency on others, whether acknowledged or denied, may be related to what researchers speculate is an "external locus of control." This term refers to people's perceptions of "the source of control in their lives," (Cox, 159) a contested measure of alcoholism on empirical tests. Although not all clinicians and alcohol theorists would agree with this finding, Levin asserts that "[a]lmost all studies of alcoholics show them to have an external locus of control" (Levin, *Counseling*, 132).

Like Blane's ideas, which I treat as metaphorical, I think this finding about an "external locus of control" is nevertheless suggestive for an understanding of Michael Henchard. Even though Henchard is an independent laborer at 21, he is nevertheless a member of a social class, a notable characteristic of which was very little control over their lives and social circumstances.[8] Members of this social class at the beginning of the nineteenth century in England were at the mercy of forces to which those males with more money were not subject.

A significant feature of many of Hardy's working poor is their insistence on fate rather than individual efforts and will. Michael Henchard's conviction of victimization by fate is exacerbated by his alcoholic inability to accept responsibility for his own behavior. Whether he is an unemployed hay trusser or the mayor of a prosperous town, Henchard cannot take responsibility for his actions; he blames his wife for the fact that he sold her (Hardy, 12). When he discovers that Elizabeth-Jane is not his own child, he is convinced that a "sinister intelligence" has decreed that he suffer (Hardy, 97). Instead of being able to recognize his own role in the fall of his corn empire, he strikes out at Jopp onto whom he projects the cause of all his problems (Hardy, 145).

Henchard's first reaction to events that do not go his way, drunk or sober, is to look to others' failures or behaviors as the cause. It is an almost impossible struggle for him to maintain contact with the fact that he is at the center of his life, not fate or another person, thus demonstrating the perceptual style termed "external locus of control."

Depression has a high correlation with alcoholism, as numerous sources attest. However, the complexity and dimensions of this correlation continue to be contested (Hamm et al., 580; Weissman and Meyers, 372–73). Alcohol is physiologically a depressive drug (Levin, *Counseling,* 17; Levin, *Treatment,* 37–39). But does prior depression predispose some to become an alcoholic? Is alcohol a "self-medication," then, to treat a pre-existing condition? Vaillant, advocating a medical model, argues that depression results from drinking (*Revisited,* 82). Her clinical work with alcoholics leads Bean to suggest that depression results from shame over the loss of control in alcoholic drinking, and from the necessity of denying the severe toll uncontrolled drinking takes on self esteem, relationships, and adult functioning capacity. While acknowledging the devastation alcoholism brings, Khantzian has consistently argued that intolerable feeling states, including depression, may lead to addiction as an alternative to such suffering (Bell and Khantzian, 274, 279).

In 1952, Frederick Lemere, a Seattle psychiatrist, surveyed the life histories of five hundred deceased alcoholic patients, discovering that 11 percent had killed themselves (695). Earlier, Menninger "conceptualized alcohol addiction as a chronic progressive suicide" (qtd. in Hamm et al., 580); an interpretation that Giordano's study of Henchard substantiates.[9] Michael Henchard is depressed to the point of suicide several times in the novel, and his return to drinking can be interpreted as a suicidal gesture of rage turned against himself (Giordano, 79, 96). In the first rapture of their friendship, the mayor tells Farfrae that his depressions were rather common and that he expected them in his life (Hardy, 60). One of his methods of handling depression is to become immobilized, as when he retreats to Jopp's lodgings and isolates himself from everyone for a time (169). He consciously contemplates suicide at least three times (97–98, 171, 226–27, 253–54); finally having decided to drown himself, he is only deterred by seeing his effigy in the weir-hole of Blackwater, a visitation that he regards as proof of "an appalling miracle" of divine intervention (227).

Henchard also handles his depressions by formulating external situations as the problem and becoming enraged about them, as for instance, when he maneuvers Farfrae into quitting (78–83). He does not want Farfrae to leave his employ, but he lacks the impulse control necessary to tolerate his feelings and to wait for an appropriate time to work things out with Farfrae in private.

After his return to drinking, Henchard moves from bouts of depression and an inability to tolerate sadness to increasingly self-destructive behaviors. Following Elizabeth-Jane's angry rejection of him, Henchard flees from this last human tie, retreating to the hovel that becomes his final resting place. Although he is attended there by Abel Whittle, Henchard seems to be too weakened to drive Whittle away, rather than to have willingly accepted the care of this impaired working man to whose mother Henchard had been so generous in former days. Henchard's homely list of requests reads more like a suicide note than a will, indicating the severe depression that hastens his alcoholic death. This list of requests (Hardy, 254) makes clear that his death is motivated by what Lemere might have interpreted as the suicidal raging despair of the still-drinking alcoholic.

So specific were Hardy's observation and understanding of the alcoholics around him that his fictional character presents a convincing portrait of an alcoholic. The creation of Michael Henchard indicates that Hardy closely observed the characteristic behaviors and sufferings of the many alcoholics he knew and used his compassionate observations to create the unforgettable figure of the mayor of Casterbridge.

NOTES

1. The British Temperance Movement was influenced by the Scottish and Irish movements (Harrison, 103–4). Thus, it is not surprising that Henchard's oath is similar to the total abstinence pledge of Irish abstainers (Bland, 24–25). For "[t]here were a variety of different pledges, rather than a standard one for the whole movement. In the 1830s and 1940s there were many battles about what was to be excluded and what was to be allowed in the pledge" (Shiman, 258 n. 160). The British Temperance Movement was factionalized between moderate drinkers and total abstainers, segregated by social class, and further divided geographically, with hostilities separating northern and southern British temperance groups (Shiman, 18–42).

   Henchard's "gospel oath" has biographical and historical precedents. As I have noted, Horace Moule tried for a time to control his drinking by total abstinence from alcohol (Millgate, 70). Further, temperance was a current topic for readers of this novel. During the early 1880s, when the novel was serialized and then published in book form, the Gospel Temperance faction of the movement was enjoying a "phenomenal" national resurgence (Shiman, 112).

   So topical was the serialized version of *The Mayor of Casterbridge* that the Church of England's temperance journal praised the novel for supporting its cause (Millgate, 269 n).
2. The reader will notice that I use current models of scientific analyses of alcoholism to substantiate my biopsychosicial interpretation of

Michael Henchard's alcoholism. I have explained my methodological arguments about my use of scientific/medical discourses of addiction rather than the AA simplified version of the medical model, my choice of mimetic rather than postmodernist modes of reading, my defense of and adoption of feminist standpoint theories in my interpretation of and reliance on some current North American medical discourses of alcoholism, my historicizing the novel at length in the introduction to my book, *Reading Alcoholisms,* and I would like to refer the reader to these substantiated assertions, as space constraints do not permit me to rehearse them here.

The reader will also notice that I use such models to discuss a nineteenth century fictional figure. I do not believe it is anachronistic to discuss the consequences of nineteenth-century male alcoholism in terms established by twentieth century North American medical literature. I assert this because the British and North American Temperance Movements developed a sophisticated understanding of alcoholism and an analysis of the interconnection of social class, male drinking, and male violence and women's lives (Sournia, 29–33, 120–26; Stivers, 34; Flexner, 185–91). Hence I do not think it is inaccurate to use twentieth-century feminist analyses of familial alcohol systems to analyze a nineteenth-century male/female working class relationship. For further discussion of Michael and Susan Henchard's alcoholic marriage, see my *Reading Alcoholisms* (27–33, 35–39, 59–60). Although I do not always agree with his categories or definitions of alcoholism and problem drinking, I am indebted to the compassionate insights of Denis Thomas who has established that drinking negatively impacted Michael Henchard.

3. For example, if Michael Henchard is analyzed according to the categories proposed in the *DSM-IV* (fourth edition of the *Diagnostic and Statistical Manual*) for substance dependence, he might be said to demonstrate tolerance, as I have discussed above when noting his physiological reactions to the rum he drank. He appears to have little or no hangover. Tolerance in the *DSM-IV* is related to the loss of control of how much one drinks (181), a symptom the medical model considers indispensable to a diagnosis of alcoholism (Miller and Chappel, 202).

If Michael Henchard is analyzed according to criteria for "substance abuse," a diagnosis that does not depend on physiological dependence, Henchard demonstrates at least two of the criteria. (1) His alcohol use impairs his social relationships. His wife had clearly worried—if not confronted him about—his drinking, as I have noted above. (2) He tries to stop drinking by taking an abstinence pledge (*DSM-IV,* 182–83).

If Michael Henchard is analyzed according to the Cahalan scale quoted in Vaillant, he demonstrates belligerence, binge drinking, marital problems, financial problems, and admits his problem with control. Further, the narrator reports that his wife worried about his drinking (qtd. in Vaillant, *Revisted,* 27).

E. M. Jellinek would diagnose Michael Henchard as a binge drinker, that is as having "*Episolon alcoholism,*" a form of alcoholism that Jellinek considered did fit the disease model (39, emphasis in original).

According to all these definitions, Michael Henchard clearly has a problem with alcohol.

4. It appears likely that genetically transmitted predisposing central nervous system disorders might be a factor in the development of alcoholism (Vaillant, *Natural,* 64–70, but see *Revisited,* 72–73; Wallace, 24–26; Miller and De Baca, 364, #16 and #42; Noble, 216; Windle, 130–35, 152–56). "The fact that alcoholism runs in families has been known for centuries" (Goodwin, 427). "By itself, the finding of familiality of an illness says nothing about mode of inheritance or transmission . . . But the absence of such a [clear] pattern [of transmission] cannot be considered absence of genetic contribution" (Dinwiddie and Cloninger, 207; see also Cloninger, Bohman, and Sigvardsson, whose study, "Inheritance," has recently been replicated, as I discuss below in note 8). In other words, the exact genetic links or link have not been clearly established, but that there are genetic links is proven by adoption studies as well as other forms of evidence.

   Summarizing the decision of the DSM-IV study group not to recommend familial alcoholism as a diagnostic category for now, Mark Schuckit nevertheless points out that "using the most restrictive criteria, between 20% and 35% of alcoholic persons who enter treatment have an alcoholic father and/or mother" (163).

5. Clinical portraits of a certain subset of male alcoholics overlap to some extent with the results of batteries of psychological and psychometric tests—such as the MMPI (Minnesota Multiphasic Personality Inventory) and the TAT (Thematic Apperception Test), among others—that continue to be administered to inpatient alcoholics as well as to those in outpatient treatment (Cox, 149–51, 153). Reviewing the literature on such tests in 1976, Neuringer and Clopton

critiqued these tests, criticisms that Barnes corroborated in his 1979 review of the literature. Discrepancies in test results due to the divergent severity of subjects' alcoholism, differences in subjects' race and social class, and differences in kinds of population tested (inpatient or outpatient) have undermined claims that such tests are "objective" and accurate assessment measures.

Nevertheless, some researchers and clinicians find that the results of the MMPI appear to substantiate two aspects of the clinical picture of a certain subset of male alcoholics that I have noted above (Cox, 150; Levin, *Counseling,* 125). Neuringer and Clopton found in reviewing MMPI results that alcoholics consistently scored high on Depression scale 2 (D) and Psychopathic Deviate scale 4 (Pd), or what might be termed antisocial interpersonal interactions (Cox, 155–56; Neuringer and Clopton, 21). Levin also cites these two MMPI scores as consistent and thus as significant (Levin, *Counseling,* 125–26).

Further, perceptual styles of certain subsets of male alcoholics resulted in controversial but interesting findings. Early research into the psychological/physiological ways alcoholics experienced themselves in the physical world suggested that alcoholics perceived differently than nonalcoholics (Cox, 158–60; Barnes, 609–11, 617–18). Obviously, chronic alcoholism causes brain damage (Levin, *Counseling,* 46–49) and might be expected to affect perception. However, current research in the area of neurobiological preconditions to alcoholism suggest the possibility that such early findings about alcoholics' perceptual differences from those of nonalcoholics may one day be substantiated (Jacobson, 188; Windle, 130–36; Noble, 216). For purposes of my discussion, however, I regard the early test results as worth citing if not entirely verifiable, and view such evidence as suggestive rather than as definitive.

6. See above, note 3.
7. Hardy cannot say this relationship with Lucetta is sexual because of the conventions of the Victorian novel, so he uses the word "intimate" to indicate that it was sexual. The relationship was "explicitly sexual in the original manuscript" (Langbaum, 127).
8. The postmodern revolution in the discipline of history has problematized the social construction of the human being in culture (Laslett et al.). Additionally, scholars debate the history of the family in England from the Renaissance to the early twentieth century, particularly interrogating the influential arguments of Lawrence

Stone (Ross, 5–9; O'Day, 163–67; Pollard, 1–69, 96–143). To place the fictional Henchard's life in historical context is therefore difficult. (For an explanation of why I think it is useful to historicize a fictional figure's "life story," see the introduction and epilogue to my *Reading Alcoholisms.*)

Social class shaped family life, particularly the extent to which parents relied on their children's labor (O'Day, 168; Ittman, 148). Henchard "was brought up as a hay trusser" (Hardy, 37), and was thus slightly above unskilled laborers in social rank (Williams and Williams, 34).

The narrative opens in the early years of the nineteenth century when Henchard was 21. He thus was born in the 1780s. At that time in rural, laboring British families, men and women died in their 40s; children went to work with their parents before puberty; and most such families lacked sufficient food, secure dwellings, and physical comforts.

In the last decade of the eighteenth century and the first thirteen years of the nineteenth century many harvests were bad (Smith, 524, 549). These economic uncertainties and the precipitous rise and fall of wages, availability of work, and high costs of food, would have added to the ordinary difficulties of a child growing up in a rural, working-class family.

The agricultural working-class family of that era is assumed by social historians to have differed significantly from the late-twentieth-century North American middle-class family. Children were expected to behave as adults. Physical punishment was ordained by church teachings and custom. The sadistic streak in Michael Henchard, exacerbated by drink but still evident when he is sober, might have arisen in part not just from the violence that alcohol often engenders (Vaillant, *Revisited,* 103; NIAAA, 20; Brown, *Adult,* 15), but from the brutalizations to which a child of his class and time would almost certainly have been subject.

The "[s]ons of alcoholics are four times more likely to be alcoholic than the sons of non-alcoholics" (Noble, 216). What follows is my speculation about the impact of alcohol on Henchard's family of origin and early life.

Given Henchard's approximate birth date, Henchard's father could have been alive during what is termed in British history as "the gin epidemic," well known from Hogarth's prints (Sournia, 20–22; Vaillant, *Causes,* 98–99). The epidemic was still virulent during the

1750s, and if Henchard were born in 1784 when his father was 30, his father would have been a young boy—and children drank gin—during the 1750s. Thus, it is possible that the congruence of parental alcoholism with social sanction for physical brutality toward children might have shadowed Henchard's childhood.

To speculate further, Sigvardsson, Bohman, and Cloninger have replicated their influential Stockholm study of male adoptees. They posit "two distinct forms of alcoholism" (681): clinically, Type 1 male alcoholics have "adult onset and rapid progression of dependence," whereas Type 2 male alcoholics have "teenage onset and recurrent social and legal problems from alcohol abuse" (681; for a discussion of this controversial division see Liskow et al.; Irwin, Schuckit, and Smith; Dinwiddie and Cloninger). Is Michael Henchard a Type 2 alcoholic? Perhaps a prequel might depict Henchard's first 21 years and answer my questions.

9. Vaillant's longitudinal studies suggest that depression is a result of alcoholism (*Revisited,* 82–85), a supposition Schuckit's analysis in the DSM-IV sourcebook substantiates ("Relationship," 54). Depression is consistently revealed by Minnesota Multiphasic Personality Inventory (MMPI) results as I noted above. Many sources agree that depression lessens for most alcoholics as they stay sober, among them Vaillant (*Revisited,* 85) and Schuckit ("Relationship," 55). In his discussion of depression as consequent to alcoholism, Vaillant reviewed Lemere's findings (*Revisited,* 150–56).

BIBLIOGRAPHY

Barnes, Gordon. "The Alcoholic Personality: A Reanalysis of the Literature." *Journal of Studies on Alcohol* 40 (1979). Pp. 571–633.

Bayog-Bean, Margaret. "Psychopathology Produced by Alcoholism." *Psychopathology and Addictive Disorders.* Ed. Roger Meyer. New York: Guilford, 1986. Pp. 334–45.

Bean, Margaret. "Denial and the Psychological Complications of Alcoholism." *Dynamic Approaches to the Understanding and Treatment of Alcoholism.* Eds. Margaret Bean and Norman Zinberg. New York: Free Press, 1981. Pp. 55–97.

Bell, Carolyn M. and Edward J. Khantizian. "Contemporary Psychodynamic Perspectives and the Disease Concept of Addiction: Complementary or Competing Models?" *Psychiatric Annals* 21.5 (1991). Pp. 273–81.

Bland, Sister Joan. *Hibernian Crusade: The Story of the Catholic Total Abstinence Union of America.* Washington, DC: Catholic University Press, 1951.

Blane, Howard T. *The Personality of the Alcoholic: Guises of Dependency.* New York: Harper and Row, 1968.

Brown, Stephanie. *Treating Adult Children of Alcoholics: A Developmental Perspective.* New York: Wiley & Sons, 1988.

———. *Treating the Alcoholic: A Developmental Model of Recovery.* New York: Wiley & Sons, 1985.

Chaudron, C. D. and D. A. Wilkinson, eds. *Theories on Alcoholism.* Toronto: Addiction Research Foundation, 1988.

Chodorow, Nancy. *The Reproduction of Mothering: Psychoanalysis and the Sociology of Gender.* Berkeley, CA: Berkeley University Press, 1978.

Cloninger, C. Robert, Michael Bohman, and Soren Sigvardsson. "Inheritance of Alcohol Abuse: Cross-Fostering Analysis of Adopted Men." *Archives of General Psychiatry* 38 (1981). Pp. 861–68.

Cox, Donald. "Personality Theory." *Theories on Alcoholism.* Ed. C. D. Chaudron and D. A. Wilkinson. Toronto: Addiction Research Foundation, 1988. Pp. 143–72.

Diagnostic and Statistical Manual of Mental Disorders. Fourth ed. Washington, DC: American Psychiatric Association, 1994.

Dinwiddie, Stephen H. and C. Robert Cloninger. "Family and Adoption Studies in Alcoholism and Drug Addiction." *Psychiatric Annals* 21.4 (1991). Pp. 206–14.

Dowling, Scott, ed. *The Psychology and Treatment of Addictive Behavior.* Madison, WI: International University Press, 1995.

Flexner, Eleanor. *Century of Struggle: The Woman's Rights Movement in the United States.* rev. ed. Cambridge, MA: Harvard University Press, 1976.

Giordano, Frank R. *"I'd Have My Life Unbe": Thomas Hardy's Self-Destructive Characters.* University, AL: University of Alabama Press, 1984.

Gittings, Robert. *Young Thomas Hardy.* Boston: Little, Brown, 1975.

Goodwin, Donald W. "Genetic Factors in the Development of Alcoholism." *Psychiatric Clinics of North America* 9.3 (1986). Pp. 427–33.

Hamm, John E., et al. "The Qualitative Measurement of Depression and Anxi[illegible] in Male Alcoholics." *American Journal of Psychiatry* 136. 4B (19[illegible] Pp. 580–82.

Hardy, Thomas. *The Mayor of Casterbridge: A Story of a Man of Character.* Ed. James K. Robinson. New York: Norton, 1977.

Harrison, Brian. *Drink and the Victorians: The Temperance Question in England, 1815–1872.* Pittsburgh: University of Pittsburgh, 1971.

Heath, Dwight B. "Emerging Anthropological Theory and Models of Alcohol Use and Alcoholism." *Theories on Alcoholism.* Ed. C. D. Chaudron and D. A. Wilkinson. Toronto: Addiction Research Foundation, 1988. Pp. 353–410.

Irwin, Michael, Mark Schuckit, and Tom L. Smith. "Clinical Importance of Age at Onset in Type 1 and Type 2 Primary Alcoholics." *Archives of General Psychiatry* 47 (1990). Pp. 320–24.

Ittman, Karl. *Gender and Family in Victorian England.* New York: New York University Press, 1990.

Jacobson, Jacob G. "The Advantages of Multiple Approaches to Understanding Addictive Behavior." Ed. Scott Dowling. *The Psychology and Treatment of Addictive Behavior.* Madison, WI: International University, 1995. Pp. 175–90.

Jellinek, E. M. *The Disease Concept of Alcoholism.* New Haven, CT: College and University Press, 1960.

Khantzian, Edward. "Self Regulation Vulnerabilities in Substance Abusers: Treatment Implications." Ed. Scott Dowling. *The Psychology and Treatment of Addictive Behavior.* Madison, WI: International University, 1995. Pp. 17–42.

Kinney, Jean and Gwen Leaton. *Loosening the Grip: A Handbook of Alcohol Information.* St. Louis: Mosby Year Book, 1991.

Langbaum, Robert. *Thomas Hardy in Our Time.* London: Macmillan, 1995.

Laslett, Barbara, et al. eds. *History and Theory: Feminist Research, Debates, Contestations.* Chicago: University of Chicago Press, 1997.

Lemere, Frederick. "What Happens to Alcoholics?" *American Journal of Psychiatry* 136 (1952). Pp. 586–88.

Levin, Jerome David. *Introduction to Alcoholism Counseling: A Bio-Psycho-Social Approach.* 2nd ed. New York: Taylor & Francis, 1995.

———. *Treatment of Alcoholism and Other Addictions: A Self Psychology Approach.* Northvale, NJ.: Jason Aronson, 1987.

Liskow, Barry, Barbara Powell, Elizabeth Nickel, and Elizabeth Penick. "Anti-Social Alcoholics: Are There Clinically Significant Diagnostic Subtypes?" *Journal of Studies on Alcohol* 53.1 (1991). Pp. 62–69.

Ludwig, Arnold. *Understanding the Alcoholic's Mind: The Nature of Craving and How to Control It.* New York: Oxford University Press, 1988.

Miller, Norman M., and John N. Chappel. "History of the Disease Concept." *Psychiatric Annals* 21.4 (April 1991). Pp. 196–205.

Miller, Norman M., and Mark S. Gold. "Dependence Syndrome: A Critical Analysis of Essential Features." *Psychiatric Annals* 21.5 (May 1991). Pp. 282–90.

Miller, William R. and Janet C'De Baca. "Alcohol Education Inventory: What Every Health Professional Should Know about Alcoholism." *Journal of Substance Abuse Treatment* 12.5 (1995). Pp. 355–65.

Millgate, Michael. *Thomas Hardy, a Biography.* New York: Random House, 1982.

Neuringer, Charles and James R. Clopton. "The Use of Psychological Tests for the Study of the Identification, Prediction, and Treatment of Alcoholism." *Empirical Studies of Alcoholism.* Eds. Gerald Goldstein and Charles Neuringer. Cambridge, MA: Ballinger, 1976. Pp. 7–35.

Noble, Ernest P. "Genetic Studies in Alcoholism: CNS Functioning and Molecular Biology." *Psychiatric Annals* 21.4 (1991). Pp. 215–29.

O'Day, Rosemary. *The Family and Family Relationships: 1500–1900.* New York: St. Martin's, 1994.

Pollard, Linda. *Forgotten Children: Parent-Child Relations from 1500–1900.* 2nd ed. Cambridge, UK: Cambridge University Press, 1985.

Real, Terence. *I Don't Want to Talk about It: Overcoming the Secret Legacy of Male Depression.* New York: Scribner, 1997.

Ross, Ellen. *Love and Toil: Motherhood in Outcast London.* New York: Oxford University Press, 1993.

Schuckit, Mark. "Familial Alcoholism." Ed. Thomas Widiger. *DSM-IV Sourcebook.* Volume 1. Washington, DC: American Psychoanalytic Association, 1994. Pp. 159–67.

———. "The Relationship between Alcohol Problems, Substance Abuse, and Psychiatric Disorders." Ed. Thomas Widiger. *DSM-IV Sourcebook.* Vol. 1. Washington, DC: American Psychoanalytic Association, 1994. Pp. 45–66.

Shiman, Lilian Lewis. *Crusade against Drink in Victorian England.* New York: St. Martin's, 1988.

Sigvardsson, Soren, Michael Bohman, and Robert C. Cloninger. "Replication of the Stockholm Adoption Study of Alcoholism: Confirmatory Cross-Fostering Analysis." *Archives of General Psychiatry* 53.8 (1996). Pp. 681–87.

Smith, Go[illegible]win. *A History of England.* 2nd rev. ed. New York: Scribner, 19[illegible]

Sournia, Jean-Charles. *A History of Alcoholism.* Tr. Nick Hindley and Gareth Stanton. London: Basil Blackwell, 1990.

Stivers, Richard. *A Hair of the Dog: Irish Drinking and American Stereotype.* University Park: Penn State University Press, 1976.

Stone, Lawrence. *The Family, Sex, and Marriage in England, 1500–1800.* New York: Harper and Row, 1977.

Syme, Leonard. "Personality Characteristics of the Alcoholic: A Critique of Current Studies." *Quarterly Journal of Alcohol Studies* 18 (November 1956). Pp. 288–301.

Thomas, Denis W. "Drunkenness in Thomas Hardy's Novels." *College Language Association Journal* 28 (December 1984). Pp. 190–209.

U.S. Department of Health and Human Services. Division of Prevention. National Institute of Alcohol Abuse and Alcoholism. *Final Report: An Assessment of the Needs of and Resources for Children of Alcoholic Parents.* Rockville, MD: NIAAA, 1975.

Vaillant, George. *The Natural History of Alcoholism: Causes, Patterns, and Paths to Recovery.* Cambridge, MA: Harvard University Press, 1983.

———. *The Natural History of Alcoholism Revisited.* Cambridge, MA: Harvard University Press, 1995.

Wallace, John. "Working with the Preferred Defense Structure of the Recovering Alcoholic." *Practical Approaches to Alcoholism Psychotherapy.* Ed. Sheldon Zimberg, et al. 2nd ed. New York: Plenum Press, 1987. Pp. 23–36.

Weissman, Myrna, and Jerome K. Meyers. "Clinical Depression in Alcoholism." *American Journal of Psychiatry* 13/3 (March 1980). Pp. 372–73.

Widiger, Thomas, et al., eds. *DSM-IV Sourcebook.* Vol. 1. Washington, DC: American Psychoanalytic Association, 1994.

Williams, Raymond and Merryn Williams. "Hardy and Social Class." *Thomas Hardy: The Writer and His Background.* Ed. Norman Page. London: Bell & Hyman, 1980. Pp. 29–40.

Windle, Michael. "Temperment and Personality Attributes of Children of Alcoholics." *Children of Alcoholics: Critical Perspectives.* Eds. Michael Windle and John Searles. New York: Guilford, 1990. Pp. 129–67.

CONTRIBUTORS

BEN ADAMS received his M.Ed. from Cambridge College in Cambridge, Massachusetts. He is an alcohol counselor who first worked at CASPAR, and who now works at St. Elizabeth's Hospital in Boston and teaches DUI classes at Bay Colony in Woburn, Massachusetts. He is actively involved in local politics in the Brighton, Massachusetts area, participates in community theater, and is the past president for the Alliance of the Mentally Ill.

NANCY TOPPING BAZIN is an Eminent Scholar and Professor of English at Old Dominion University in Norfolk, VA. She has directed Women's Studies programs at Rutgers, Pittsburgh, and Old Dominion and, from 1985 to 1989, chaired the ODU English Department. In 1994, Dr. Bazin was one of eleven in the Commonwealth of Virginia to be honored with an Outstanding Faculty Award, and, in 1996, she received The Charles O. and Elisabeth Burgess Faculty Research and Creativity Award. Dr. Bazin has published two books—*Virginia Woolf and the Androgynous Vision* and *Conversations with Nadine Gordimer*—and forty articles.

MATTS G. DJOS is Professor of English at Mesa State College in Grand Junction, Colorado, where he has taught American literature, modernist poets, and seventeenth century British literature for the past 23 years. Dr. Djos has published and presented numerous papers on the subject of American alcoholic writers, and he continues to conduct special courses and workshops on the field of literature and addiction. He was awarded a Ph.D. in American and seventeenth century British literature from Texas A&M University in 1975. Prior to his work at Mesa State College, he taught at the secondary level in western Washington State for 17 years, where he was involved in special education, the teaching of high school English, and the development of innovative strategies for programs in remedial education.

LAWRENCE DRISCOLL completed his Ph.D. in 1995 at the University of Southern California. His book, *Desiring Drugs,* is forthcoming from St. Martin's Press. He has also published on contemporary English cinema and culture and is now assistant professor of literature at Santa Monica College.

ROGER DANIELS FORSETH is Professor Emeritus of English of the University of Wisconsin-Superior as well as former, and founding, editor of *Dionysos: The Literature and Addiction TriQuarterly.* He received his Ph.D. in 1956 from Northwestern University. Dr. Forseth has received sabbatical leaves for research at the British Museum and the Beinecke and Bancroft libraries, and his teaching specialties include the Enlightenment and Romanticism, in addition to Shakespeare, Matthew Arnold and James Joyce. Furthermore, he has a strong interest in computers, having received the Burlington Northern Teacher of the Year Award for converting the university's freshman English curriculum to computers.

GREGG FRANZWA is Professor of Philosophy at Texas Christian University. His research and teaching interests center on issues treated under the heading of "theories of human nature." He has published articles on a variety of topics, recently including "Cultural Theory and the Problem of Moral Relativism."

STEPHEN C. INFANTINO received his Ph.D. in French literature at the University of Southern California in 1986. He has published articles on Marcel Proust, Marguerite Duras and surrealism, as well as a book, *Photographic Vision in Proust.* Ongoing research pursues the relationship between verbal and visual elements of narrative.

EDWARD J. KHANTZIAN, M.D. is Clinical Professor of Psychiatry, Harvard Medical School, and a founding member of the Department of Psychiatry at the Cambridge Hospital. He has spent more than 20 years studying the psychological causes of drug a[illegible]hol abuse. Dr. Khantzian is a practicing psychiatrist and psy[illegible]a[illegible]yst, a participant in numerous clinical research studies on substance abuse, and a lecturer and writer on psychiatry, psychoanalysis, and substance abuse problems. A former chairman of the Massachusetts' Governor's Drug Rehabilitation Advisory Board and consultant to the National Institute on Drug Abuse, Dr. Khantzian is currently Associate Chief of Psychiatry for Substance Abuse Disorders in the Cambridge Hospital Department of Psychiatry. From its inception in 1986 to 1991, he was a consultant and supervising physician for the National Football League Institute on Drug Abuse (NIDA). Dr. Khantzian received his M.D. from Albany Medical School (NY). He is a founding member of the American Academy of Addiction Psychiatry (AAAP), founding chairperson for the Group for the Advancement of Psychiatry (GAP) Committee on Alcoholism and the Addictions, and a founding member and Chairman of the Board of Directors of the Massachusetts Medical Society's affiliated program, Physician Health Services, Inc. His studies, publications, and teaching have gained him recognition for his contributions on self-medication factors and self-care deficits in substance use disorders and the importance of modified techniques in group therapy for substance abusers.

ELLEN LANSKY was born in Minneapolis and grew up in Overland Park, Kansas. She attended the College of St. Catherine in St. Paul (B.A.), State University of New York at Binghamton (M.A.), and the University of Minnesota (Ph.D.). She now lives in Minneapolis, where she writes fiction and teaches literature and composition. Her scholarly work on literature and alcoholism has appeared in *Dionysos, Literature and Medicine,* and at several regional and national conferences.

JANE LILIENFELD is an Associate Professor of English at Lincoln University, an historically black college located in Jefferson City, Missouri. Her essay, "Mother Love and Mother Hate in *To the Lighthouse*" has been widely cited and anthologized. She has published essays on Willa Cather, Colette, Margaret Atwood, James Joyce, Virginia Woolf, Charlotte Bronte, Elizabeth Gaskell, mothers and daughters in myth and literature, and feminist theory. She is the author of *Reading Alcoholisms: Theorizing Character and Narrative in Selected Novels of Hardy, Joyce, and Woolf.*

KATHRYNE SLATE MCDORMAN received her Ph.D. in British history from Vanderbilt University in 1977. Since then she has taught history at Texas Christian University and, since 1994, has served as the director of the TCU Honors Program. In 1991, she published a full length study of Ngaio Marsh that appeared in the Twayne English Author's series.

SANDY MOREY NORTON teaches Victorian literature and in the Women's Study Program at Eastern Michigan University. Owing to her interest in Mikhail Bakhtin, the primary focus of her research, her work has covered a wide range of topics from mother/child bonding as the basis of sympathy (in her dissertation), to epic in George Elliot's Middlemarch, to Stephen Spielberg's undermining of Alice Walker's feminism in his filming of *The Color Purple.*

JEFFREY OXFORD, Assistant Professor of Spanish and Assistant Chair of the Department of Foreign Languages at the University of North Texas in Denton, Texas, received his Ph.D. in Spanish from Texas Tech University. Previously, he taught at McNeese State University in Lake Charles, Louisiana. His primary area of expertise is Naturalism and the Generation of '98, and he is the author of *Vicente Blasco Ibáñez: Color Symbolism in Selected Novels.*

KRISTA RATCLIFF is Associate Professor at Marquette University. She teaches composition, rhetorical theory, and women's literature. She has published *Anglo-American Feminist Challenges to the Rhetorical Traditions* and articles in *Style, Rhetoric Review, Studies in the Literary Imagination* and *The Writing Instructor.* She is currently working on a manuscript entitled *Rhetorical Listening,* which examines women's multicultural autobiographies to build a theory of listening as a code of cross-cultural conduct.

INDEX